Vegan Italiano

COOKBOOKS BY DONNA KLEIN

The Mediterranean Vegan Kitchen
The PDQ (Pretty Darn Quick) Vegetarian Cookbook
Vegan Italiano

Vegan *Italiano*

MEAT-FREE ▪ EGG-FREE ▪ DAIRY-FREE DISHES FROM SUN-DRENCHED ITALY

DONNA KLEIN

HOME

A HOME BOOK
Published by the Penguin Group
Penguin Group (USA) Inc.
375 Hudson Street, New York, New York 10014, USA
Penguin Group (Canada), 90 Eglinton Avenue East, Suite 700, Toronto, Ontario M4P 2Y3, Canada
(a division of Pearson Penguin Canada Inc.)
Penguin Books Ltd., 80 Strand, London WC2R 0RL, England
Penguin Group Ireland, 25 St. Stephen's Green, Dublin 2, Ireland (a division of Penguin Books Ltd.)
Penguin Group (Australia), 250 Camberwell Road, Camberwell, Victoria 3124, Australia
(a division of Pearson Australia Group Pty. Ltd.)
Penguin Books India Pvt. Ltd., 11 Community Centre, Panchsheel Park, New Delhi—110 017, India
Penguin Group (NZ), Cnr. Airborne and Rosedale Roads, Albany, Auckland 1310, New Zealand
(a division of Pearson New Zealand Ltd.)
Penguin Books (South Africa) (Pty.) Ltd., 24 Sturdee Avenue, Rosebank, Johannesburg 2196,
South Africa

Penguin Books Ltd., Registered Offices: 80 Strand, London WC2R 0RL, England

While the author has made every effort to provide accurate telephone numbers and Internet addresses at the time of publication, neither the publisher nor the author assumes responsibility for errors, or for changes that occur after publication. Further, publisher does not have any control over and does not assume any responsibility for author or third-party websites or their content.

Copyright © 2006 by Donna Klein.
Cover design by Dorothy Wachtensheim.
Cover photo by Stock Food.
Text design by Kristin del Rosario.

First edition: October 2006

Library of Congress Cataloging-in-Publication Data

Klein, Donna.
    Vegan Italiano : meat-free, egg-free, dairy-free dishes from the sun-drenched regions of italy /
Donna Klein.
        p. cm.
    Includes bibliographical references and index.
    ISBN 1-55788-494-3 (alk. paper)
  1. Vegan cookery. 2. Cookery, Italian. I. Title.
    TX837.K548 2006
    641.5'6360945—dc22
                                                                2006014786

PRINTED IN THE UNITED STATES OF AMERICA

10   9   8   7   6   5   4

PUBLISHER'S NOTE: The recipes contained in this book are to be followed exactly as written. The publisher is not responsible for your specific health or allergy needs that may require medical supervision. The publisher is not responsible for any adverse reactions to the recipes contained in this book.

Most Home Books are available at special quantity discounts for bulk purchases for sales promotions, premiums, fund-raising, or educational use. Special books, or book excerpts, can also be created to fit specific needs. For details, write: Special Markets, The Berkley Publishing Group, 375 Hudson Street, New York, New York 10014.

To Trevor, a gift from above,
and all the dogs at
the Montgomery County Humane Society of Maryland
in need of loving homes.

Contents

Acknowledgments

First and foremost, I thank my literary agent, Linda Konner, for her tireless efforts on behalf of my writing projects.

As always, many thanks to John Duff, and to Jeanette Egan, for her invaluable editing skills.

Loving thanks to my daughters, Emma and Sarah, who tested many of the recipes and ate them all with pleasure.

Heartfelt thanks to Mary Lee Barker, whose friendship, support, and prayers helped make this book possible.

Thank you to Don Beck, whose enthusiasm for Italian cuisine rubbed off over the years and onto these pages.

Finally, special thanks to St. Francis of Assisi, who watches over Trevor and all dogs, big and small.

Introduction

Italian Cuisine
A Delicious Brand of the Mediterranean Diet

Garlic-rubbed bread with vine-ripened tomatoes lightly drizzled with olive oil and garnished with fresh basil. A lentil soup enriched with pastina. A salad of arugula, fennel, and radicchio tossed with raisins and pine nuts. Panini sandwiches filled with grilled eggplant and roasted red bell peppers. Pizza topped with wild mushrooms and caramelized onions. Linguine coated with artichoke-marinara sauce. Pears poached in grappa. Strawberries marinated in wine. These are the staples of Italian cooking, which are increasingly appearing on dinner tables and restaurant menus everywhere as the goodness and simplicity of the Mediterranean diet continues to captivate the world.

High in fiber and low in saturated fat, Italian cuisine is a marvelous combination of vegetables, fruits, grains, legumes, fish, cheeses, and a scattering of meats, fowl, and game. Many consider it to be the most delicious brand of the Mediterranean diet—not surprisingly, pasta and pizza consistently rank among America's favorite foods. The single most important feature that unites Italian cooking with other cuisines under the wide umbrella of the Mediterranean diet is olive oil, the primary source of fat. Not only is olive oil a heart-healthy monounsaturated fat that has been shown to lower the bad cholesterol (the LDLs) while raising the good (the HDLs), it also contains beneficial phytonutrients and antioxidants that contribute to overall good health. Yet perhaps the most significant contribution of this miracle oil to the cooking of Italy is that it enhances the flavor of its most popular fruit, the tomato (yes, tomatoes are technically a fruit), and countless vegetables, grains, and legumes, thus promoting the passionate consumption of good-for-you plant-based foods—in effect, a veritable vegan-friendly diet.

An Italian meal, of course, would not be complete without red wine. Modern science continues to establish what Italians have always known—that moderate consumption of red wine can be beneficial to your health. Each bottle of wine contains the concentrated phytonutrients and antioxidants of approximately six hundred grapes. Put it all together—the olive oil, the fruits, the vegetables, the grains, the legumes, the red wine, and you have a sinfully delicious yet virtuous diet that promises a long, happy, healthy life. Come join me on a quick culinary tour of the regions of Italy, and I will show you in the following recipes how it's done. *Saluti* (to your health)!

The Regional Cooking of Italy

PIEDMONT

A fertile area located near the French and Swiss Alps, the cooking of the Piedmont and the Valla d'Aosta region is strongly influenced by that of nearby France. Butter is the preferred cooking fat, yet olive oil is used to dress salads and various vegetables. While rice and polenta are eaten more frequently than pasta and other wheat dishes, the capital of Turin is the home of the thin breadsticks called *grissini*. The region is also known for its white truffles and chocolate desserts, and is the proud producer of world-class wines, namely Barolo, Barbaresco, and Asti, either still or sparkling (*spumante*).

LOMBARDY

Often called the garden of Italy, Lombardy is also the most industrialized region, with the bustling city of Milan as its capital. Rice trumps pasta, and butter, not olive oil, is the preferred cooking fat, though the latter is used in many salads, soups, and vegetable dishes. From this area comes *minestrone alla Milanese*, a variation of the famous Italian vegetable soup made with rice instead of pasta, *risotto alla Milanese*, a creamy saffron-scented rice dish, and *panettone*, a tall sweet bread containing raisins and candied orange peel traditionally eaten around the Christmas holidays.

TRENTINO AND THE ALTO ADIGE

This fertile region of mountains and valleys produces various grains, namely barley, corn, oats, rye, and wheat. Grapes, raspberries, and fruit trees also grow well here. Heavily influenced by German and Austro-Hungarian cuisine, cabbage, potatoes, turnips, dumplings, pancakes, and strudels are popular foods among the locals.

VENETO

Largely influenced by the capital of Venice, the most affluent city in Europe during the Middle Ages, the cuisine of the Veneto is refined and elegant. Rice and risotto dishes abound and are served with the wide variety of vegetables grown in the region, namely artichokes, asparagus, cabbage, mushrooms, onions, peas, pumpkins, tomatoes, and zucchini. The town of Treviso is famous for its *radicchio rosso* (red chicory), which is served raw in salads, grilled with other vegetables, or sautéed in risottos. For dessert, many Venetians enjoy a *sgroppino*, an after-dinner drink made from vodka, Prosecco, and lemon sorbet. Grapes thrive here, and some of the best wines in Italy, namely Valpolicella, Bardolino, Amarone, and Soave, come from the district of Verona.

FRIULI AND VENEZIA GIULIA

Bordering Austria and Slovenia, this bucolic region is conducive to grape-growing and many esteemed wines, such as Ribolla, Picolit, Pignolo, and Pinot Grigio are produced here. Vegetable risottos, similar to those of the nearby Veneto, are popular, and fruits—cherries, peaches, apricots, plums, figs, apples, and pears—appear in savory dishes, as well as desserts, namely strudels and *sorbetti*.

LIGURIA

Stretching from the French border to Tuscany, this narrow coastal region is home to the famous Italian Riviera. Its capital city, Genoa, blessed the world with pesto, a rich basil-and-pine-nut sauce that is tossed with pasta and vegetables, and stirred into soups. Genoa is also famous for its Easter fruitcake known as *pandolce*. Stuffed vegetables, vegetable tarts, *focaccia*, and sweet pizzas made with walnuts, chestnuts, and candied fruit are other regional specialties. Olive groves, vineyards, and orchards are abundant, and flowers are grown on an industrial scale.

TUSCANY

A land of low-lying hills and vineyards under a limpid light, Tuscany possesses a pastoral beauty that has inspired much of the world's greatest art. It has also inspired one of the world's greatest cuisines. Indeed, many food historians agree that this is where Italian cooking was born, under the court of the Medici, with the lovely city of Florence as its capital. A few of the dishes for which the region is famous include assorted *bruschetta* and *crostini*; *panzanella*, a hearty bread salad; *ribollita*, a rib-sticking bread and bean soup; and *panforte*, a spiced fruit cake from Siena. Some of the best olive oil in the world comes from Lucca. Tuscan wines, such as Chianti, Vernaccia di San Geminiano, and Brunello, to name a few, are savored worldwide.

EMILIA-ROMAGNA

Emilia-Romagna is a fabled culinary region that contains the cities of Parma, Modena (home of balsamic vinegar), and Bologna, esteemed by many to be the gastronomic capital of Italy. A major producer of wheat, the area is famous for its pasta, namely ravioli and lasagna, the latter of which is said to have been invented here. Fruits and vegetables are abundant, and the region is well-known for its liqueurs and fruit-flavored brandies. Lambrusco, a fruity, sparkling red wine with universal appeal, is produced here.

UMBRIA

One of the smallest and most tranquil regions in Italy, Umbria contains the town of Assisi, the birthplace of St. Francis, who is honored by the Roman Catholic Church as the patron saint of animals and the environment. Wheat, figs, mushrooms, olives, plums, and many other fruits and vegetables thrive here. The area is known for its truffles, which appear in various *bruschetta*, salads, pasta, and rice dishes—risotto with truffles is a regional specialty. The capital city of Perugia is famous for its chocolate and hosts the Eurochocolate festival each year.

LE MARCHE

Bordering the Adriatic Sea with the port city of Ancona as its capital, the Marches is a largely agricultural region of fruit and olive trees, grapes, vegetables, and wheat. While pasta is preferred over rice, a favorite regional dish is risotto with mushrooms. Other local specialties include a potato soup with greens and farro (the ancestor of modern wheat) and chestnut ravioli. The Marches is also known for its aniseed biscuits, made with the local aniseed liqueur called Mistà.

ROME AND THE LAZIO

Located in the center of Italy, the cooking of Rome and the Lazio is a delightful union of the cuisines of northern and southern Italy. Vegetables grow in profusion, and are often dressed with an *agrodolce*, or sweet and sour, sauce. *Carciofi alla Romana*, artichokes stewed with olive oil, garlic, and mint, and *carciofi alla giudea*, deep-fried artichokes, are two of the region's most famous dishes. Pasta dishes prevail, but gnocchi, polenta, and rice croquettes are widely eaten as well. Italian ices are the quintessential dessert for many Romans and tourists alike.

ABRUZZI AND THE MOLISE

Although situated between northern and southern Italy along the Adriatic Sea, the cooking of the Abruzzi and the Molise region belongs to the south, where pasta and olive oil rule. Hot peppers lend flavor to many dishes— pepper is even used in a local cookie called *pepatelli*. Chickpeas are so popular that there is a local dessert ravioli filled with chickpeas, chocolate, and walnuts.

CAMPANIA

The Campania region is one of the most beautiful and fertile regions in Italy, with the lively city of Naples, the birthplace of pizza, as its capital. Naples is also famous for its rich tomato sauces. *Alla Napoletana* usually signifies that a recipe contains such a sauce. Vegetables grow year-round, and some of Italy's most delicious vegetable dishes are made here. Pasta and gnocchi are immensely popular, as are *babas*, rum-soaked yeast cakes, and *zeppole*, fried pastry rings covered in powdered cinnamon sugar. The huge lemons of the Amalfi Coast are used to make Limoncello, a refreshing liqueur.

BASILICATA

Located between Campania and Calabria, Basilicata has an almost entirely mountainous terrain and is one of the poorest regions in Italy. Even so, citrus fruits, figs, nuts, olive trees, wine grapes, and wheat are grown at a sustainable level. The cuisine is simple and frugal, with fresh herbs, hot peppers, capers, and garlic used for flavoring. A favorite local dish is pasta with a spicy lentil sauce. Fresh, dried, or roasted figs are popular for dessert.

CALABRIA

With its rugged landscape and frequent water shortages, Calabria, once one of the wealthiest regions in Italy, now ranks among the poorest. Despite its poverty, almonds, artichokes, citrus fruits, eggplant, figs, grapes, olives, peppers, and tomatoes are grown by thrifty farmers and appear in many delectable regional dishes. Local favorites include *ciambatta*, a hearty vegetable stew, and tomatoes stuffed with pasta and mint.

APULIA

The easternmost region of Italy, Puglia, or Apulia as it is often called in English, is "the heel" of the Italian boot. Though poor, the region is a significant producer of olive oil, upon which the cuisine is based. Wheat is the major grain crop, and bread and pasta are staples. Artichokes, asparagus, citrus fruits, eggplant, fava beans, fennel, grapes, greens, melons, onions, and potatoes also grow well here. From Apulia comes *la capriata*, a bean puree served with cooked greens; *pizza rustica*, a two-crust pizza; and *tiella*, a layered potato, onion, and vegetable casserole.

SICILY

The largest of the Mediterranean islands, with Palermo as its capital, Sicily is the largest producer of citrus fruits in Italy and also grows a substantial amount of the country's wheat. Artichokes, broccoli, capers, eggplant, fennel, figs, grapes, nuts, peppers, tomatoes, and zucchini thrive here, and bread and pasta dishes are staples. Sicily offers *caponata*, the famous sweet-and-sour eggplant, celery, and olive appetizer, and *impanata*, a delicious bread pie stuffed with spinach or broccoli. It is also renowned for its almond marzipan pastries called *frutta de martorana* (or *pasta reale*), which are colored and shaped to resemble real fruit, and Marsala wine, a fortified dessert wine used frequently in cooking.

SARDINIA

Another Mediterranean island, Sardinia is only slightly smaller than Sicily yet considerably less populated. Artichokes, cauliflower, eggplant, fava beans, nuts, peas, tomatoes, and fruits of various kinds grow well here. Gnocchi flavored with saffron, and ravioli stuffed with spinach are regional specialties. Sardinia is also known for its cauliflower soups, vegetable *tortas*, and sweet pastries.

About the Ingredients

As this is an authentic Italian cookbook, no tofu or other food substitutes are required for any of the recipes. Fortunately, there are many meat-free, egg-free, and dairy-free dishes that are eaten each and every day throughout Italy, particularly in the south where vegetables and olive oil rule, and in the poorer regions where frugality is an economic necessity. Therefore, you will not find a recipe for mock veal scaloppini or eggplant Parmesan among these pages. Instead, you will find lots of naturally vegan dishes that are good for you and delicious to boot. But should you decide every now and again to sprinkle a cheese substitute on your pasta or add one to your pesto, vegan cheese substitutes are not recommended, as they do not melt well. Unfortunately, the only acceptable cheese substitutes contain casein, a milk derivative.

About the Nutritional Numbers

All of the nutritional analyses in this book were compiled using MasterCook Deluxe 4.06 Software, from SierraHome. However, as certain ingredients (potato gnocchi, *caponata*) were unknown to the software at the time of compilation, substitutes of equivalent caloric and nutritional value were used in their place. Also, approximations based on the analysis of total ingredients used have been given for a few of the recipes, namely the Caramelized Vegetable Broth on page 15, whose solid ingredients are overwhelmingly discarded after cooking.

All of the recipes using broth have been analyzed using canned low-sodium vegetable broth. All the recipes using rinsed and drained canned beans have been analyzed using freshly cooked dried beans. Unless salt is listed as a measured ingredient (versus to taste, with no preceding suggested measurement) in the recipe, or unless otherwise indicated, no salt has been included in the analysis; this applies to other seasonings (black pepper, cayenne) as well. None of the recipes' optional ingredients, unless otherwise indicated, have been included in the nutritional analyses. If there is a choice of two or more ingredients in a recipe (for example, arugula or spinach), the first ingredient has been used in the analysis. Likewise, if there is a choice in the amounts of a particular ingredient in a recipe (for example, 1 to 2 tablespoons pine nuts), the first amount has been used in the analysis. If there is a range in the number of servings a recipe yields (for example, 4 to 6 main-dish servings), the analysis has been based on the first amount.

Appetizers

Italian cuisine offers some of the tastiest appetizers around. From Asparagus Bruschetta to Zucchini a Scapici, *antipasto*, which literally means "before the meal," is meant to tease the palate as well as appeal to the eyes and prepare the stomach for the other courses to come. Despite the literal translation, you don't need to serve dinner to enjoy these delectable little dishes. Indeed, *antipasti* are so diverse and numerous that they can also become the meal—often a delicious option for vegetarians when dining at an Italian restaurant. But if about to sit down to a typical supper, Italian families wouldn't serve too many and risk spoiling the appetite—just two or three offerings would suffice. While probably no two Italian cooks would agree on the best antipasto plate to prepare, most would agree that it should incorporate fresh seasonal fruits and vegetables whenever possible and that it should complement the planned meal. Everyone would agree that, as with all great culinary art, less is more. When you have a vine-ripened tomato, garden-fresh basil, and extra-virgin olive oil, all you need is some garlic-rubbed bread to create a memorable *antipasto*. *Basta* (that's enough).

Artichoke Hearts with Garlic, Olive Oil, and Mint

MAKES 4 TO 6 SERVINGS

Serve this popular Roman antipasto with cocktail forks or in small bowls accompanied by crusty bread. It is also wonderful tossed with rice or orzo.

3 tablespoons extra-virgin olive oil
4 large cloves garlic, chopped
2 tablespoons finely chopped fresh mint
1 (12-ounce) package frozen artichoke hearts, thawed
¼ cup low-sodium vegetable broth
2 tablespoons dry white wine (optional)
Salt and freshly ground black pepper, to taste

In a large nonstick skillet with a lid, heat the oil over medium heat. Add the garlic and 1 table-spoon of the mint; cook, stirring constantly, until garlic starts to sizzle but is not browned, about 1 minute. Add the artichokes and stir to coat. Add the broth, wine (if using), salt, and pepper; bring to a brisk simmer over medium-high heat. Reduce the heat to low and simmer, covered, until the artichokes are tender, about 10 minutes. Uncover and cook over medium heat, stirring occasionally, until the juices thicken and coat the artichokes, 2 to 3 minutes.

Transfer to a serving bowl and let cool to room temperature. (At this point, the mixture may be covered and refrigerated up to 2 days before returning to room temperature and serving.) Sprinkle with the remaining mint and serve.

PER SERVING
Calories 130 ■ Protein 3g ■ Total Fat 11g ■
Sat. Fat 2g ■ Cholesterol 0mg ■ Carbohydrate 8g ■
Dietary Fiber 4g ■ Sodium 74mg

Crostini with Artichokes and Hearts of Palm

MAKES 4 TO 6 SERVINGS

Perfect for carefree entertaining, this sophisticated crostini topping can be made several days in advance and stored, covered, in the refrigerator before returning to room temperature and serving. To turn this into a bruschetta, use toasted slices of Italian bread, rubbed on one side with a halved clove of garlic, instead of the baguette rounds.

½ cup marinated quartered artichoke hearts, drained and 1 tablespoon marinade reserved
½ cup canned sliced hearts of palm, drained
2 tablespoons cocktail onions, drained
1 tablespoon extra-virgin olive oil
1 teaspoon fresh lemon juice
½ teaspoon dried thyme leaves
½ teaspoon coarse salt
¼ teaspoon freshly ground black pepper
Baguette rounds or slices Italian bread, toasted (see Cook's Tip, page 4), halved crosswise, to serve

Place the artichokes, hearts of palm, onions, reserved artichoke marinade, olive oil, lemon juice, thyme, salt, and pepper in a food processor fitted with the knife blade; pulse until smooth but slightly chunky. Serve at room temperature, accompanied by the toasted bread.

PER SERVING (WITHOUT BREAD)

Calories 78 ■ Protein 1g ■ Total Fat 7g ■ Sat. Fat 1g ■
Cholesterol 0mg ■ Carbohydrate 4g ■
Dietary Fiber 2g ■ Sodium 345mg

Roman-Style Marinated Broccoli

MAKES 4 TO 6 APPETIZER OR SIDE-DISH SERVINGS

Called *flammifero*, which means matches, this marinated appetizer from Rome typically calls for raw broccoli stalks cut into thin, matchstick-size pieces. Ready-made broccoli slaw is an ideal time-saving substitute.

- **12 ounces broccoli slaw**
- **6 ounces plum tomatoes (about 3 medium), chopped**
- **¼ cup extra-virgin olive oil**
- **1 tablespoon red wine vinegar**
- **1 tablespoon fresh lemon juice**
- **1 teaspoon sugar**
- **¼ teaspoon coarse salt, or to taste**
- **Freshly ground black pepper, to taste**

Place all ingredients in a large bowl; toss well to combine. Cover and refrigerate 3 hours or up to 2 days, and serve chilled.

PER SERVING

Calories 148 ■ Protein 2g ■ Total Fat 14g ■
Sat. Fat 2g ■ Cholesterol 0mg ■ Carbohydrate 6g ■
Dietary Fiber 2g ■ Sodium 135mg

Asparagus Bruschetta

MAKES 6 SERVINGS

This is a lovely bruschetta to serve in the spring, when asparagus is in season. The optional white truffle oil is available in gourmet markets and specialty shops.

- **1 pound medium asparagus, trimmed**
- **2 tablespoons extra-virgin olive oil**
- **½ teaspoon coarse salt, or to taste**
- **Freshly ground black pepper, to taste**
- **2 tablespoons balsamic vinegar**
- **1 to 2 teaspoons white truffle oil (optional)**
- **6 large slices Italian bread (about 1¼ ounces each), preferably Tuscan pane**
- **1 clove garlic, halved**

Preheat the oven to 425F (220C).

Place the asparagus on a baking sheet with sides and toss with the olive oil, salt, and pepper. Roast 10 to 15 minutes, or until tender and lightly browned, turning once or twice. Remove from oven and toss with the vinegar and truffle oil (if using). Let cool to room temperature, and then cut into ½-inch pieces.

Toast the bread (see Cook's Tip, page 4) and rub each slice on one side with the garlic while still hot. Place equal portions of asparagus on each bread slice, garlic rubbed–side up. Serve at room temperature.

PER SERVING

Calories 140 ■ Protein 4g ■ Total Fat 6g ■ Sat. Fat 1g ■
Cholesterol 0mg ■ Carbohydrate 19g ■
Dietary Fiber 2g ■ Sodium 351mg

PER SERVING (WITHOUT BREAD)
Calories 115 ■ Protein 6g ■ Total Fat 4g ■
Sat. Fat 1g ■ Cholesterol 0mg ■ Carbohydrate 15g ■
Dietary Fiber 5g ■ Sodium 23mg

Apulian-Style Bruschetta with Cherry Tomatoes and Basil

MAKES 16 SERVINGS

This peasant-style bruschetta from Apulia is the perfect choice for serving a crowd. If halving the recipe, store the unused bread loaf half in the freezer for up to one month. Trader Joe's rustic *pane bello* is excellent here.

- 1 round or oblong loaf Italian bread (about 16 ounces), sliced horizontally in half
- 1 clove garlic, halved
- 2 cups (1 pint) cherry tomatoes, preferably vine-ripened, cut into eighths
- ½ cup loosely packed fresh basil leaves, finely chopped
- ¼ cup extra-virgin olive oil
- 1 teaspoon salt, preferably the coarse variety, or to taste
- Freshly ground black pepper, to taste

Preheat the oven to 350F (175C).

Place the bread halves, cut sides up, on the center rack and bake 15 minutes, or until crispy and golden, taking care that the bread doesn't burn. While still warm, rub the top of each half with a halved garlic clove. Set aside to cool.

Meanwhile, add the tomatoes, basil, oil, salt, and pepper to a medium bowl; toss well to com-

Italian-Style Butter Bean Dip

MAKES 4 SERVINGS

This is a simple yet delicious party spread. Use baby lima beans if butter beans are not available. The recipe easily doubles or triples to serve a crowd.

- 1 (16-ounce) can butter beans, rinsed and drained
- 1 tablespoon extra-virgin olive oil
- ½ tablespoon fresh lemon juice
- Salt and freshly ground black pepper, to taste
- 1 to 2 tablespoons chopped red onion
- 1 to 2 tablespoons chopped green and/or black olives
- Baguette rounds or slices Italian bread, toasted (see Cook's Tip above), halved crosswise, to serve

Process the beans, oil, lemon juice, salt, and pepper in a food processor fitted with the knife blade, or in a blender, until smooth. Transfer to a serving dish and garnish with the onion and olives. Serve at room temperature, accompanied by the bread.

bine. Let stand about 10 minutes to allow the flavors to blend; toss again. Distribute the tomatoes and their dressing evenly over the top of the bread halves. Cut each bread half into 8 wedges. Serve within 1 hour.

PER SERVING
Calories 113 ■ Protein 3g ■ Total Fat 5g ■ Sat. Fat 1g ■
Cholesterol 0mg ■ Carbohydrate 16g ■
Dietary Fiber 1g ■ Sodium 286mg

Cherry Tomato and Roasted Red Pepper Bruschetta

MAKES 4 SERVINGS

For a delicious side dish, toss the bruschetta topping with sautéed zucchini or steamed green beans.

1 (7.25-ounce) jar roasted red bell peppers, drained and chopped
1 cup cherry tomatoes, chopped
¼ cup finely chopped fresh basil leaves
1 tablespoon extra-virgin olive oil
1 large clove garlic, finely chopped
½ teaspoon balsamic or red wine vinegar
Salt, preferably the coarse variety, and freshly ground black pepper, to taste
Slices Italian bread, toasted (see Cook's Tip, opposite page), rubbed on one side with a halved clove garlic, to serve

In a medium bowl, toss all the ingredients except the bread until thoroughly combined. Let stand about 15 minutes at room temperature to allow the flavors to blend. Toss again and serve at room

temperature, accompanied by the bread. Alternatively, the topping can be covered and refrigerated up to 24 hours before returning to room temperature and serving.

PER SERVING (WITHOUT BREAD)
Calories 57 ■ Protein 1g ■ Total Fat 4g ■ Sat. Fat 1g ■
Cholesterol 0mg ■ Carbohydrate 6g ■
Dietary Fiber 2g ■ Sodium 6mg

Eggplant and Black Olive Crostini

MAKES 4 SERVINGS

This tangy eggplant and black olive spread is also tasty tossed with steamed asparagus.

1½ cups water
½ cup red wine vinegar
2 peppercorns
1 bay leaf
1 clove garlic, peeled
¼ teaspoon salt, plus additional to taste
1 cup cubed, peeled eggplant
¾ cup pitted kalamata or other good-quality black olives
2 tablespoons extra-virgin olive oil
Freshly ground black pepper, to taste
Baguette rounds or slices Italian bread, toasted (see Cook's Tip, opposite page), halved crosswise, to serve

Combine the water, vinegar, peppercorns, bay leaf, garlic, and ¼ teaspoon salt in a medium saucepan. Bring to a boil over high heat; reduce heat and simmer, uncovered, 15 minutes. Add the eggplant and return to a boil over medium-high heat; reduce heat to medium and cook, stirring occasionally, until eggplant is tender when pierced with a knife, about 3 minutes. Drain well, then pat dry between paper towels. Let cool slightly.

Place the eggplant, olives, oil, salt, and pepper in a food processor fitted with the knife blade. Pulse until combined but slightly chunky. Serve at room temperature, accompanied by the toasted bread.

PER SERVING (WITHOUT BREAD)
Calories 107 ▪ Protein 1g ▪ Total Fat 10g ▪
Sat. Fat 1g ▪ Cholesterol 0mg ▪ Carbohydrate 6g ▪
Dietary Fiber 2g ▪ Sodium 490mg

Marinated Grilled Eggplant

MAKES 6 SERVINGS

A scapici essentially refers to an ancient Italian technique of marinating very thin slices of meat, fish, or vegetables in olive oil and vinegar or lemon juice. Grilled eggplant strips prepared in this simple fashion are meltingly tender, and a Sicilian favorite. Here, rolled up and secured with toothpicks, accompanied with cherry tomatoes and assorted olives, they are the stars of an easy yet impressive summertime *antipasti* platter.

1 (1-pound) eggplant
Salt
4 tablespoons extra-virgin olive oil
2 teaspoons fresh lemon juice
2 teaspoons red wine vinegar
1 clove garlic, finely chopped
Dried oregano, to taste
Freshly ground black pepper, to taste
Cherry tomatoes (optional)
Assorted olives (optional)

Trim both ends of the eggplant and stand upright on the flattest end. Remove a thin slice of skin from two opposite sides and discard. Cut lengthwise into 2 equal halves. Place one half, cut side down, on a cutting board. With one hand resting on top of eggplant, cut lengthwise into 4 equal slices with a large sharp knife. Repeat with other half. (You should have a total of 8 long eggplant slices about ½ inch in thickness.) Sprinkle the eggplant slices liberally with salt, and place in a colander to drain for 30 minutes. Rinse under cold-running water and drain well between paper towels.

Meanwhile, prepare a medium-hot charcoal or gas grill, or preheat a broiler. If broiling, position oven rack 4 inches from heat source; lightly oil a large baking sheet and set aside. Alternatively, place a stovetop grilling pan with grids over medium-high heat.

Brush both sides of the eggplant evenly with half of the oil. If broiling, arrange eggplant on the prepared baking sheet. Otherwise, place eggplant directly on the grill. Grill or broil until lightly browned, 2 to 3 minutes per side; if grilling, rotate clockwise with a wide metal spatula a few times on each side to prevent scorch marks. Remove from heat source and transfer to a work surface.

Remove the skin from the eggplant (it should peel off rather easily), and cut the flesh into long thin strips about ½ inch in width. Place in a long shallow dish. Combine the remaining oil, lemon juice, vinegar, and garlic in a small pouring jar; drizzle over the eggplant. Season with oregano and pepper (do not add salt). Turn the eggplant gently in the marinade a few times. Cover and let marinate at room temperature a minimum of 30 minutes, or up to 1 hour, turning occasionally. (Alternatively, cover and refrigerate up to 2 days before returning to room temperature and proceeding.) Shortly before serving, roll each strip up, securing with toothpicks. Transfer to a serving plate and serve at room temperature, garnished with the cherry tomatoes and olives (if using).

PER SERVING
Calories 97 ■ Protein 1g ■ Total Fat 9g ■
Sat. Fat 1 ■ Cholesterol 0mg ■
Carbohydrate 4g ■ Dietary Fiber 2g ■ Sodium 2mg

VARIATION: *To make Zucchini a Scapici: Substitute 2 (8-ounce) zucchini for the eggplant, slicing each one lengthwise into 4 equal strips, but omit salting before cooking. Season with salt and pepper after cooking.*

❧ COOK'S TIP ❧

Salting the eggplant before cooking is highly recommended in this particular recipe. The rapid cooking over high heat tends to concentrate the eggplant's natural bitterness in its surface; salting will draw out much of this acerbity. For another method that is longer but won't tie up your kitchen sink, place the liberally salted eggplant slices in a bowl and add water to cover. Set a plate inside the bowl and weight with a large can of tomatoes to hold all the eggplant slices under the water. Set aside 1 to 2 hours before draining and drying well between paper towels.

Crostini with Garlic Cream

MAKES 4 SERVINGS

Of course, there's no cream here, just creamy roasted garlic puree. The puree is also delicious spread over grilled eggplant slices.

2 large heads garlic
1 tablespoon extra-virgin olive oil

⅛ **teaspoon dried thyme leaves**
Salt and freshly ground black pepper, to taste
½ **teaspoon fresh thyme leaves (optional)**
Baguette rounds or slices Italian bread, toasted (see Cook's Tip, page 4), halved crosswise, to serve

Preheat oven to 400F (205C).

Wrap the heads of garlic in aluminum foil and roast 45 to 50 minutes, or until soft. Remove the foil and set the garlic aside to cool slightly. Peel the cloves and transfer to a food processor fitted with the knife blade. Add the oil, dried thyme, salt, and pepper, and process until smooth and pureed. Transfer the mixture to a small serving bowl or crock. (At this point, the mixture can be stored, covered, in the refrigerator up to 3 days.) Sprinkle with the fresh thyme leaves (if using). Serve at room temperature, accompanied by the toasted bread.

PER SERVING (WITHOUT BREAD)
Calories 60 ■ Protein 1g ■ Total Fat 4g ■ Sat. Fat 1g ■
Cholesterol 0mg ■ Carbohydrate 7g ■
Dietary Fiber 0g ■ Sodium 3mg

Marinated Olives

MAKES 12 SERVINGS

Straight from the pantry, this tangy appetizer is always a crowd-pleaser.

⅓ cup extra-virgin olive oil

¼ cup white wine vinegar

½ tablespoon garlic powder

1 teaspoon dried basil

1 teaspoon dried thyme leaves

1 teaspoon sugar

½ teaspoon dried oregano

¼ teaspoon fennel seed

Freshly ground black pepper, to taste

3 cups assorted pitted olives, drained

In a medium bowl, whisk together all the ingredients, except the olives, until thoroughly blended. Add the olives and toss well to coat. Cover and refrigerate a minimum of 8 hours or up to 5 days, stirring occasionally. Let come to room temperature before serving.

PER SERVING
Calories 155 ▪ Protein 0g ▪ Total Fat 16g ▪
Sat. Fat 1g ▪ Cholesterol 0mg ▪ Carbohydrate 4g ▪
Dietary Fiber 0g ▪ Sodium 619mg

Sautéed Olives

MAKES 10 TO 12 SERVINGS

Here is a quick and delicious appetizer you can make using fresh herbs in the warm-weather months or the dried varieties any time of the year.

2 tablespoons extra-virgin olive oil

1 teaspoon chopped fresh oregano leaves, or
¼ teaspoon dried

1 teaspoon whole fresh thyme leaves, or ¼
teaspoon dried

Pinch crushed red pepper flakes, or to taste

2 cups pitted gaeta, kalamata, or other good-
quality black olives, drained

In a large nonstick skillet, heat the oil over medium heat. Add the oregano, thyme, and red pepper flakes; cook, stirring, 1 minute. Add the olives and cook, stirring, until heated through, about 3 minutes. Serve warm, with wooden picks.

PER SERVING
Calories 150 ▪ Protein 0g ▪ Total Fat 15g ▪
Sat. Fat 0g ▪ Cholesterol 0mg ▪ Carbohydrate 3g ▪
Dietary Fiber 0g ▪ Sodium 754mg

⸰ COOK'S TIP ⸰
For easy olive pitting, place each olive on its side and place the flat side of a large knife over top; using your palm, strike the knife swiftly—the olive usually splits in half and the pit pops out.

Roasted Bell Peppers

MAKES 6 SERVINGS

An Italian cookbook wouldn't seem complete without including a recipe for roasted bell peppers, arguably the most popular antipasto of all. For a hotter variation, you can add some seeded and chopped pepperoncini to the seasonings.

> **4 large bell peppers (about 8 ounces each), preferably 2 red and 2 green, cored, seeded, and ribbed, each cut into sixths or eighths**
> **½ cup finely chopped fresh flat-leaf parsley**
> **¼ cup extra-virgin olive oil**
> **2 cloves garlic, finely chopped**
> **Salt, preferably the coarse variety, and freshly ground black pepper, to taste**

Preheat the oven to broil. Position the oven rack 4 inches from heat source. Lightly oil a large baking sheet.

Place bell peppers, skin sides up, on the baking sheet; flatten peppers with your hand. Broil until skins are partially charred and puffy, about 5 minutes. Transfer to a paper bag and twist to seal. Alternatively, place in a self-sealing plastic bag and seal. Let rest 15 to 20 minutes.

Remove bell peppers from bag; peel away and discard the skins. Slice lengthwise into ½-inch wide strips. Transfer pepper strips to a large bowl and toss with the remaining ingredients. Let stand 15 minutes at room temperature to allow the flavors to blend. Toss again and serve at room temperature. Alternatively, cover and refrigerate a minimum of 3 hours, or up to 2 days, and serve chilled or return to room temperature.

PER SERVING
Calories 116 ▪ Protein 1g ▪ Total Fat 9g ▪ Sat. Fat 1g ▪ Cholesterol 0mg ▪ Carbohydrate 9g ▪ Dietary Fiber 2g ▪ Sodium 5mg

Sicilian Olive Salad

MAKES 8 SERVINGS

This antipasto is especially popular with fans of green olives. Caperberries can be found in most major supermarkets next to the capers. If unavailable, substitute with the latter.

> **2½ cups pitted large green olives (about 1 pound), drained**
> **3 stalks celery, thinly sliced**
> **1 medium carrot (about 4 ounces), thinly sliced**
> **1 small red onion (about 4 ounces), thinly sliced**
> **1 large clove garlic, finely chopped**
> **½ cup caperberries, drained**
> **1 teaspoon dried oregano**
> **½ teaspoon freshly ground black pepper, or to taste**
> **½ cup extra-virgin olive oil**

In a medium bowl, toss all ingredients until well combined. Cover and marinate in the refrigerator 1 to 3 days, stirring occasionally. Return to room temperature before serving.

PER SERVING
Calories 183 ▪ Protein 1g ▪ Total Fat 18g ▪ Sat. Fat 2g ▪ Cholesterol 0mg ▪ Carbohydrate 6g ▪ Dietary Fiber 1g ▪ Sodium 456mg

Sautéed Red Bell Peppers with Olives and Capers

MAKES 6 SERVINGS

Popular throughout southern Italy, this simple yet versatile dish can be served cold or at room temperature as an antipasto, or warm as a side dish.

- ¼ cup extra-virgin olive oil
- 6 large red bell peppers (about 8 ounces each), cored, seeded, ribbed, and quartered
- ¼ cup pitted good-quality black olives, such as kalamata
- 3 tablespoons capers, drained
- 1 large clove garlic, finely chopped
- Salt and freshly ground black pepper, to taste
- Pinch cayenne pepper, or to taste (optional)
- 1 to 2 tablespoons finely chopped fresh flat-leaf parsley

In a large nonstick skillet, heat the oil over medium heat until hot. Add the bell peppers and cook, stirring, until softened but not colored, about 5 minutes. Add the olives, capers, and garlic; reduce heat to medium-low and cook, stirring, until bell peppers are lightly colored, 5 to 6 minutes. Season with salt, black pepper, and cayenne (if using).

Serve warm, chilled, or at room temperature. (Completely cooled peppers can be refrigerated, covered, up to 2 days before serving chilled or returning to room temperature.) Sprinkle with parsley just before serving.

PER SERVING
Calories 149 ▪ Protein 2g ▪ Total Fat 10g ▪ Sat. Fat 1g ▪ Cholesterol 0mg ▪ Carbohydrate 15g ▪ Dietary Fiber 5g ▪ Sodium 93mg

Pinzimonio

MAKES 6 TO 8 SERVINGS

Pinzimonio is a classic springtime antipasto that is usually served with very young vegetables, but any fresh veggies can be used here. The following list is more a suggestion than a recipe.

- ½ cup extra-virgin olive oil, in a cruet
- ½ cup red wine vinegar, in a cruet
- Coarse salt, to taste
- Freshly ground black pepper, to taste
- 6 cups fresh vegetables (cauliflower, broccoli, bell peppers, carrots, celery, cherry tomatoes, radishes), cut into bite-size pieces or strips

Set the cruets of olive oil and vinegar on the table, along with the coarse salt and pepper. Provide each guest with a small bowl in which to create a sauce with the olive oil and vinegar, seasoning with the salt and pepper. Serve with the vegetables for dipping.

PER SERVING
Calories 205 ▪ Protein 2g ▪ Total Fat 19g ▪ Sat. Fat 3g ▪ Cholesterol 0mg ▪ Carbohydrate 11g ▪ Dietary Fiber 2g ▪ Sodium 44mg

Polenta Canapés with Black Olive and Sun-Dried Tomato Paste

MAKES 18 APPETIZERS

I use Trader Joe's cooked organic polenta to make these savory canapés, which can be assembled and refrigerated up to one day before baking for easy entertaining.

1 cup pitted kalamata, gaeta, or other good-quality black olives
¼ cup marinated sun-dried tomatoes, drained and chopped, and ½ tablespoon marinade reserved
1 large clove garlic, finely chopped
Freshly ground black pepper, to taste
1 (18-ounce) package cooked polenta
9 small pimiento-stuffed green olives, halved

Preheat the oven to 350F (175C). Lightly oil a baking sheet and set aside.

In a food processor fitted with the knife blade, process the black olives, tomatoes, reserved marinade, garlic, and black pepper until a smooth paste forms.

Cut the polenta into 18 slices, about ⅓ inch in thickness. Arrange on the prepared baking sheet and spread each slice with equal portions (about ½ tablespoon) of the olive mixture. Top each with half a green olive. Bake 30 minutes. Serve hot.

PER CANAPÉ
Calories 36 ▪ Protein 1g ▪ Total Fat 2g ▪ Sat. Fat 0g ▪
Cholesterol 0mg ▪ Carbohydrate 5g ▪
Dietary Fiber 1g ▪ Sodium 134mg

Polenta Crostini with Pesto

MAKES 24 PIECES

These tasty crostini are terrific party appetizers, as they can be assembled and refrigerated a day before baking.

3 cups low-sodium vegetable broth
1½ cups polenta or coarse-ground yellow cornmeal
½ tablespoon extra-virgin olive oil
2 large cloves garlic, finely chopped
Salt and freshly ground black pepper, to taste
1 recipe Ligurian Basil Pesto (page 71)

Lightly oil a 13 × 9-inch baking pan and set aside.

In a large stockpot, bring the broth to a boil over high heat. Slowly add the polenta, stirring constantly with a long-handled wooden spoon. Reduce the heat to low and add the oil, garlic, salt, and pepper, stirring well to combine. Cover and cook, stirring occasionally, until polenta is tender, about 15 minutes. Remove from heat and let stand, covered, 5 minutes.

Preheat the oven to 350F (175C).

Spread the polenta mixture evenly in the prepared baking pan. Let stand until firm, 20 minutes. Spread evenly with the pesto. Transfer to center rack of oven and bake 15 minutes, or until just heated. Cut into 24 squares and serve at once.

PER CROSTINI
Calories 78 ▪ Protein 3g ▪ Total Fat 4g ▪ Sat. Fat 1g ▪
Cholesterol 0mg ▪ Carbohydrate 9g ▪
Dietary Fiber 2g ▪ Sodium 105mg

Radicchio Strudel

MAKES 6 TO 12 SERVINGS

Serve this savory strudel from Friuli as an impressive first course for six to eight or as an appealing appetizer for up to twelve. Chopped fresh fennel can be substituted for half of the radicchio, if desired.

2 tablespoons extra-virgin olive oil

1 small red onion (4 ounces), finely chopped

2 medium heads radicchio (about 5 ounces each), cored and chopped

2 cloves garlic, finely chopped

Salt and freshly ground black pepper, to taste

½ (about 17-ounce) package frozen puff pastry (1 sheet), thawed according to package directions

Preheat the oven to 375F (190C).

In a large nonstick skillet, heat the oil over medium heat. Add the onion and cook, stirring, until softened, about 3 minutes. Add the radicchio and cook, stirring frequently, until tender and wilted, about 8 minutes, adding the garlic the last few minutes of cooking. Remove from the heat and season with salt and pepper. Let cool slightly.

Unfold pastry onto an ungreased baking sheet. Line the middle third of pastry with half the radicchio filling. Fold the third of the pastry to your left over the filling; line with remaining filling. Fold the third of the pastry to your right as far over to the other side as it will comfortably stretch, pressing the dough together where it meets to seal. (Do not seal the ends.) Cut about 6 (1-inch long) slits across the top. Bake in center of oven about 25 minutes, or until golden. Cool on baking sheet on wire rack 15 minutes. Serve warm.

PER SERVING
Calories 258 ▪ Protein 4g ▪ Total Fat 16g ▪ Sat. Fat 3g ▪ Cholesterol 0mg ▪ Carbohydrate 27g ▪ Dietary Fiber 3g ▪ Sodium 145mg

Crostini with Rapini and Cannellini Beans

MAKES 6 SERVINGS

This topping is also delicious over polenta and makes an excellent pasta sauce, as well. Rapini (see Cook's Tip, opposite page), a cruciferous green rich in cancer-fighting antioxidants, is available at Italian grocers, health-food stores, gourmet markets, and, increasingly, major supermarkets. Broccoli can be substituted, if desired.

1 large bunch rapini (about 1 pound), rinsed, trimmed, and coarsely chopped

1 tablespoon extra-virgin olive oil

1 medium onion (about 6 ounces), chopped

2 cloves garlic, finely chopped

4 to 5 large plum tomatoes (about 3 ounces each), chopped

1 tablespoon balsamic vinegar

Salt and freshly ground black pepper, to taste

1 (19-ounce) can cannellini or other white beans, rinsed and drained

Baguette rounds or slices Italian bread, toasted (see Cook's Tip, page 4), halved crosswise, to serve

Boil the rapini in a large stockpot filled with boiling, salted water, 3 minutes. Drain in a colander and immediately rinse under cold-running water. Drain well, pressing with the back of a wooden spoon to remove excess water.

In a large deep-sided nonstick skillet, heat the oil over medium heat. Add the onion and garlic and cook, stirring, until softened but not browned, about 3 minutes. Stir in the tomatoes, vinegar, salt, and pepper; bring to a gentle simmer over medium-high heat. Reduce the heat and simmer, uncovered, 10 minutes, stirring occasionally. Stir in the rapini and beans and cook until rapini is tender and beans are heated through, 3 minutes.

Serve at once, accompanied by the toasted baguette rounds.

PER SERVING (WITHOUT BREAD)
Calories 148 ▪ Protein 9g ▪ Total Fat 3g ▪ Sat. Fat 0g ▪
Cholesterol 0mg ▪ Carbohydrate 24g ▪
Dietary Fiber 9g ▪ Sodium 30mg

◦⁘ COOK'S TIP ⁘◦

When shopping for rapini, also known as broccoli rabe, broccoli di rape, or broccoletti, select only bunches with firm, small stems and bright green leaves and buds. Unlike broccoli, whose leaves and most of the stems are discarded before cooking, rapini is essentially cooked in its entirety, with only discolored leaves and tough stem ends thrown away. As a rule of thumb, any stem much thicker than a pencil should be discarded when trimming the rapini.

Sicilian-Style Tomato Spread

MAKES 4 SERVINGS

This simple topping of tomato paste dressed up with fresh herbs is delicious spread on toasted baguette rounds, bread sticks, or a crusty Italian loaf. It can be stored, covered, in the refrigerator up to one week.

½ **cup tomato paste**
1 **tablespoon extra-virgin olive oil**
1 **teaspoon red wine vinegar**
1 **teaspoon capers, drained (optional)**
1 **large clove garlic, finely chopped**
½ **teaspoon chopped fresh thyme leaves**
¼ **teaspoon chopped fresh oregano leaves**
Salt, preferably the coarse variety, and freshly ground black pepper, to taste
Baguette rounds or slices Italian bread, toasted (see Cook's Tip, page 4), halved crosswise, or bread sticks, to serve

Place all ingredients (except the bread) in a small bowl and stir until thoroughly blended. Transfer to a small crock and serve at room temperature, accompanied by the bread rounds.

PER SERVING (WITHOUT BREAD)
Calories 59 ▪ Protein 1g ▪ Total Fat 4g ▪ Sat. Fat 1g ▪
Cholesterol 0mg ▪ Carbohydrate 7g ▪
Dietary Fiber 2g ▪ Sodium 259mg

Soups

The history of Italian soup is probably as old as the history of Italian cuisine. Since early Roman times, combining various ingredients in a large pot to create a nutritious, filling, digestible, simple-to-prepare, easy-to-serve food made it the perfect choice for both the rich and peasant classes, the healthy and the infirm. Cooking great Italian soups isn't hard, and it doesn't have to be time-consuming if you use canned vegetable broth. For the more ambitious, there is delicious Caramelized Vegetable Broth, which is suitable for use in all the recipes requiring low-sodium vegetable broth.

To help distinguish among the wide variety of Italian soups, *zuppe* are thick soups that do not contain pasta or rice, are not creamed, and are usually ladled over toasted bread or garnished with croutons. *Minestre* are vegetable soups that typically contain pasta, barley, or rice, and whose consistency can be light or thick. *Minestrine* are thin broths containing tiny pasta, such as pastina. *Minestrone* is thick vegetable soup often containing pasta or rice and served either with pesto, olive oil, or Parmesan cheese. *Passati* are pureed vegetable soups, generally thickened with potato or cream. But don't get too caught up in the distinctions—there's a soup for everyone among the following soul-warming recipes.

Light Soups

Caramelized Vegetable Broth

MAKES ABOUT 8 CUPS

This flavorful broth can be used throughout the book in any of the recipes requiring low-sodium vegetable broth. Add some tiny pasta such as pastina, and serve this on its own as a *minestrina*.

2 tablespoons extra-virgin olive oil

4 medium carrots (about 4 ounces each), cut into 3-inch lengths

3 large leeks (about 8 ounces each), white parts chopped, green tops reserved, coarsely chopped

3 large stalks celery, cut into 3-inch lengths, leaves reserved

2 large onions (about 8 ounces each), peeled and quartered

1 small turnip (about 4 ounces), peeled and quartered

3 large cloves garlic, peeled and halved

10 cups water

1 cup coarsely chopped fresh parsley, stems included

¼ cup coarsely chopped fresh thyme sprigs, stems included

1 tablespoon sugar

1 large bay leaf

¼ teaspoon whole black peppercorns

¼ teaspoon whole allspice

Salt and freshly ground black pepper, to taste

In a large stockpot, heat the oil over medium-low heat. Add the carrots, leeks, celery, onions, turnip,

and garlic; cook, covered, stirring occasionally, until vegetables are fragrant and softened, about 45 minutes. Uncover and increase heat to medium. Cook, stirring occasionally, about 15 minutes, or until vegetables are light golden and brown bits are forming on the bottom of the pot.

Add water and the remaining ingredients, including the reserved leek tops and reserved celery leaves. Bring to a boil over high heat, scrapping the bottom to release the browned bits. Reduce the heat and simmer gently, uncovered, 1½ hours, stirring occasionally.

Strain the stock into a bowl through a sieve or colander, pressing firmly on the solids to extract as much of the liquid as possible, then discard vegetables. Season with salt and pepper, to taste. Let cool to room temperature before covering and refrigerating up to 5 days, or transferring to freezer bags and storing in the freezer up to 3 months.

PER SERVING

Calories 78 ▪ Protein 1g ▪ Total Fat 4g ▪ Sat. Fat 1g ▪
Cholesterol 0mg ▪ Carbohydrate 11g ▪
Dietary Fiber 2g ▪ Sodium 27mg

Cauliflower Soup with Parsley

MAKES 6 SERVINGS

This garlicky cauliflower soup is particularly popular in the island of Sardinia. You can control its heat by adjusting the amount of crushed red pepper flakes, or omitting them entirely.

1 large head cauliflower (about 2 pounds), cored and separated into florets, cut into ½-inch pieces
¼ cup extra-virgin olive oil
4 large cloves garlic, finely chopped
¼ teaspoon crushed red pepper flakes, or to taste
4 cups low-sodium vegetable broth
½ teaspoon salt
Freshly ground black pepper, to taste
¼ cup finely chopped fresh flat-leaf parsley

Bring a medium stockpot filled with salted water to a boil over high heat. Add the cauliflower and cook until just tender, 4 to 5 minutes. Drain well and set aside.

Place the oil in the stockpot and heat over medium heat. Add the garlic and red pepper flakes and cook, stirring constantly, 1 minute. Reduce the heat to medium-low and add the cauliflower; cook, stirring often, until just beginning to brown, about 5 minutes. Add the broth, salt, and black pepper; bring to a boil over medium-high heat. Reduce the heat to low and simmer, covered, 10 minutes. Transfer about two-thirds of the soup to a food processor fitted with a knife blade, or to a blender. Process until smooth and pureed. Return mixture to the pot and stir in the parsley. Cook over low heat until heated through. Serve hot.

PER SERVING

Calories 155 ▪ Protein 11g ▪ Total Fat 9g ▪ Sat. Fat 1g ▪ Cholesterol 0mg ▪ Carbohydrate 10g ▪ Dietary Fiber 6g ▪ Sodium 570mg

VARIATIONS: *To make* **Cauliflower Soup with Pesto:** *Omit the parsley and prepare ½ recipe Ligurian Basil Pesto (page 71). Garnish each serving with an equal dollop of pesto.*

To make **Cauliflower Soup with Tomatoes:** *Add 1 (14.5-ounce) can stewed tomatoes with their juices when you add the broth.*

To make **Cauliflower Soup with Pasta and Tomatoes:** *Add 1 (14.5-ounce) can stewed tomatoes as directed above. Cook ½ cup small elbow macaroni or other similar pasta according to package directions until just al dente; add to the soup when you return the pureed mixture to the pot.*

Pizza Soup

MAKES 4 SERVINGS

This soup is wonderful served with Skillet Garlic Bread (page 138). If you don't have pizza seasoning, substitute with a combination of dried oregano and basil and a pinch of cayenne or crushed red pepper flakes.

2 tablespoons extra-virgin olive oil
1 cup chopped onion
1 cup chopped green bell pepper
1 cup sliced fresh mushrooms
2 large cloves garlic, finely chopped

2 cups low-sodium vegetable broth

1 (14.5-ounce) can diced tomatoes, juices included

1 (8-ounce) can pizza sauce

½ cup water

½ teaspoon pizza seasoning

Salt and freshly ground black pepper, to taste

In a medium stockpot, heat the oil over medium heat. Add the onion, bell pepper, and mushrooms; cook, stirring often, until softened, about 5 minutes. Add the garlic and cook, stirring constantly, 1 minute. Add the broth, tomatoes and their juices, pizza sauce, water, pizza seasoning, salt, and pepper; bring to a boil over medium-high heat. Reduce the heat and simmer, covered, stirring occasionally, until vegetables are tender, about 10 minutes. Serve warm.

PER SERVING

Calories 173 ▪ Protein 9g ▪ Total Fat 9g ▪ Sat. Fat 1g ▪
Cholesterol 0mg ▪ Carbohydrate 18g ▪
Dietary Fiber 4g ▪ Sodium 837mg

Chilled Tomato-Basil Soup

MAKES 4 SERVINGS

This is the quintessential summer soup. Serve with crusty bread and a tossed salad for a light but satisfying meal.

2½ pounds ripe tomatoes, peeled, seeded, and chopped

2 cups low-sodium vegetable broth

¼ cup finely chopped fresh basil

2 cloves garlic, finely chopped

1 teaspoon sugar

½ teaspoon salt

Freshly ground black pepper, to taste

2 tablespoons extra-virgin olive oil

1 tablespoon red wine vinegar

½ tablespoon balsamic vinegar

Whole basil leaves for garnish (optional)

Puree the tomatoes in a food processor fitted with the knife blade, or in a blender. Transfer to a large saucepan or medium stockpot and add the broth, chopped basil, garlic, sugar, salt, and pepper; bring to a brisk simmer over medium-high heat. Reduce the heat to low and simmer gently 20 minutes, stirring occasionally. Remove from heat and stir in the oil and vinegars. Let cool to room temperature. Cover and refrigerate a minimum of 4 hours, or up to 2 days. Serve chilled, garnished with the whole basil leaves (if using).

PER SERVING

Calories 147 ▪ Protein 8g ▪ Total Fat 8g ▪
Sat. Fat 1g ▪ Cholesterol 0mg ▪ Carbohydrate 15g ▪
Dietary Fiber 5g ▪ Sodium 549mg

Roasted Tomato Soup with Basil Puree

MAKES 4 SERVINGS

This *passata* is restaurant-quality soup, ideal to serve in the summer as a first course or light lunch with crusty Italian bread and a green salad. For an even lighter soup, omit the basil puree and garnish with freshly chopped basil instead.

> 6 large, ripe yet firm tomatoes (about 8 ounces each), peeled, cut in half
> 3 large cloves garlic, peeled, left whole
> Salt, preferably the coarse variety, and freshly ground black pepper, to taste
> 2 tablespoons extra-virgin olive oil
> 6 large basil leaves, torn in half
> 2 cups low-sodium vegetable broth
> 2 cups water
> 1 large russet potato (about 8 ounces), peeled and cut into chunks
> 1 tablespoon tomato paste
> Basil Puree (right)

Preheat the oven to 400F (205C). Lightly oil a shallow baking dish large enough to hold the tomatoes in a single layer.

Place the tomato halves, cut sides up, and the garlic in the prepared baking dish. Sprinkle with salt and pepper. Drizzle with the oil, and then top each tomato half with half a basil leaf, turning each piece of leaf over to coat with the oil. Bake 50 to 60 minutes, or until the edges of the tomato halves are slightly blackened.

Meanwhile, in a medium saucepan, bring the broth, water, potato, and tomato paste to a boil over high heat. Reduce the heat slightly and boil until the potato is tender, about 20 minutes. Transfer half of the mixture to a food processor fitted with the knife blade, or to a blender. Add half the roasted tomato mixture; process until smooth but still a bit chunky. Transfer to a medium stockpot. Repeat with remaining potato and roasted tomato mixture. Stir over medium-low heat until heated through. Serve hot, garnished with equal portions of basil puree.

PER SERVING
Calories 261 ▪ Protein 10g ▪ Total Fat 15g ▪ Sat. Fat 2g ▪
Cholesterol 0mg ▪ Carbohydrate 26g ▪
Dietary Fiber 6g ▪ Sodium 441mg

Basil Puree

MAKES ABOUT ⅓ CUP

A bit lighter than classic Ligurian Basil Pesto (page 71), basil puree can be used in the same way—as a sauce for pasta and vegetables, and garnish for countless soups.

> 1 cup packed fresh basil leaves
> 2 tablespoons extra-virgin olive oil
> 1 teaspoon balsamic vinegar
> ¼ teaspoon coarse salt
> Freshly ground black pepper, to taste

Process all the ingredients in a food processor fitted with knife blade until smooth. Serve at room temperature.

PER SERVING (ABOUT 4 TEASPOONS)
Calories 70 ▪ Protein 1g ▪ Total Fat 7g ▪ Sat. Fat 1g ▪
Cholesterol 0mg ▪ Carbohydrate 2g ▪
Dietary Fiber 0g ▪ Sodium 119mg

Tomato Florentine Soup

MAKES 6 SERVINGS

For a Milanese-style variation, substitute rice for the pasta. If fresh spinach is not available, use a 10-ounce package of frozen chopped spinach and add it along with the broth and tomatoes.

- **2 tablespoons extra-virgin olive oil**
- **1 small onion (about 4 ounces), finely chopped**
- **1 small carrot (about 2 ounces), finely chopped**
- **2 stalks celery, finely chopped**
- **3 large cloves garlic, finely chopped**
- **8 cups low-sodium vegetable broth**
- **2 (14.5-ounce) cans diced tomatoes, juices included**
- **1 teaspoon dried oregano**
- **1 teaspoon dried thyme leaves**
- **Salt and freshly ground black pepper, to taste**
- **1 cup ditalini or other small pasta**
- **1 (10-ounce) bag washed spinach leaves, coarsely chopped**
- **3 tablespoons chopped fresh basil**

In a large stockpot, heat the oil over medium heat. Add the onion, carrot, and celery and cook, stirring, until softened but not browned, 3 to 5 minutes. Add the garlic; cook, stirring constantly, 1 minute. Add the broth, tomatoes with their juices, oregano, thyme, salt, and pepper; bring to a boil over high heat.

Add the pasta and let return to a boil. Reduce the heat to medium and simmer, uncovered, stirring occasionally, until pasta is cooked al dente, about 10 minutes, adding the spinach and basil the last 5 minutes of cooking. Serve hot.

PER SERVING
Calories 225 ▪ Protein 20g ▪ Total Fat 5g ▪ Sat. Fat 1g ▪ Cholesterol 0mg ▪ Carbohydrate 27g ▪ Dietary Fiber 8g ▪ Sodium 1026mg

Tomato and Red Pepper Soup with Arugula

MAKES 4 SERVINGS

If desired, you can omit the arugula and this quick and easy first-course soup will still be quite delicious and nutritious.

- **1 tablespoon extra-virgin olive oil**
- **1 small onion (about 4 ounces), chopped**
- **1 stalk celery, chopped**
- **2 cloves garlic, finely chopped**
- **1 (28-ounce) can diced tomatoes, juices included**
- **2 cups low-sodium vegetable broth**
- **1 (6-ounce) jar sweet red pepper spread or puree (see Cook's Tip page 146)**
- **⅛ teaspoon crushed red pepper flakes, or to taste**
- **Pinch sugar, or more to taste (optional)**
- **Salt and freshly ground black pepper, to taste**
- **2 cups loosely packed arugula or baby spinach leaves, coarsely chopped**
- **Olive Croutons (page 34) or Herbed Croutons (page 45) (optional)**

In a medium stockpot, heat oil over medium heat. Add the onion and celery and cook, stirring, until softened but not browned, about 5 minutes. Add garlic and cook, stirring constantly, 1 minute. Add tomatoes and their juices, broth, red pepper spread, crushed red pepper flakes, sugar (if using), salt, and black pepper; bring to a brisk simmer over medium-high heat. Reduce the heat and simmer gently, uncovered, about 10 minutes, stirring occasionally, adding the arugula the last 5 minutes of cooking. Serve hot, with croutons (if using).

PER SERVING

Calories 127 ■ Protein 9g ■ Total Fat 4g ■ Sat. Fat 1g ■
Cholesterol 0mg ■ Carbohydrate 17g ■
Dietary Fiber 6g ■ Sodium 695mg

Meal-in-a-Bowl Soups

Barley Soup with Roasted Red Peppers and Mushrooms

MAKES 4 SERVINGS

This *minestra* is an excellent soup to serve in the fall when there's a nip in the air.

> 2 tablespoons extra-virgin olive oil
> 12 ounces fresh mushrooms, sliced
> 1 medium onion (about 6 ounces), chopped
> 2 large cloves garlic, finely chopped
> 3 cups low-sodium vegetable broth
> 1 (12-ounce) jar roasted red bell peppers, drained and chopped
> ½ cup quick-cooking barley
> 2 tablespoons finely chopped fresh sage, or 1 teaspoon dried ground sage
> Pinch cayenne pepper, or to taste (optional)
> Salt and freshly ground black pepper, to taste

In a medium stockpot, heat the oil over medium-low heat. Add the mushrooms and onion and cook, stirring often, until lightly browned, about 15 minutes, adding the garlic the last few minutes of cooking.

Add the broth, roasted peppers, barley, sage, cayenne (if using), salt, and black pepper; bring to a boil over high heat. Reduce the heat, cover, and simmer, stirring a few times, until the barley is tender, about 25 minutes. Serve hot.

Baked Vegetable Soup

MAKES 6 SERVINGS

From Abruzzi, this homey casserole-style *zuppa* is a meal in itself with a tossed green salad.

6 tablespoons extra-virgin olive oil

2 medium onions (about 6 ounces each), thinly sliced

2 large cloves garlic, finely chopped

½ teaspoon salt, preferably the coarse variety, plus additional to taste

¼ teaspoon dried oregano leaves

¼ teaspoon dried thyme leaves

Freshly ground black pepper, to taste

2 (15-ounce) cans sliced potatoes, rinsed and drained

2 medium tomatoes (about 6 ounces each), thinly sliced

1 (12-ounce) jar roasted red bell peppers, drained and cut into 1-inch wide strips

1 large zucchini (about 8 ounces), thinly sliced

2 cups low-sodium vegetable broth

6 pieces Italian bread (about 6 ounces), lightly toasted (see Cook's Tip, page 4)

Preheat oven to 350F (175C). Lightly oil an 11 × 7-inch casserole.

In a large nonstick skillet, heat 2 tablespoons of the oil over medium heat. Add the onions and cook, stirring, until softened, about 5 minutes. Add the garlic, salt, oregano, thyme, and black pepper; cook,

stirring, 1 minute. Remove from heat and set aside.

Layer the vegetables in the following manner: half the potatoes, the tomatoes, the onion mixture, the bell peppers, and zucchini, ending with the potatoes. Season the layers with salt and pepper. Pour the remaining oil evenly over top, followed by the broth. Bake, uncovered, about 45 minutes, or until the top is lightly browned. Transfer to a stockpot or soup tureen and stir well to combine.

To serve, arrange a piece of bread in the bottom of each soup bowl. Ladle with equal portions of the vegetables and broth and serve at once.

Chickpea and Pasta Soup

MAKES 4 SERVINGS

This hearty soup from the Abruzzi region is delicious. For a Tuscan-style variation, substitute white beans for the chickpeas and sage for the rosemary.

- 2 tablespoons extra-virgin olive oil
- 3 large cloves garlic, finely chopped
- 4 cups low-sodium vegetable broth
- 1 (15-ounce) can chickpeas, rinsed and drained
- 1 (14-ounce) can stewed tomatoes, juices included
- 1 tablespoon chopped fresh rosemary, or 1 teaspoon dried
- Salt and freshly ground black pepper, to taste
- 2 ounces ditalini or any small pasta (about ½ cup)

In a medium stockpot, heat the oil over medium heat. Add the garlic and cook, stirring, 1 minute. Add the broth, chickpeas, tomatoes and their juices, rosemary, salt, and pepper; bring to a boil over high heat. Reduce the heat, cover, and simmer 5 minutes.

Transfer about two-thirds of the mixture to a food processor fitted with the knife blade, or to a blender. Process until smooth and pureed. Return to the pot and bring to a boil over high heat. Add the pasta and let return to a boil. Reduce the heat, cover, and simmer, stirring a few times, until pasta is cooked al dente, about 10 minutes. Serve hot.

PER SERVING

Calories 293 ▪ Protein 19g ▪ Total Fat 9g ▪ Sat. Fat 1g ▪ Cholesterol 0mg ▪ Carbohydrate 37g ▪ Dietary Fiber 5g ▪ Sodium 775mg

(Almost) Fat-Free Minestrone

MAKES 5 TO 6 SERVINGS

Not one drop of oil is used in this virtually fat-free version of minestrone, the flavor of which is rounded out nicely with the addition of red wine.

- 6 cups low-sodium vegetable broth
- 3 cups water
- 1 cup dry red wine
- 1 (28-ounce) can plum tomatoes, coarsely chopped, juices included
- 2 medium carrots (about 4 ounces each), thinly sliced
- 1 medium onion (about 6 ounces), chopped
- 1 medium zucchini (about 6 ounces), chopped
- 2 stalks celery, chopped
- 2 large cloves garlic, finely chopped
- 1 teaspoon dried basil
- 1 teaspoon dried oregano
- 1 teaspoon dried thyme leaves
- Salt and freshly ground black pepper, to taste
- 1 (16-ounce) can kidney beans, rinsed and drained
- 2 cups shredded cabbage
- ½ cup ditalini or other small pasta

In a large pot, combine all the ingredients except the beans, cabbage, and pasta. Bring to a boil over high heat. Reduce the heat to medium-low and simmer, partially covered, 1 hour, stirring occasionally.

Stir in the beans and cabbage and cook, covered, 10 minutes. Uncover and bring to a boil over medium-high heat. Stir in the pasta and let return to a boil. Reduce heat and simmer briskly, uncovered, stirring occasionally, until pasta is cooked al dente, about 10 minutes. Serve hot.

PER SERVING
Calories 281 ▪ Protein 23g ▪ Total Fat 1g ▪ Sat. Fat 0g ▪
Cholesterol 0mg ▪ Carbohydrate 41g ▪
Dietary Fiber 12g ▪ Sodium 1,027mg

Ligurian Minestrone with Pesto

MAKES 4 MAIN-DISH SERVINGS

Liguria gave the world pesto sauce, which is often stirred into minestrone and other vegetable soups. The addition of eggplant, though optional, is a nice touch during the summer months, when in Italy this soup would be served barely warm or at room temperature. If using the eggplant, don't bother with salting and draining it, as any bitterness will be masked by the other ingredients.

½ cup dried white beans, such as cannellini, navy, Great Northern, or borlotti (cranberry) beans, soaked overnight in water to cover and drained
5 cups low-sodium vegetable broth
1 tablespoon extra-virgin olive oil
1 large onion (about 8 ounces), finely chopped
4 ounces eggplant (about ½ small), peeled and cubed (optional)
1 small carrot (about 2 ounces), finely chopped
1 stalk celery, finely chopped
2 cloves garlic, finely chopped
1 (14.5-ounce) can diced tomatoes, juices included
Salt and freshly ground black pepper, to taste
6 ounces boiling potatoes, peeled and cut into ½-inch cubes
1 medium zucchini (about 6 ounces), quartered lengthwise, then cut into ½-inch pieces
2 ounces fresh green beans, trimmed and cut into 1-inch pieces
¼ cup finely broken spaghetti
½ recipe Ligurian Basil Pesto (page 71)

In a large saucepan, bring the white beans and half of the broth to a boil over medium-high heat. Reduce the heat, cover, and simmer gently until the beans are tender but not falling apart, 45 minutes to 1 hour, depending upon the age of the beans. Remove from heat and set aside in the cooking liquid.

In a medium stockpot, heat the oil over medium-low heat. Add the onion, eggplant (if using), carrot, and celery; cook, stirring occasionally, until softened, about 10 minutes. Add the garlic and cook, stirring, 2 minutes. Add the remaining broth, tomatoes and their juices, salt, and pepper; bring to a boil over high heat. Reduce the heat, cover, and simmer gently 20 minutes. Add the potatoes, zucchini, green beans, and spaghetti; bring to a boil over high heat. Reduce the heat, cover, and simmer gently 10 minutes.

Add the white beans and their cooking liquid. Cover, adjust the heat to maintain a gentle simmer, and cook, stirring occasionally, until the vegetables are tender, the pasta is cooked al dente, and the beans are heated through, 5 to 10 minutes. Serve hot, with each serving garnished with an equal dollop of pesto.

PER SERVING
Calories 388 ▪ Protein 26g ▪ Total Fat 14g ▪ Sat. Fat 2g ▪
Cholesterol 0mg ▪ Carbohydrate 45g ▪
Dietary Fiber 13g ▪ Sodium 1,015mg

Lentils and Pastina Soup

MAKES 4 SERVINGS

This iron-rich *minestra* from Umbria is delicious accompanied by a tossed spinach salad. If you don't have pastina or other tiny pasta shapes, grind spaghetti in a food processor fitted with a knife blade until it's reduced to very short lengths.

- 2 tablespoons extra-virgin olive oil
- 1 medium onion (about 6 ounces), chopped
- 1 medium carrot (about 4 ounces), chopped
- 1 stalk celery, chopped
- 1 tablespoon finely chopped fresh rosemary, or 1 teaspoon dried
- 2 large cloves garlic, finely chopped
- 6 cups water and/or low-sodium vegetable broth
- ½ pound dried lentils, rinsed and picked over
- ½ teaspoon salt, or to taste
- ¼ teaspoon freshly ground black pepper
- ¼ cup pastina, orzo, or other tiny pasta
- 2 tablespoons chopped fresh flat-leaf parsley (optional)

In a medium stockpot, heat the oil over medium heat. Add the onion, carrot, and celery; cook, stirring, until fragrant and softened, about 5 minutes. Add the rosemary and garlic and cook, stirring, 1 minute. Add the water, lentils, salt, and pepper; bring to a boil over high heat. Reduce the heat, cover, and simmer, stirring occasionally, until the lentils are just tender, about 30 minutes. Uncover and return to a boil over high heat. Add the pastina, reduce the heat, cover, and simmer, stirring occasionally, until the pasta is tender yet firm

to the bite, 10 to 15 minutes. Serve hot, sprinkled with the parsley (if using).

PER SERVING
Calories 306 ▪ Protein 18g ▪ Total Fat 8g ▪ Sat Fat 1g ▪ Cholesterol 0mg ▪ Carbohydrate 44g ▪ Dietary Fiber 19g ▪ Sodium 293mg

Three-Bean Soup with Vegetables

MAKES 4 SERVINGS

Feel free to use any variety or combination of beans you desire here—the results will invariably be delicious. Also, if you would like to use freshly cooked dried beans, versus canned, see the Cook's Tip on the opposite page.

- 1½ tablespoons extra-virgin olive oil
- 1 medium onion (about 6 ounces), chopped
- 1 medium carrot (about 4 ounces), chopped
- 1 stalk celery, chopped
- 4 cups low-sodium vegetable broth
- 2 cups water
- 1 (14-ounce) can sliced stewed tomatoes, juices included
- 2 cups shredded cabbage
- 1 medium boiling potato (about 4 ounces), peeled and cubed
- 1 small zucchini (about 4 ounces), sliced
- 1 teaspoon dried oregano
- ½ teaspoon dried thyme leaves
- Salt and freshly ground black pepper, to taste
- ½ cup elbow macaroni or other small pasta, uncooked
- ½ cup rinsed and drained canned chickpeas

½ cup rinsed and drained canned navy or other white beans

½ cup rinsed and drained canned kidney beans

In a medium stockpot, heat the oil over medium heat. Add the onion, carrot, and celery; cook, stirring, until softened and fragrant, about 5 minutes. Add the broth, water, tomatoes and their juices, cabbage, potato, zucchini, oregano, thyme, salt, and pepper; bring to a boil over high heat. Add the remaining ingredients and let return to a boil.

Reduce the heat slightly and cook, uncovered, until pasta is tender yet firm to the bite, about 15 minutes, stirring occasionally. Serve hot.

PER SERVING

Calories 323 ■ Protein 22g ■ Total Fat 7g ■ Sat. Fat 1g ■ Cholesterol 0mg ■ Carbohydrate 48g ■ Dietary Fiber 11g ■ Sodium 800mg

> ## ✃ COOK'S TIP ✃
>
> *To cook dried beans, use ¼ cup dried for every ½ cup canned beans called for in the recipe and prepare separately. Pick through them to find any small stones, then rinse well. Soak a minimum of 8 hours in unsalted water equaling 2 to 3 times their volume. (Alternatively, use this quick-soak method: In a large saucepan or medium stockpot, bring the beans and enough unsalted water to cover by at least 2 inches to a boil over high heat. Boil 2 minutes. Remove from the heat, cover, and let stand 1 hour.) Drain the beans and replace in fresh water to cover by at least 2 inches. Bring to a brisk simmer over medium-high heat, reduce the heat to medium-low, and simmer 1 to 2 hours, stirring occasionally, or until the beans are tender, depending on the age and type of the beans (generally, chickpeas will take longer to cook than kidney beans). Drain and proceed as directed in the recipe.*

Turnip and Potato Soup with Basil

MAKES 4 SERVINGS

Turnips are one of Europe's oldest vegetables, the food of the poor, which was most of the population during the Middle Ages. At some point, after the discovery of the Americas, the turnip relinquished its role as everyday vegetable to the potato. This winter-warming soup from Trentino is a delicious and nutritious combination of the old world root and the New World tuber.

3 tablespoons extra-virgin olive oil

2 medium onions (about 6 ounces each), thinly sliced

1½ pounds turnips, peeled and thinly sliced

¾ pound russet potatoes, peeled and thinly sliced

3 cups low-sodium vegetable broth

Salt and freshly ground black pepper, to taste

Pinch nutmeg (optional)

2 tablespoons finely chopped fresh basil

In a medium stockpot, heat the oil over medium heat. Add the onions and cook, stirring, until softened but not browned, about 5 minutes. Add the turnips and potatoes and stir to coat with the oil. Cover and reduce heat to low; cook, stirring occasionally, until the vegetables are tender, about 20 minutes.

Stir in the broth, salt, and pepper; bring to a brisk simmer over medium-high heat. Reduce the heat to medium and cook, partially covered, until the vegetables are very tender, about 10 minutes.

Working in batches, puree the soup in a food

processor fitted with the knife blade, or in a blender. Return to the pot and season with salt and pepper, if necessary, and the nutmeg (if using). Reheat over low heat if necessary. Serve hot, garnished with the basil.

PER SERVING

Calories 256 ▪ Protein 12g ▪ Total Fat 11g ▪ Sat. Fat 1g ▪ Cholesterol 0mg ▪ Carbohydrate 31g ▪ Dietary Fiber 8g ▪ Sodium 509mg

Tuscan-Style Baked Bread and Tomato Soup with Basil

MAKES 6 MAIN-DISH OR 8 TO 10 SIDE-DISH SERVINGS

More like stuffing or bread pudding than soup, this rustic dish is an excellent accompaniment to vegetarian sausages or as a filling for grilled or baked portobello mushrooms. Try to use good-quality Tuscan pane and vine-ripened tomatoes here. If you don't have an ovenproof skillet, transfer the tomato-and-bread-cube mixture to a shallow casserole instead.

1 (16-ounce) loaf day-old peasant bread, preferably Tuscan pane, cubed

3 tablespoons extra-virgin olive oil

2 cloves garlic, finely chopped

Salt, preferably the coarse variety, and freshly ground black pepper, to taste

1½ pounds ripe tomatoes, preferably vine-ripened, cut into chunks

1 cup loosely packed fresh basil leaves, chopped

2 cups low-sodium vegetable broth

2 tablespoons dry white wine (optional)

Preheat the oven to 350F (175C).

Arrange the bread cubes in a single layer on a large (or two standard-size) ungreased baking sheet. Bake about 20 minutes, or until just golden, stirring and turning halfway through cooking. Remove from the oven and, using a wide spatula, toss with 1 tablespoon of the oil, half the garlic, salt, and pepper. Return to the oven and bake 2 to 3 minutes, or until golden. Remove from oven and set aside. (Do not turn off oven.)

Meanwhile, in a large deep-sided ovenproof skillet, heat the remaining oil over medium heat. Add the remaining garlic and cook, stirring constantly, 30 seconds. Add the tomatoes, half of the basil, half of the broth, the wine (if using), salt, and pepper; bring to a simmer over medium-high heat. Reduce the heat to medium-low and simmer, uncovered, about 20 minutes, or until thickened, stirring occasionally.

Add the bread cubes to the skillet, along with the remaining basil and broth, stirring well to combine. Transfer the skillet to the oven and bake 10 minutes, or until the bread has absorbed the liquids and the mixture is hot. Serve at once.

PER SERVING

Calories 311 ▪ Protein 12g ▪ Total Fat 10g ▪ Sat. Fat 2g ▪ Cholesterol 0mg ▪ Carbohydrate 45g ▪ Dietary Fiber 6g ▪ Sodium 624mg

Classic Tuscan White Bean Soup

MAKES 4 SERVINGS

A Tuscan classic, this simple yet delicious bean soup becomes a complete meal when served with a green salad. If serving as a first course, the garlic-rubbed bread can be omitted from the recipe, if desired.

> **2 tablespoons extra-virgin olive oil**
>
> **2 scallions (white and green parts), chopped**
>
> **1 cup low-sodium vegetable broth or water, plus additional as necessary**
>
> **2 (16-ounce) cans cannellini or other white beans, rinsed and drained**
>
> **1 teaspoon whole fresh thyme leaves, or ¼ teaspoon dried**
>
> **1 teaspoon chopped fresh rosemary, or ¼ teaspoon dried**
>
> **¼ teaspoon dried oregano**
>
> **⅛ teaspoon ground sage**
>
> **¼ teaspoon salt, preferably the coarse variety, or to taste**
>
> **Freshly ground black pepper, to taste**
>
> **4 slices day-old Italian bread, about 1 ounce each**
>
> **1 clove garlic, halved**

In a large stockpot, heat the oil over medium heat. Add the scallions and cook, stirring, until softened and fragrant, about 3 minutes. Add the broth, beans, thyme, rosemary, oregano, sage, salt, and pepper; bring to a boil over medium-high heat. Reduce the heat and simmer, covered, about 15 minutes, stirring occasionally and mashing about half the beans against the sides of the pot with the back of a large wooden spoon. For a thinner soup, add more broth or water as necessary.

Meanwhile, toast the bread and rub on one side with the halved garlic. Place the bread on the bottom of each of 4 soup bowls and pour the soup evenly over the bread. Serve hot.

PER SERVING
Calories 341 ▪ Protein 19g ▪ Total Fat 8g ▪ Sat Fat 1g ▪ Cholesterol 0mg ▪ Carbohydrate 49g ▪ Dietary Fiber 9g ▪ Sodium 540mg

Tomato and Bread Stew with Pasta

MAKES 4 SERVINGS

Made from canned plum tomatoes, this hearty stew is ideal to make during the cold-weather months when good-quality fresh tomatoes are hard to come by. For best results, use a good-quality Tuscan pane—I use Trader Joe's brand.

> **3 pieces day-old Italian bread (about 3 ounces), preferably Tuscan *pane***
>
> **4 large cloves garlic, 1 halved, 3 finely chopped**
>
> **¼ cup extra-virgin olive oil**
>
> **2 medium onions (about 6 ounces each), finely chopped**
>
> **1 (28-ounce) can whole peeled plum tomatoes, juices included**
>
> **1 cup low-sodium vegetable broth**
>
> **½ cup dry white wine**
>
> **1 teaspoon dried oregano**
>
> **Salt, preferably the coarse variety, and freshly ground black pepper, to taste**
>
> **3 tablespoons orzo, pastina, or other tiny pasta**

Lightly toast the bread and rub on one side with the halved garlic. Tear into bite-size pieces and set aside.

In a large deep-sided nonstick skillet with a lid, heat the oil over medium heat. Add the onions and cook, stirring, until softened and translucent, 5 to 8 minutes. Add the remaining garlic and cook, stirring, 1 minute. Add the tomatoes and their juices, broth, wine, oregano, salt, and pepper; bring to a brisk simmer over medium-high heat, stirring occasionally and breaking up the tomatoes with a wooden spoon. Stir in the pasta and bread, reduce heat to medium-low, cover, and simmer, stirring occasionally, until the pasta is tender yet firm to the bite, about 15 minutes. Serve at once.

PER SERVING

Calories 302 ▪ Protein 8g ▪ Total Fat 15g ▪ Sat Fat 2g ▪
Cholesterol 0mg ▪ Carbohydrate 31g ▪
Dietary Fiber 5g ▪ Sodium 681mg

Split-Pea and Tomato Soup with Spinach

MAKES 6 SERVINGS

This rib-sticking *minestra*, enlivened with a little cayenne, is proof that Italian home cooks really do make superb split-pea soup fit to rival that of France's. To make it even heartier, cooked ditalini, small elbow macaroni, or other similar pasta is often added toward the end of the cooking time.

2 tablespoons extra-virgin olive oil
2 medium onions (about 6 ounces each), chopped
2 small carrots (about 2 ounces each), chopped
2 stalks celery, chopped
3 to 4 cloves garlic, finely chopped
1 (28-ounce) can whole plum tomatoes, drained, seeded, and chopped
3 cups low-sodium vegetable broth, plus additional as necessary
2 cups water, plus additional as necessary
1 cup dried split peas
2 tablespoons finely chopped fresh flat-leaf parsley

½ teaspoon dried thyme leaves
1 bay leaf
⅛ teaspoon cayenne, or to taste
Salt and freshly ground black pepper, to taste
1 cup coarsely chopped fresh spinach
1 cup ditalini or other small pasta, cooked according to package directions until just al dente (optional)

In a medium stockpot, heat the oil over medium-low heat. Add the onions, carrots, celery, and garlic and cook, stirring occasionally, until softened, about 10 minutes.

Add the tomatoes, broth, water, split peas, parsley, thyme, bay leaf, cayenne, salt, and black pepper; bring to a boil over medium-high heat. Reduce the heat, cover, and simmer gently, stirring occasionally, until the peas are tender, about 1½ hours.

Stir in the spinach and the pasta (if using). Cook, stirring, until the spinach is wilted and the pasta is heated through, about 5 minutes. If the soup seems too thick, thin it with a little broth or water as necessary. Serve hot.

PER SERVING (WITHOUT PASTA)

Calories 239 ▪ Protein 16g ▪ Total Fat 5g ▪ Sat Fat 1g ▪
Cholesterol 0mg ▪ Carbohydrate 34g ▪
Dietary Fiber 13g ▪ Sodium 573mg

Salads

Nothing short of superlatives describe Italian salads. Only the freshest and best seasonal ingredients are bought or picked and, regardless of how the salad is made, it is always dressed at the table, just before serving, to guarantee optimal flavor.

The most basic salad is the *insalata verde*, or green salad, consisting predominately of one variety of lettuce, such as romaine, plus one or two other greens, usually of a bitter or sharp variety, such as curly endive, escarole, arugula, Belgian endive, or radicchio. An *insalata mista*, or mixed salad, usually combines a variety of lettuce and greens with tomato, onion, olives and, sometimes, cooked vegetables such as artichokes, asparagus, beets, green beans, and potatoes. To ensure success for these types of salads, toss with wooden utensils to help avoid bruising the tender prime greens, and make sure the dressing is at room temperature.

There are other types of Italian salads that require less care. Cold, cooked vegetables, dressed with vinegar or lemon juice and olive oil, also qualify as salads. A mixture of several cooked vegetables together in a salad is called *in-*

salatone. While there are also hearty rice salads, potato salads, bean salads, and grain salads, pasta salads are rarely served, except perhaps in the hottest of months—and even then, they are really pasta dishes served at room temperature. Fortunately, you don't need to wait for a sweltering day to enjoy Florentine Pasta Salad with Lemon, which is as appropriate to serve at a Fourth of July picnic as it is on a New Year's Eve buffet—*delizioso!*

First-Course and Side Salads

Artichoke Heart, Lima Bean, and Fennel Salad

MAKES 4 TO 6 SERVINGS

This first-course salad takes advantage of both fresh and frozen vegetables, making it as easy to prepare as it is elegant to serve.

1 (10-ounce) package frozen baby lima beans, thawed

1 (8-ounce) package quartered frozen artichoke hearts, thawed

1 medium fennel bulb (about 12 ounces), trimmed, cored, cut vertically into ½-inch-wide strips, and 2 tablespoons feathery fronds reserved and finely chopped

1 bunch (6 to 8) scallions (green and white parts), thinly sliced

2 tablespoons extra-virgin olive oil

2 tablespoons white wine vinegar

½ teaspoon sugar

Salt and freshly ground black pepper, to taste

Fill a medium stockpot or saucepan large enough to accommodate a 9-inch steaming basket with about 1 inch of water. Place the steaming basket in the pot and add the lima beans and artichokes. Bring to a boil over high heat. Cover tightly, reduce heat to medium, and steam 6 to 8 minutes, or until tender. Carefully remove the steaming basket and let the lima beans and artichokes cool to room temperature.

Place the lima beans, artichokes, fennel strips, reserved fennel fronds, and scallions in a large shallow serving bowl. In a small bowl or pouring container, whisk together the oil, vinegar, sugar, salt, and pepper. Add to the lima bean mixture, tossing thoroughly to combine.

Serve at room temperature. Alternatively, cover and refrigerate a minimum of 1 hour, or overnight, and serve chilled.

PER SERVING
Calories 213 ▪ Protein 9g ▪ Total Fat 8g ▪ Sat Fat 1g ▪
Cholesterol 0mg ▪ Carbohydrate 31g ▪
Dietary Fiber 9g ▪ Sodium 113mg

Arugula, Fennel, and Radicchio Salad with Raisins and Pine Nuts

MAKES 6 SERVINGS

This is a wonderful salad to enjoy during the winter months when all of the ingredients are in season. In a pinch, drained canned mandarin orange segments can be used in lieu of the fresh navel variety, if desired.

3 tablespoons pine nuts

¼ cup fresh orange juice

3 tablespoons extra-virgin olive oil

1½ tablespoons red wine vinegar

Salt and freshly ground black pepper, to taste

6 tablespoons golden raisins

1 medium fennel bulb (about 12 ounces), trimmed, quartered, cored, and thinly sliced

1 (10-ounce) bag arugula

1 medium head radicchio (about 6 ounces), cored and torn into bite-size pieces

3 large seedless navel oranges, peeled and segmented

Heat a small heavy-bottomed skillet over medium heat. Add the pine nuts and cook, stirring constantly, until lightly browned and fragrant, about 3 minutes. Immediately remove the nuts from the skillet and set aside.

In a large bowl, whisk together the orange juice, oil, vinegar, salt, and pepper until thoroughly blended. Stir in the raisins and let stand about 10 minutes to soften. Stir again. Add the fennel, arugula, and radicchio; toss well to combine.

Divide evenly among 6 serving plates and gar-

nish with equal portions of the orange segments and reserved pine nuts. Serve at once.

PER SERVING

Calories 189 ▪ Protein 5g ▪ Total Fat 10 ▪ Sat. Fat 2 ▪
Cholesterol 0mg ▪ Carbohydrate 25g ▪
Dietary Fiber 2g ▪ Sodium 50mg

Bean Salad with Balsamic Vinaigrette

MAKES 6 SERVINGS

Any combination of cooked beans will work in this protein-packed salad. It is actually better the next day, returned to room temperature. To create an impressive first-course salad, serve in radicchio and/or Belgian endive leaves.

1 (16-ounce) can chickpeas, rinsed and drained

1 (16-ounce) can light red kidney beans, rinsed and drained

⅔ cup chopped red onion

¼ cup chopped fresh flat-leaf parsley

3 tablespoons extra-virgin olive oil

2 tablespoons balsamic vinegar

1 tablespoon chopped fresh basil (optional)

1 teaspoon sugar (optional)

Salt and freshly ground black pepper, to taste

Place all the ingredients in a medium bowl and toss well to combine. Let stand 30 minutes at room temperature before tossing again and serving. Alternatively, cover and refrigerate up to 2 days, and return to room temperature before serving.

VARIATION: *To make* **Tuscan-Style White Bean Salad:** *Substitute cannellini or other white beans for both the chickpeas and red kidney beans, and use 1 tablespoon chopped fresh sage in lieu of the optional basil. Serve over fresh spinach leaves instead of radicchio or Belgian endive, if desired.*

Celeriac and Radicchio Salad with Walnuts

MAKES 4 SERVINGS

Celeriac is a variety of celery prized for its turniplike root instead of for its stalks. Like celery, it can be served cooked or raw.

3 tablespoons extra-virgin olive oil
1½ tablespoons balsamic vinegar
Salt, preferably the coarse variety, and freshly ground black pepper, to taste
2 medium or 1 large celeriac (about 1 pound without leaves), trimmed, peeled, and cut into thin strips
⅓ cup walnut pieces
1 medium head radicchio (about 6 ounces), cored and leaves separated

In a large salad bowl, whisk together the oil, vinegar, salt, and pepper until thoroughly blended. Add the celeriac and walnuts and toss well to combine. Divide the radicchio leaves equally among 4 serving plates. Top with equal portions of the celeriac mixture and serve at once.

Bruschetta Salad with Olive Croutons

MAKES 6 SERVINGS

This outstanding salad is perfect for easy summertime entertaining, as it can be assembled twenty-four hours ahead, then tossed with the croutons and served.

4 tablespoons extra-virgin olive oil
1½ tablespoons red wine vinegar
6 medium vine-ripened tomatoes (about 6 ounces each), cut into 1-inch pieces
½ cup chopped red onion
¼ cup finely chopped fresh basil leaves
1 tablespoon drained capers (optional)
Salt, preferably the coarse variety, and freshly ground black pepper, to taste
Olive Croutons (page 34)

In a large bowl, whisk together the oil and vinegar. Add the tomatoes, onion, basil, capers (if using), salt, and pepper; toss well to thoroughly combine. Let stand about 15 minutes to let the flavors blend, tossing occasionally. Just before serving, add the croutons, tossing well to thoroughly combine. Serve at once.

Olive Croutons

MAKES ABOUT 3 CUPS

These croutons are excellent served with soups as well as salads. If you don't have garlic-flavored olive oil, use extra-virgin olive oil and replace the coarse salt with garlic salt, to taste.

- ¼ cup pitted kalamata or other good-quality black olives
- 1 tablespoon garlic-flavored olive oil
- ¼ teaspoon dried oregano and/or crumbled thyme leaves
- ¼ teaspoon coarse salt
- 4 ounces day-old ciabatta, Tuscan pane, or other Italian-style bread, crusts removed, cut into small cubes

Preheat the oven to 375F (190C). Lightly oil a baking sheet and set aside.

Puree the olives in a food processor fitted with the knife blade, or in a blender. Transfer to a large bowl and add the oil, oregano, and salt; stir well to combine. Add the bread cubes and toss well to thoroughly coat. Arrange in a single layer on the prepared baking sheet.

Bake on the center oven rack, stirring and turning halfway through cooking time, 8 to 10 minutes, or until lightly browned. Let cool to room temperature. If not using immediately, place in an airtight container and store a few days at room temperature.

PER SERVING (ABOUT ½ CUP OR ⅙ RECIPE)
Calories 78 ■ Protein 2g ■ Total Fat 4g ■ Sat. Fat 1g ■ Cholesterol 0mg ■ Carbohydrate 10g ■ Dietary Fiber 1g ■ Sodium 238mg

Carrot Salad with Green Peppers and Raisins

MAKES 6 SERVINGS

A delightful Italian alternative to standard mayonnaise-based carrot and raisin slaw, this crunchy salad is ideal to serve any time of year.

- 3 tablespoons extra-virgin olive oil
- 2 tablespoons red wine vinegar
- 1 teaspoon sugar, or more to taste
- Salt and freshly ground black pepper, to taste
- 16 ounces shredded carrots
- 1 small green bell pepper (about 4 ounces), finely chopped
- 4 scallions (white and green parts), thinly sliced
- 6 tablespoons golden or dark raisins, soaked in warm water to cover for 10 minutes, drained

In a large bowl, whisk together the oil, vinegar, sugar, salt, and pepper. Let stand about 5 minutes to allow the sugar to dissolve; whisk again.

Add the remaining ingredients, tossing well to combine. Cover and refrigerate a minimum of 3 hours, or up to 2 days. Serve chilled or return to room temperature.

PER SERVING
Calories 132 ■ Protein 2g ■ Total Fat 7g ■ Sat. Fat 1g ■ Cholesterol 0mg ■ Carbohydrate 18g ■ Dietary Fiber 3g ■ Sodium 27mg

VARIATION: *To make **Cucumber, Red Onion, and Tomato Salad:** Omit 1 cucumber and replace with 12 ounces plum tomatoes, quartered.*

Cucumber and Red Onion Salad

MAKES 6 SERVINGS

This crunchy cucumber salad is a cool accompaniment to many of the book's spicier dishes.

- **3 cucumbers (about 12 ounces each), peeled and halved lengthwise**
- **3 tablespoons extra-virgin olive oil**
- **1½ tablespoons distilled white or white wine vinegar**
- **¾ teaspoon sugar**
- **½ teaspoon coarse salt**
- **¼ teaspoon freshly ground black pepper**
- **1 small red onion (about 4 ounces), finely chopped**

With a teaspoon, scrape out and discard the seeds from each cucumber half. Cut each cucumber half crosswise into ¼-inch-thick slices.

In a large bowl, whisk together the oil, vinegar, sugar, salt, and pepper until well blended. Add the cucumber and the onion; toss well to combine. Cover with plastic wrap and let stand at room temperature a minimum of 30 minutes to allow the flavors to blend. Toss again and serve. Alternatively, refrigerate a minimum of 1 hour or up to 1 day, and serve chilled or return to room temperature.

PER SERVING

Calories 91 ▪ Protein 1g ▪ Total Fat 7g ▪ Sat. Fat 1g ▪ Cholesterol 0mg ▪ Carbohydrate 7g ▪ Dietary Fiber 2g ▪ Sodium 161mg

Fennel, Pear, and Endive Salad

MAKES 4 SERVINGS

The French influence is apparent in this easy yet elegant first-course salad from northern Italy, ideal for holiday entertaining. If you don't have tarragon vinegar, substitute with white wine vinegar and add a pinch of dried tarragon leaves.

- **2 tablespoons extra-virgin olive oil**
- **2 tablespoons tarragon vinegar**
- **½ tablespoon Dijon mustard**
- **Salt and freshly ground black pepper, to taste**
- **2 large, ripe yet firm Bosc pears, cored and cut into thin wedges**
- **1 large fennel bulb (about 1 pound), trimmed, quartered, cored, and thinly sliced, 2 tablespoons feathery fronds reserved and chopped**
- **2 medium heads Belgian endive, leaves separated**
- **⅓ cup walnuts, coarsely chopped**

In a large bowl, whisk together the oil, vinegar, mustard, salt, and pepper. Let stand about 5 minutes to allow the flavors to blend. Add the pears and fennel slices; toss gently to combine. Serve at once, over the endive, sprinkled with the reserved fennel fronds and the walnuts.

PER SERVING

Calories 253 ▪ Protein 8g ▪ Total Fat 14g ▪ Sat. Fat 1g ▪ Cholesterol 0mg ▪ Carbohydrate 31g ▪ Dietary Fiber 12g ▪ Sodium 139mg

Fresh Tomato and Basil Salad

MAKES 4 TO 6 SERVINGS

Vine-ripened tomatoes work best in this quick and delicious recipe from Calabria in southern Italy.

 3 tablespoons extra-virgin olive oil
 1 large clove garlic, finely chopped (optional)
 ½ teaspoon coarse salt
 6 medium ripe tomatoes (about 6 ounces each), sliced
 6 to 8 fresh basil leaves, shredded

In a large bowl, gently toss all ingredients until well combined. Let stand about 15 minutes at room temperature to allow the flavors to blend. Toss again and serve at room temperature. Alternatively, cover and refrigerate a minimum of 1 hour or overnight and serve chilled, or return to room temperature.

PER SERVING

Calories 139 ▪ Protein 2g ▪ Total Fat 11g ▪ Sat. Fat 2g ▪
Cholesterol 0mg ▪ Carbohydrate 11g ▪
Dietary Fiber 3g ▪ Sodium 256mg

Green Bean Salad

MAKES 4 TO 6 SERVINGS

This is a reliable company salad, as it can be made a day ahead. The addition of sun-dried tomatoes, though optional, lends it pretty flecks of color for the holidays.

 1¼ pounds fresh green beans, trimmed
 2 tablespoons extra-virgin olive oil (less 1 teaspoon if using optional sun-dried tomatoes)
 1 tablespoon red wine vinegar
 1 large clove garlic, finely chopped
 Salt, preferably the coarse variety, and freshly ground black pepper, to taste
 2 tablespoons finely chopped fresh flat-leaf parsley
 2 tablespoons chopped drained oil-packed sun-dried tomatoes (optional)

Bring a large stockpot filled with salted water to a boil over high heat. Prepare a large bowl of ice water. Add the beans to the boiling water and boil until crisp-tender, 3 to 5 minutes. Drain and immediately place in ice water about 5 minutes. Drain well.

Meanwhile, in a large bowl, whisk together the oil, vinegar, garlic, salt, and pepper. Stir in the parsley and let stand about 5 minutes to allow the flavors to blend. Add the drained green beans and tomatoes (if using); toss gently yet thoroughly to combine. Cover and refrigerate a minimum of 1 hour, or up to 1 day. Serve chilled or return to room temperature.

PER SERVING

Calories 106 ▪ Protein 3g ▪ Total Fat 7g ▪ Sat. Fat 1g ▪
Cholesterol 0mg ▪ Carbohydrate 11g ▪
Dietary Fiber 5g ▪ Sodium 10mg

Grilled Radicchio and Fresh Vegetable Salad

MAKES 6 SERVINGS

This is a marvelous salad from the Veneto that everyone seems to enjoy. The key to its success is saving all the accumulated cooking juices and adding them to the tossed salad—yum!

3 small heads radicchio (about 4 ounces each), halved

3 Japanese or Italian eggplants (about 4 ounces each), halved lengthwise

2 medium zucchini or yellow squash (about 6 ounces each), halved lengthwise

1 large red bell pepper (about 8 ounces), halved

1 large red onion (about 8 ounces), cut into ½-inch-thick slices

1 large tomato (about 8 ounces), halved and seeded

6 tablespoons extra-virgin olive oil

Salt, preferably the coarse variety, and freshly ground black pepper, to taste

¼ cup balsamic vinegar

¼ cup low-sodium vegetable broth

3 tablespoons finely chopped fresh basil

3 large cloves garlic, finely chopped

6 cups romaine lettuce leaves

Prepare a medium-hot charcoal grill or gas grill. Position the grill rack 4 to 6 inches from heat source. Or, heat a large nonstick stovetop grilling pan with ridges over medium-high heat.

Rub the radicchio, eggplant, zucchini, bell pep- per, onion, and tomato with 2 tablespoons of the oil. Season with salt and pepper. Grill the vegetables until browned and tender, working in batches as necessary. As a general rule, cook the bell pepper for 4 to 5 minutes per side; the eggplant, zucchini, and onion for 3 to 4 minutes per side; and the radicchio and tomato, 2 to 3 minutes per side. Place the vegetables on a large baking sheet with sides as they finish cooking.

When vegetables are cool enough to handle, cut into bite-size pieces, working directly on the baking sheet and reserving all accumulated juices. Transfer vegetables and juices to a large bowl and add the remaining oil, vinegar, broth, basil, garlic, salt, and pepper; toss well to combine. Let stand 5 minutes to allow flavors to blend; toss again. Serve slightly warm or at room temperature, over the lettuce leaves.

PER SERVING

Calories 198 ▪ Protein 4g ▪ Total Fat 14g ▪ Sat. Fat 2g ▪
Cholesterol 0mg ▪ Carbohydrate 17g ▪
Dietary Fiber 5g ▪ Sodium 46mg

Grilled Portobello Mushroom and Romaine Salad

MAKES 4 SERVINGS

Serve this outstanding salad with lots of crusty Italian bread to sop up the delicious juices.

- ¼ cup extra-virgin olive oil
- 2 tablespoons water or low-sodium vegetable broth
- 2 tablespoons balsamic vinegar
- 3 cloves garlic, finely chopped
- 1½ teaspoons finely chopped fresh thyme leaves, or ½ teaspoon dried
- ½ teaspoon onion powder
- Salt and freshly ground black pepper, to taste
- 6 large portobello mushroom caps (about 2 ounces each)
- 10 ounces romaine lettuce or spinach leaves

In a small bowl, whisk together the oil, water, vinegar, garlic, thyme, onion powder, salt, and pepper. Place mushrooms in a large resealable plastic bag and add the oil and vinegar mixture, turning the bag to evenly coat the mushrooms. Marinate at room temperature 1 hour, turning the bag once or twice.

Prepare a medium-hot charcoal grill or gas grill. Position the grill rack 4 to 6 inches from heat source. Alternatively, heat a large nonstick stovetop grilling pan with ridges over medium-high heat.

Remove mushrooms from marinade, reserving marinade. Grill 2 to 3 minutes, gill-sides down. Turn over and grill until tender and light browned, 2 to 3 minutes. Transfer mushrooms to a baking sheet with sides. Thinly slice, and then cover with foil to keep warm.

To serve, divide the lettuce among 4 plates. Top with equal portions of the sliced mushrooms, drizzling with reserved marinade and any accumulated juices on the baking sheet. Serve at once.

PER SERVING

Calories 155 ■ Protein 3g ■ Total Fat 14g ■ Sat. Fat 2g ■ Cholesterol 0mg ■ Carbohydrate 7g ■ Dietary Fiber 2g ■ Sodium 9mg

Spinach Salad with Oranges

MAKES 4 SERVINGS

This colorful salad is ideal to serve during the bleak, cold-weather months. Arugula can replace the spinach.

- 2 tablespoons extra-virgin olive oil
- 2 tablespoons red wine vinegar
- 2 tablespoons fresh orange juice
- Salt and freshly ground black pepper, to taste
- 1 (10-ounce) bag fresh baby spinach
- 2 large navel oranges, peeled and segmented
- ½ small red onion (about 2 ounces), very thinly sliced, soaked in cold water to cover 10 minutes, and drained well
- 2 tablespoons pine nuts, toasted if desired (see Cook's Tip, opposite page)

In a large bowl, whisk together the oil, vinegar, juice, salt, and pepper. Add the spinach, oranges, onion, and pine nuts; toss gently yet thoroughly to combine. Serve at once.

4 tablespoons white wine vinegar

Salt and freshly ground black pepper, to taste

5 to 6 medium vine-ripened tomatoes (about 6 ounces), cut into ¼-inch-thick slices

1 tablespoon capers (optional)

½ cup pitted kalamata or other good-quality black olives, chopped (optional)

2 tablespoons chopped fresh basil leaves

> ### ❧ COOK'S TIP ❧
> To toast pine nuts or other small nut shapes or pieces in the oven: *Preheat the oven to 350F (175C). Spread the nuts in a single layer on an ungreased, light-colored baking sheet. Bake until light golden, about 5 minutes, stirring halfway through the cooking time. Immediately remove from the baking sheet and set aside briefly to cool.*
>
> To toast on the stovetop: *Heat a small skillet over medium heat. Add the nuts and cook, stirring constantly, until lightly golden, 3 to 5 minutes. Immediately remove from the skillet and set aside briefly to cool. For larger whole nuts and nut pieces, increase the cooking time by a few minutes.*

In a medium nonstick skillet, heat the oil over medium heat. Add the bay leaves and cook, stirring, until fragrant, about 2 minutes. Remove and discard bay leaves; reduce heat to medium-low. Add the onion and cook, stirring occasionally, until softened and translucent but not browned, about 8 minutes. Add the vinegar, salt, and pepper, and increase heat to medium-high; cook, stirring constantly, 1 minute. Remove skillet from heat and allow mixture to cool.

Arrange the tomatoes in a circular fashion on a platter. Top with the cooled onion mixture, along with the optional ingredients (if using). Let stand about 15 minutes to allow the flavors to blend. Or, cover and refrigerate a minimum of 1 hour, or overnight, and serve chilled or return to room temperature. Sprinkle with the basil just before serving.

Marinated Tomato, Onion, and Basil Salad

MAKES 4 TO 6 SERVINGS

This salad is a delicious dairy-free alternative to *insalata caprese*, a tomato and basil salad that also contains fresh mozzarella cheese. Like the latter, it is always a crowd-pleaser. If you can't find a sweet variety of onion, use a red one instead.

¼ cup extra-virgin olive oil

2 bay leaves

1 large sweet onion (about 8 ounces), such as Vidalia, very thinly sliced

PER SERVING
Calories 184 ▪ Protein 2g ▪ Total Fat 14g ▪ Sat. Fat 2g ▪
Cholesterol 0mg ▪ Carbohydrate 15g ▪
Dietary Fiber 3g ▪ Sodium 19mg

Mixed Baby Greens with Balsamic Vinaigrette

MAKES 4 SERVINGS

Any mix of young greens—arugula, radicchio, curly endive, dandelion, oak leaf lettuce—will work well in this lovely spring salad.

    3 tablespoons extra-virgin olive oil
    1½ tablespoons balsamic vinegar
    ¼ teaspoon salt, preferably the coarse variety,
        or to taste
    ⅛ teaspoon freshly ground black pepper, or to
        taste
    10 ounces mixed baby greens

In a large bowl, whisk together the oil, vinegar, salt, and pepper. Let stand about 5 minutes to allow the flavors to blend, then whisk again. Add the greens and toss well to combine. Serve at once.

PER SERVING
Calories 109 ▪ Protein 2g ▪ Total Fat 10g ▪ Sat. Fat 1g ▪
Cholesterol 0mg ▪ Carbohydrate 4g ▪
Dietary Fiber 1g ▪ Sodium 135mg

Potato and Chickpea Salad

MAKES 6 TO 8 SERVINGS

This unusual potato salad is a terrific choice for a potluck or picnic.

    1½ pounds small red-skin potatoes, scrubbed,
        left whole
    ¼ cup low-sodium vegetable broth
    2 tablespoons extra-virgin olive oil
    2 tablespoons red wine vinegar
    4 cloves garlic, finely chopped
    ½ teaspoon coarse salt
    ¼ teaspoon freshly ground black pepper
    3 medium plum tomatoes (about 6 ounces),
        chopped
    ½ medium red onion (about 3 ounces), finely
        chopped
    1 (16-ounce) can chickpeas, rinsed and drained
    ¼ pound fresh spinach or arugula leaves,
        chopped (optional)

Place the potatoes in a large saucepan or medium stockpot with salted water to cover; bring to a boil over high heat. Reduce the heat to a gentle boil and cook until the potatoes are just tender, about 15 minutes, depending on size. Drain and set aside to cool slightly.

Meanwhile, in a large bowl, whisk together the broth, oil, vinegar, garlic, salt, and pepper. Stir in the tomatoes and onion. Let stand a few minutes to allow the flavors to blend.

As soon as the potatoes are cool enough to handle, yet still quite warm, cut them in half or in quarters, depending on size. Stir the dressing a few times, and then add the warm potato halves along with the chickpeas and spinach (if using). Toss gently until the potatoes are thoroughly coated. Serve warm or at room temperature. Alternatively, let cool to room temperature and refrigerate a minimum of 3 hours, or up to 2 days (or overnight if using the spinach), and serve chilled or return to room temperature.

PER SERVING

Calories 220 ▪ Protein 8g ▪ Total Fat 6g ▪ Sat Fat 1g ▪
Cholesterol 0mg ▪ Carbohydrate 36g ▪
Dietary Fiber 3g ▪ Sodium 228mg

PER SERVING

Calories 189 ▪ Protein 2g ▪ Total Fat 13g ▪ Sat. Fat 1g ▪
Cholesterol 0mg ▪ Carbohydrate 18g ▪
Dietary Fiber 3g ▪ Sodium 181mg

> ### ❧ COOK'S TIP ❧
> *Soaking raw onion rings in cold water for 10 minutes helps minimize their pungency.*

Sicilian Orange Salad

MAKES 4 SERVINGS

Sicily is orange country—not surprisingly, *insalata de arance* is one of the region's most popular salads. While there are many variations—some add fennel and celery, others omit the olives and onion—I prefer the following for its delicious simplicity.

- 4 large seedless blood or navel oranges, peeled and segmented
- ½ small red onion (about 2 ounces), thinly sliced into half-rings, soaked in cold water to cover 10 minutes, and drained well
- 3 tablespoons extra-virgin olive oil
- Salt and freshly ground black pepper, to taste
- 2 tablespoons chopped fresh flat-leaf parsley or mint (optional)
- 12 pitted kalamata or other good-quality black olives

Place the orange segments, onion, oil, salt, and pepper in a medium bowl; toss gently yet thoroughly to combine. Let stand about 10 minutes to allow the flavors to blend; toss again. (At this point, the salad can be refrigerated, covered, up to 8 hours before continuing with the recipe.) Divide evenly among 4 serving plates and sprinkle with the parsley (if using). Garnish with the olives and serve at once.

Potato and Green Bean Salad

MAKES 6 SERVINGS

While you could cook the potatoes and green beans together to save a pot, the following method allows the beans to retain their bright green color by being refreshed in an ice-water bath.

- 1 pound small red-skin potatoes, scrubbed, left whole
- 1 pound fresh green beans, trimmed and halved lengthwise
- ¼ cup low-sodium vegetable broth
- 2 tablespoons white wine vinegar
- ½ teaspoon dried oregano
- Salt, preferably the coarse variety, and freshly ground black pepper, to taste
- ¼ cup extra-virgin olive oil

Place the potatoes in a large saucepan or medium stockpot with salted water to cover; bring to a boil over high heat. Reduce the heat to a gentle boil and cook until the potatoes are just tender, about 15 minutes, depending on size. Drain and set aside to cool slightly.

Meanwhile, bring a large stockpot filled with salted water to a boil over high heat. Prepare a large bowl of ice water. Add the beans to the boiling water and boil until crisp-tender, 3 to 5 minutes. Drain and immediately place in ice water for about 5 minutes. Drain well.

When the potatoes are cool enough to handle but still quite warm, cut in half or quarters, depending on size. Transfer to a large bowl and toss with the broth, vinegar, oregano, salt, and pepper. Let stand a few minutes to allow the broth and vinegar to be absorbed; toss again. Add the green beans and olive oil; toss gently yet thoroughly to combine. Season with salt and pepper as necessary. Serve slightly warm or at room temperature. Alternatively, cover and refrigerate a minimum of 3 hours, or up to 1 day, and serve chilled or return to room temperature.

PER SERVING
Calories 151 ■ Protein 3g ■ Total Fat 9g ■ Sat. Fat 1g ■
Cholesterol 0mg ■ Carbohydrate 16g ■
Dietary Fiber 4g ■ Sodium 30mg

Roasted Tomato and Basil Salad

MAKES 6 SERVINGS

This is one of my favorite ways to eat tomatoes. Lots of crusty bread is essential for sopping up their scrumptious juices.

6 large tomatoes (about 8 ounces each), peeled (see Cook's Tip on opposite page) and cut in half
2 large cloves garlic, finely chopped
Salt, preferably the coarse variety, and freshly ground black pepper, to taste

4 tablespoons extra-virgin olive oil
6 large fresh basil leaves, torn in half, plus additional for garnish (optional)
2 tablespoons low-sodium vegetable broth
2 tablespoons balsamic vinegar
Crusty Italian bread slices, to serve

Preheat the oven to 400F (205C). Lightly oil a shallow baking dish large enough to hold the tomatoes in a single layer.

Place the tomato halves in the prepared baking dish, cut sides up. Sprinkle evenly with the garlic, salt, and pepper. Drizzle with half of the oil, and then top each with half a basil leaf, turning each piece of leaf over to coat with the oil. Bake 50 to 60 minutes or until the edges of the tomato halves are slightly blackened. Let cool to room temperature. (At this point, tomatoes may be stored, covered, in the refrigerator up to 24 hours before returning to room temperature and proceeding with the recipe.)

In a small bowl, whisk together the remaining oil, broth, and vinegar. Drizzle over the tomatoes and serve at room temperature, garnished with fresh basil leaves (if using), accompanied with the bread.

PER SERVING (WITHOUT BREAD)
Calories 127 ■ Protein 2g ■ Total Fat 10g ■ Sat. Fat 1g ■
Cholesterol 0mg ■ Carbohydrate 10g ■
Dietary Fiber 2g ■ Sodium 30mg

> ❧ **COOK'S TIP** ❧
> *To peel the tomatoes, bring a medium stockpot filled with water to a boil over high heat; drop in the tomatoes and boil 20 seconds. Drain and rinse under cold-running water. Peel off the skins.*

Potato Salad with Italian Parsley

MAKES 6 SERVINGS

This is a popular method of preparing potato salad in southern Italy, particularly during the warm summer months. To ensure its success, select new potatoes of relatively the same size so that they cook at the same rate. If you don't have Italian-style flat-leaf parsley, use the curly-leaf variety instead.

1¾ pounds small new potatoes, preferably red-skinned, unpeeled, scrubbed

3 tablespoons extra-virgin olive oil

1 tablespoon red wine vinegar

1 teaspoon dried oregano

½ teaspoon coarse salt, or to taste

Freshly ground black pepper, to taste

¼ cup finely chopped fresh flat-leaf parsley

1 large clove garlic, finely chopped

Place the potatoes in a large saucepan or medium stockpot with salted water to cover; bring to a boil over high heat. Reduce the heat to a gentle boil and cook until the potatoes are just tender, about 15 minutes, depending on size. Drain and set aside to cool slightly.

Meanwhile, in a large bowl, whisk together the oil, vinegar, oregano, salt, and pepper. Stir in the parsley and garlic. Let stand about 5 minutes to allow the flavors to blend.

As soon as the potatoes are cool enough to handle, yet still quite warm, cut them in half or in quarters, depending on size. Stir the reserved dressing a few times, and add the warm potato halves. Toss gently until the potatoes are thoroughly coated. Serve warm or at room tempera-

ture. Alternatively, let cool to room temperature and refrigerate a minimum of 3 hours, or up to 2 days, and serve chilled or return to room temperature.

PER SERVING

Calories 141 ▪ Protein 2g ▪ Total Fat 7g ▪ Sat. Fat 1g ▪ Cholesterol 0mg ▪ Carbohydrate 19g ▪ Dietary Fiber 2g ▪ Sodium 164mg

Vine-Ripened Tomato Salad with Parsley Vinaigrette

MAKES 4 SERVINGS

Serve this perfect summer salad with lots of crusty Italian bread to sop up the delicious juices.

¼ cup extra-virgin olive oil

2 tablespoons white wine vinegar

½ tablespoon Dijon mustard

1 large clove garlic, finely chopped

1 teaspoon coarse salt

1 teaspoon sugar

Freshly ground black pepper, to taste

¼ cup finely chopped fresh flat-leaf parsley

6 small vine-ripened tomatoes (about 4 ounces each), cut into ½-inch-thick slices

In a large bowl, whisk together the oil, vinegar, mustard, garlic, salt, sugar, and pepper; stir in the parsley. Let stand about 5 minutes to allow the sugar to dissolve. Add the tomatoes and toss gently yet thoroughly to combine. Let stand at room temperature about 15 minutes to allow the flavors to blend. Toss again and serve. Alternatively, cover and refrigerate a minimum of 3 hours, or overnight, and serve chilled or return to room temperature.

Main-Dish Salads

Italian Bread Salad

MAKES 4 SERVINGS

Any salad green can replace the romaine in this tasty Italian bread salad.

¼ cup extra-virgin olive oil
2 tablespoons red wine vinegar
½ teaspoon sugar
Salt, preferably the coarse variety, and freshly ground black pepper, to taste
1 cup cherry or grape tomatoes, halved or quartered, depending on size
½ cup chopped, seeded, peeled cucumber
¼ cup chopped red onion
1 tablespoon finely chopped fresh basil or flat-leaf parsley
4 cups romaine lettuce, spinach, or other lettuce leaves, torn into bite-size pieces
Herbed Croutons (see page 45)

In a large bowl, whisk together the oil, vinegar, sugar, salt, and pepper. Add the tomatoes, cucumbers, onion, and basil; toss gently yet thoroughly to combine. Set aside for a minimum of 15 minutes or up to 1 hour to allow the flavors to blend. Toss again before adding the remaining ingredients; toss gently yet thoroughly to combine. Serve at once.

Herbed Croutons

MAKES ABOUT 3 CUPS

Stir these zesty homemade croutons into soups, as well.

- **2 tablespoons extra-virgin olive oil**
- **½ teaspoon dried oregano**
- **¼ teaspoon dried parsley**
- **¼ teaspoon dried thyme leaves**
- **Freshly ground black pepper, to taste**
- **3 ounces slightly stale Italian or French bread, with crusts, cut into ¾-inch cubes**
- **Garlic salt, to taste**

Preheat the oven to 325F (165C). Lightly oil a baking sheet and set aside.

In a large bowl, whisk together the oil, oregano, parsley, thyme, and pepper. Working quickly, add the bread cubes and toss well to coat.

Arrange seasoned bread cubes in a single layer on prepared baking sheet. Sprinkle lightly with garlic salt. Bake on center rack, stirring and turning a few times, about 20 minutes, or until lightly browned and crisp. Remove from baking sheet and let cool to room temperature. If not using immediately, place in an airtight container and store up to 1 week at room temperature.

PER SERVING (PER ¼ CUP)
Calories 40 ▪ Protein 1g ▪ Total Fat 3g ▪ Sat. Fat 0g ▪
Cholesterol 0mg ▪ Carbohydrate 4g ▪
Dietary Fiber 0g ▪ Sodium 41mg

Italian Grain and Tomato Salad

MAKES 4 MAIN-DISH OR 6 TO 8 SIDE-DISH SERVINGS

Farro, often called emmer or spelt, is an ancient grain similar to barley, which can be used in this hearty salad, called *farinella*, instead. If using barley, skip the soaking process and rinse under cold-running water before proceeding.

- **1 cup farro, soaked overnight in water to cover**
- **6 to 7 cups water**
- **4 tablespoons extra-virgin olive oil**
- **2 tablespoons red-wine vinegar**
- **Salt, preferably the coarse variety, and freshly ground black pepper, to taste**
- **½ small red onion (about 2 ounces), chopped**
- **4 medium tomatoes (about 6 ounces each), seeded and chopped**
- **1 medium cucumber (about 8 ounces), peeled, seeded, and chopped**
- **½ cup chopped fresh basil leaves**
- **2 tablespoons chopped fresh parsley or mint leaves**

Drain the farro.

In a medium stockpot, bring 6 cups of salted water and the farro to a boil over high heat. Reduce the heat to between medium and medium-low and simmer, uncovered, until the farro is tender, stirring occasionally, about 40 minutes, adding water if necessary to prevent the farro from drying out. Drain the farro in a colander and rinse with cold water. Drain well.

Meanwhile, in a large bowl, whisk together the

oil, vinegar, salt, and pepper; stir in onion and let stand about 15 minutes at room temperature to allow the flavors to blend.

Add the farro and remaining ingredients to the onion mixture; toss well to combine. Let stand about 15 minutes at room temperature to allow the flavors to blend. Season with salt and pepper if necessary. Toss again and serve. Alternatively, cover and refrigerate a minimum of 3 hours, or overnight, and serve chilled or return to room temperature.

PER SERVING

Calories 349 ▪ Protein 7g ▪ Total Fat 15g ▪ Sat. Fat 2g ▪
Cholesterol 0mg ▪ Carbohydrate 51g ▪
Dietary Fiber 11g ▪ Sodium 22mg

Orzo Salad
with Zucchini and Basil

**MAKES 4 MAIN-DISH
OR 6 TO 8 SIDE-DISH SERVINGS**

This is always a refreshing pasta salad to bring to a potluck or picnic. Orzo is a rice-shaped pasta that can be found in most major supermarkets.

½ pound orzo

2 medium zucchini (about 6 ounces each), preferably 1 green and 1 yellow, finely diced

4 tablespoons extra-virgin olive oil

4 tablespoons fresh lemon juice (the juice of 1 large lemon)

2 cups loosely packed fresh basil leaves

¼ cup fresh flat-leaf parsley

3 cloves garlic, peeled

1 teaspoon salt, preferably the coarse variety, or to taste

½ teaspoon dried oregano

Freshly ground black pepper, to taste

In a large stockpot filled with boiling salted water, cook the orzo according to package directions until just al dente. While orzo is cooking, place the zucchini in a colander in a sink. When orzo is finished cooking, slowly drain over the zucchini. Stir a few times in the colander, then return the hot mixture to the pot and toss with 1 tablespoon of the oil and 1 tablespoon of the lemon juice. Cover and let stand 10 minutes.

Meanwhile, in a food processor fitted with the knife blade, process the basil, parsley, remaining oil, remaining lemon juice, garlic, salt, oregano, and pepper until smooth. Add to the orzo mixture; toss well to thoroughly combine. Serve at room temperature, or cover and refrigerate a minimum of 3 hours, or overnight, and serve chilled or return to room temperature.

PER SERVING

Calories 371 ▪ Protein 11g ▪ Total Fat 15g ▪ Sat. Fat 2g ▪
Cholesterol 0mg ▪ Carbohydrate 51g ▪
Dietary Fiber 3g ▪ Sodium 482mg

Florentine Pasta Salad
with Lemon

**MAKES 4 TO 6 MAIN-DISH
OR 8 SIDE-DISH SERVINGS**

This tangy pasta salad is perfect for picnics or buffets, as it can be served chilled or at room temperature.

¼ cup extra-virgin olive oil

¼ cup low-sodium vegetable broth

Juice of 1 medium lemon (about 3 tablespoons)

1 tablespoon Dijon mustard

1 large clove garlic, finely chopped

¼ teaspoon lemon-pepper seasoning

Pinch crushed red pepper flakes, or to taste
(optional)

Salt, preferably the coarse variety, and freshly
ground black pepper, to taste

12 ounces fusilli, rotelle, penne, or other short
pasta

4 cups loosely packed spinach leaves, finely
shredded

1 cup cherry or grape tomatoes, halved or
quartered, depending on size

In a small bowl, whisk the oil, broth, lemon juice, mustard, garlic, lemon-pepper seasoning, red pepper flakes (if using), salt, and black pepper until thoroughly blended. Let stand at room temperature about 5 minutes to allow the flavors to blend, then whisk again.

Meanwhile, in a large stockpot filled with boiling salted water, cook the pasta according to package directions until al dente. Drain well and return to the pot. Add the spinach and toss until wilted. While still quite hot, add the dressing, along with the tomatoes; toss well to thoroughly combine. Let come to room temperature before serving. Alternatively, cover and refrigerate a minimum of 3 hours, or overnight, and serve chilled or return to room temperature.

PER SERVING
Calories 462 ▪ Protein 13g ▪ Total Fat 15g ▪ Sat. Fat 2g ▪
Cholesterol 0mg ▪ Carbohydrate 68g ▪
Dietary Fiber 3g ▪ Sodium 117mg

Toasted Barley Salad with Roasted Red Bell Peppers

MAKES 4 SERVINGS

Toasting the barley adds a nutty flavor to this tasty grain salad, a favorite in my household.

1 cup pearl barley

3 cups low-sodium canned vegetable broth

½ cup water, plus additional if necessary

Salt and freshly ground black pepper,
to taste

1 (7.25-ounce) jar roasted red bell peppers,
drained and chopped

3 large plum tomatoes (about 3 ounces each),
chopped

½ cup chopped fresh flat-leaf parsley

4 scallions (white and green parts), thinly
sliced

3 tablespoons extra-virgin olive oil

1½ tablespoons fresh lemon juice

Romaine lettuce or spinach leaves (optional)

In a medium deep-sided skillet with a lid, cook barley over medium heat until lightly browned, stirring and shaking pan occasionally, about 5 minutes. Add broth, water, salt, and pepper; bring to a boil over high heat. Reduce heat to between low and medium-low, cover, and simmer until barley is tender and liquids are absorbed, about 45 minutes, stirring occasionally and adding more water if necessary to prevent barley from drying out. (If barley is tender but liquid remains, cook, uncovered, over medium heat, stirring often, until liquid has evaporated.) Uncover and let cool to just warm.

Place barley, bell peppers, tomatoes, parsley, scallions, oil, lemon juice, salt, and pepper in a large bowl; toss well to combine. Serve at room temperature, over lettuce (if using).

PER SERVING
Calories 350 ■ Protein 15g ■ Total Fat 11g ■ Sat. Fat 2g ■
Cholesterol 0mg ■ Carbohydrate 51g ■
Dietary Fiber 14g ■ Sodium 407mg

Pasta

Pasta recipes abound. With the exception of the far north, where rice (in the form of creamy risottos) or corn (in the form of hearty polenta) is often the grain of choice, there are so many delicious wheat-based pasta dishes in every region of Italy that even the vegetarian ones alone could fill a book. In the interest of space, this chapter brings a selection that hopefully will round out your current file and offer some tasty combinations you've never thought of.

The pasta noodle itself comes in an amazing array of shapes, sizes, and colors, some of which are common throughout Italy, and some of which are limited to a particular region, such as Apulia's orecchiette or "little ears." There are also specialty shapes (tennis raquets, snowmen, to name a few) produced by individual pasta makers. As a general rule, sturdy pasta is paired with full-bodied sauces, while delicate pasta is matched with light sauces.

To cook pasta, use enough boiling water to cover the pasta over one and one-half times (about 4 to 6 quarts of water per pound of pasta) and add a bit of salt when adding the pasta to the water. Except for use in some pasta salads, don't rinse the pasta after cooking, as the starchiness helps the sauce adhere to the pasta. Pasta cooking times vary among the different kinds of dried pasta; on average, the dried variety takes about nine or ten minutes to reach al dente, or "firm to the bite." Typically, fresh pasta cooks in about half the time as dried. But not to worry—if you can't tell by looking how done the pasta is, just take a piece and *mangia* (eat)!

Bucatini with Eggplant and Roasted Peppers

MAKES 4 TO 5 MAIN-DISH
OR 6 TO 8 PASTA-COURSE SERVINGS

This delicious Sicilian pasta dish is ideal to serve in the summer months when eggplant, bell peppers, and tomatoes are plentiful. If you can't find bucatini, a long, hollow pasta, use linguine or spaghetti instead.

1 medium eggplant (about ¾ pound), peeled, cut into ½-inch cubes
Table salt
2 large green and/or red bell peppers (about 8 ounces each), cut in half lengthwise
2 tablespoons extra-virgin olive oil
2 large cloves garlic, finely chopped
2 cups low-sodium vegetable broth
1 pound plum tomatoes, chopped
2 tablespoons capers, drained
1 teaspoon dried oregano
½ teaspoon dried thyme leaves
½ teaspoon salt, preferably the coarse variety
Freshly ground black pepper, to taste
12 ounces bucatini or linguine

Sprinkle the eggplant with table salt and set in a colander to drain for 30 minutes. Rinse the eggplant under cold-running water and drain well between paper towels.

Preheat the oven to broil. Lightly oil a baking sheet.

Place the bell pepper halves, skin sides up, on prepared baking sheet; flatten with your hand. Broil 6 to 8 inches from heating element until peppers are blackened, about 10 minutes. Transfer to a paper bag and twist to seal, or place in a self-sealing plastic bag and seal. Let rest about 15 minutes. Remove bell peppers from bag; peel away and discard the skins. Cut the peppers into thin strips.

In a large nonstick skillet with a lid, heat the oil over medium heat. Add the eggplant and cook, stirring, until softened, about 5 minutes. Add the garlic and cook, stirring, 1 minute. Stir in the broth, bell peppers, tomatoes, capers, oregano, thyme, salt, and black pepper; bring to a brisk simmer over medium-high heat. Reduce heat, cover, and simmer, stirring occasionally, until eggplant is tender, about 15 minutes.

Meanwhile, in a large stockpot filled with boiling salted water, cook the pasta according to package directions until al dente. Drain and return to pot. Add eggplant mixture, tossing well to thoroughly combine. Serve at once.

PER SERVING
Calories 469 ▪ Protein 19g ▪ Total Fat 9g ▪ Sat. Fat 1g ▪
Cholesterol 0mg ▪ Carbohydrate 80g ▪
Dietary Fiber 8g ▪ Sodium 584mg

Eggplant Cacciatore

MAKES 5 TO 6 MAIN-DISH
OR 8 PASTA-COURSE SERVINGS

Meaty eggplant stands in nicely for traditional chicken in this tasty rendition of the perennial favorite.

1 large eggplant (1 to 1¼ pounds), peeled and
   cubed
Table salt
2 tablespoon extra-virgin olive oil
1 cup chopped onion
1 cup chopped red bell pepper
1 cup chopped green bell pepper
3 large cloves garlic, finely chopped
1 (26-ounce) jar marinara sauce
1 teaspoon dried oregano
½ teaspoon dried thyme leaves
¼ teaspoon dried basil
Salt and freshly ground black pepper, to taste
12 ounces linguine, cooked according to
   package directions until al dente, drained

Sprinkle the eggplant with table salt and set in a colander to drain for 30 minutes. Rinse the eggplant under cold-running water and drain well between paper towels.

In a large saucepan or medium stockpot, heat half the oil over medium heat. Add the onion and bell peppers; cook, stirring often, until softened, 3 minutes. Add the garlic and cook, stirring constantly, 1 minute. Add the sauce, oregano, thyme, basil, salt, and pepper; bring to a brisk simmer over medium-high heat. Reduce the heat and simmer gently, partially covered, 15 minutes, stirring occasionally.

Meanwhile, in a large nonstick skillet, heat the remaining oil over medium-high heat. Add the eggplant and cook, stirring, until lightly browned, 5 minutes. Add the sauce mixture; let come to a brisk simmer. Reduce heat and simmer gently, uncovered, 10 minutes, or until eggplant is tender, stirring occasionally. Serve hot, over linguine.

PER SERVING
Calories 447 ▪ Protein 13g ▪ Total Fat 12g ▪ Sat. Fat 2g ▪
Cholesterol 0mg ▪ Carbohydrate 77g ▪
Dietary Fiber 5g ▪ Sodium 936mg

> ### ❧ COOK'S TIP ❧
> *Salting helps draw out the eggplant's bitter juices. However, if you are short on time, the step can be omitted here and in other recipes where the eggplant is to be simmered or baked with several ingredients, as any bitterness is typically masked by the other flavors.*

Farfalle with Fennel and Lima Beans

MAKES 6 TO 8 MAIN-DISH
OR 12 PASTA-COURSE SERVINGS

Crisp fennel and tender lima beans offer a nice counterbalance of texture as well as flavor in this hearty pasta dish from Tuscany. Aniseed can be substituted for the fennel seed.

3 tablespoons extra-virgin olive oil
2 medium fennel bulbs (about 12 ounces each),
   trimmed, quartered, cored, and thinly sliced
2 large carrots (about 4 ounces each), chopped
1 large onion (about 8 ounces), chopped

3 cloves garlic, finely chopped

½ teaspoon fennel seed

Pinch crushed red pepper flakes, or to taste
  (optional)

3 cups low-sodium vegetable broth

1 (10-ounce) package frozen baby lima beans

Salt and freshly ground black pepper, to taste

1 pound farfalle (bow ties) or other similar
  pasta

In a large, deep-sided nonstick skillet, heat the oil over medium-low heat. Add fennel, carrots, onion, garlic, fennel seed, and red pepper flakes (if using); cook, stirring occasionally, until vegetables are crisp-tender, about 10 minutes. Add broth, lima beans, salt, and pepper; bring to a boil over high heat. Reduce heat to medium-low and simmer, uncovered, stirring occasionally, until beans are tender, about 10 minutes.

Meanwhile, in a large stockpot, cook the pasta in boiling salted water according to package directions until al dente. Drain and return to the pot. Add the lima bean mixture and toss well to combine. Serve at once.

PER SERVING

Calories 495 ▪ Protein 21g ▪ Total Fat 9g ▪ Sat. Fat 1g ▪
Cholesterol 0mg ▪ Carbohydrate 84g ▪
Dietary Fiber 11g ▪ Sodium 361mg

Farfalle with Sun-Dried Tomato–Mint Pesto

**MAKES 4 TO 6 MAIN-DISH
OR 8 PASTA-COURSE SERVINGS**

Sun-dried tomatoes are a staple in southern Italian cuisine, and mint grows everywhere, like weeds. Processed into a paste with walnuts and garlic, pesto never tasted any better. It's also wonderful tossed with rice or green beans.

⅓ cup oil-packed sun-dried tomatoes, drained

¼ cup walnuts

¼ cup packed fresh mint leaves

2 tablespoons extra-virgin olive oil

2 tablespoons tomato paste

2 large cloves garlic, finely chopped

1 teaspoon coarse salt, or to taste

Freshly ground black pepper, to taste

12 ounces farfalle, rotelle, or other short pasta

Combine the tomatoes, walnuts, mint, oil, tomato paste, garlic, salt, and pepper in a food processor fitted with the knife blade; process until fairly smooth. Set aside.

In a large stockpot, cook the pasta in boiling salted water according to package directions until al dente. Drain well and return to pot. Add the sun-dried tomato mixture, tossing well to combine. Serve warm.

PER SERVING

Calories 454 ▪ Protein 14g ▪ Total Fat 14g ▪ Sat. Fat 2g ▪
Cholesterol 0mg ▪ Carbohydrate 69g ▪
Dietary Fiber 3g ▪ Sodium 567mg

Farfalle with Zucchini, Mint, and Almonds

MAKES 5 TO 6 MAIN-DISH

OR 8 PASTA-COURSE SERVINGS

This tasty specialty from Calabria is easy to make with the help of a food processor. The Vine-Ripened Tomato Salad with Parsley Vinaigrette (page 43) is a nice accompaniment.

> **2 medium zucchini (about 6 ounces each), cut into ½-inch cubes**
> **½ cup loosely packed fresh mint or basil leaves**
> **¼ cup extra-virgin olive oil**
> **¼ cup blanched almonds**
> **2 large cloves garlic, peeled**
> **1 teaspoon coarse salt, plus additional to taste**
> **Freshly ground black pepper, to taste**
> **1 pound farfalle (bow ties), cooked according to package directions until al dente, drained**

Place the zucchini in a medium saucepan with salted water to cover; bring to a boil over high heat. Reduce the heat to medium and cook until tender, about 3 minutes. Drain.

Place the mint, oil, almonds, garlic, salt, and pepper in a food processor fitted with the knife blade; process until smooth. Add about three-fourths of the drained zucchini and process until pureed but still slightly chunky.

Place the hot cooked pasta in a large bowl and add the zucchini puree and remaining zucchini; toss well to thoroughly combine. Serve warm or at room temperature.

PER SERVING
Calories 490 ■ Protein 14g ■ Total Fat 16g ■ Sat. Fat 2g ■ Cholesterol 0mg ■ Carbohydrate 72g ■ Dietary Fiber 4g ■ Sodium 388mg

Fettuccine with Basil-Pea Cream

MAKES 5 TO 6 MAIN-DISH

OR 8 PASTA-COURSE SERVINGS

Incredibly, not one drop of cream has been used in this creamy sauce. If the resulting pasta dish is a bit too thick, thin with additional vegetable broth.

> **3 tablespoons extra-virgin olive oil**
> **½ cup chopped onion**
> **2½ cups low-sodium vegetable broth**
> **16 ounces frozen green peas**
> **½ teaspoon salt**
> **Freshly ground black pepper, to taste**
> **1 cup loosely packed fresh basil leaves, torn in half**
> **1 pound fresh cultivated white button mushrooms, sliced**
> **2 large cloves garlic, finely chopped**
> **12 ounces egg-free fettuccine**

In a large nonstick skillet with a lid, heat 1 tablespoon of the oil over medium heat. Add the onion and cook, stirring often, until softened, about 3 minutes. Stir in 1 cup of the broth, the peas, salt, and pepper; bring to a boil over high heat. Reduce heat to medium-low and simmer, covered, 5 minutes. Place 1½ cups of the pea mixture, remaining broth, and basil leaves in a food processor fitted with the knife blade, or in a blender; process until smooth. Transfer to a large bowl and add remaining pea mixture, stirring well to combine.

Add the remaining oil to the skillet and heat over medium heat. Add the mushrooms and cook, stirring often, until the mushrooms begin to release their liquid, 4 to 5 minutes. Add the garlic and cook, stirring constantly, 1 minute. Stir in the pea mixture; reduce the heat to low and cook, stirring, until heated through, seasoning with salt and pepper if necessary.

Meanwhile, in a large stockpot, cook the fettuccine in boiling salted water according to package directions until al dente. Drain and return to pot. Add pea and mushroom mixture, tossing well to combine. Serve at once.

PER SERVING

Calories 457 ▪ Protein 22g ▪ Total Fat 10g ▪ Sat. Fat 1g ▪
Cholesterol 0mg ▪ Carbohydrate 71g ▪
Dietary Fiber 9g ▪ Sodium 584mg

Fettuccine with Mushrooms and Marsala

MAKES 3 TO 4 MAIN-DISH
OR 6 PASTA-COURSE SERVINGS

I recommend using only white cultivated mushrooms here, as wild mushrooms may overwhelm the sweet and nutty flavor of the Marsala wine. If you don't have Marsala, use port or Madeira instead.

3 tablespoons extra-virgin olive oil
2 large cloves garlic, finely chopped
¾ pound fresh cultivated white button
    mushrooms, sliced
¼ cup Marsala wine

2 tablespoons fresh lemon juice
½ teaspoon salt, preferably the coarse variety
⅛ teaspoon crushed red pepper flakes, or to
    taste
Freshly ground black pepper, to taste
8 ounces egg-free fettuccine, cooked
    according to package directions, drained
1 tablespoon finely chopped fresh flat-leaf
    parsley

In a large deep-sided nonstick skillet, heat half of the oil over medium heat. Add the garlic and cook, stirring, 30 seconds. Add the mushrooms and cook, stirring often, until they begin to release their liquid, 4 to 5 minutes. Add the wine, lemon juice, salt, red pepper flakes, and black pepper; let come to a simmer and cook, stirring occasionally, until most of the liquids have evaporated, about 10 minutes. Remove from heat and add the fettuccine, remaining oil, and parsley. Return to low heat and toss until thoroughly combined and heated through. Serve at once.

PER SERVING

Calories 447 ▪ Protein 12g ▪ Total Fat 15g ▪ Sat. Fat 2g ▪
Cholesterol 0mg ▪ Carbohydrate 63g ▪
Dietary Fiber 3g ▪ Sodium 367mg

Fusilli with Beets

**MAKES 4 TO 6 MAIN-DISH
OR 8 PASTA-COURSE SERVINGS**

Though optional, chopped chives lend this tasty pasta dish attractive flecks of color.

  3 tablespoons extra-virgin olive oil
  1 medium red onion (about 6 ounces), chopped
  2 large cloves garlic, finely chopped
  1 (16-ounce) jar beets, drained well and cubed
  Salt, preferably the coarse variety, and freshly
      ground black pepper, to taste
  12 ounces fusilli or other short spiral pasta,
      cooked according to package directions
      until al dente, drained
  ½ cup low-sodium vegetable broth
  Chopped fresh chives (optional)

In a large deep-sided nonstick skillet, heat the oil over medium heat. Add the onion and cook, stirring, until softened, 3 to 4 minutes. Add the garlic and cook, stirring, 30 seconds. Add the beets, salt, and pepper, and cook, stirring, until heated through, about 2 minutes.

Add the pasta and broth, and toss to thoroughly combine. Serve at once, garnished with the chopped chives (if using).

PER SERVING
Calories 463 ▪ Protein 14g ▪ Total Fat 12g ▪ Sat. Fat 2g ▪
Cholesterol 0mg ▪ Carbohydrate 76g ▪
Dietary Fiber 5g ▪ Sodium 370mg

Fusilli with Caramelized Onions and Walnuts

**MAKES 4 TO 5 MAIN-DISH
OR 6 PASTA-COURSE SERVINGS**

The fragrance of caramelized onions is nothing short of tantalizing. If possible, do not use a nonstick skillet, as the onions will take longer to caramelize.

  2 tablespoons extra-virgin olive oil
  4 cups thinly sliced yellow onions (about 1
      pound)
  ½ teaspoon salt, or to taste
  2 large cloves garlic, finely chopped
  10 ounces fusilli or other spiral pasta, cooked
      according to package directions until al
      dente, drained
  ½ cup low-sodium vegetable broth
  ⅓ cup chopped fresh basil
  3 tablespoons chopped walnuts
  Freshly ground black pepper, to taste

In a large skillet with a lid, heat the oil over medium heat. Add the onions and salt and cook, stirring, until softened, about 5 minutes. Cover, reduce the heat to medium-low, and cook 15 minutes, stirring occasionally. Uncover and cook, stirring frequently, until onions turn deep golden, about 15 minutes, adding the garlic the last few minutes of cooking.

Add the pasta, broth, basil, walnuts, and pepper to the skillet; toss well to combine. Season with salt if necessary. Serve at once.

Fusilli with Lentil Sauce

**MAKES 5 TO 6 MAIN-DISH
OR 8 PASTA-COURSE SERVINGS**

Lentils lend this iron-rich sauce from Basilicata a meaty texture without the fat and cholesterol. It is also wonderful tossed with rice or barley.

2 tablespoons extra-virgin olive oil

1 large onion (about 8 ounces), chopped

1 medium carrot (about 4 ounces), chopped

4 large cloves garlic, finely chopped

2 cups low-sodium vegetable broth

½ cup lentils, rinsed

1 teaspoon chopped fresh rosemary, or ¼
    teaspoon dried

1 teaspoon fresh thyme leaves, or ¼ teaspoon
    dried

½ teaspoon salt, or to taste

⅛ teaspoon cayenne pepper, or to taste

Freshly ground black pepper, to taste

1 (14.5-ounce) can diced tomatoes, juices
    included

4 cups arugula or spinach leaves, torn into
    bite-size pieces

12 ounces fusilli, rotini, or other twist pasta

In a large deep-sided skillet with a lid, heat the oil over medium heat. Add the onion, carrot, and garlic; cook, stirring often, until softened, about 3 minutes. Add the broth, lentils, rosemary, thyme, salt, cayenne, and black pepper; bring to a boil over high heat. Reduce heat to low and simmer, covered, 15 minutes. Add tomatoes and their juices and increase heat to medium-high; cover and bring to a brisk simmer. Reduce the heat to low and simmer, covered, until the lentils are tender, 15 to 20 minutes, stirring occasionally. Stir in the arugula and cook, covered, until the arugula is wilted, about 5 more minutes.

Meanwhile, in a large stockpot, cook the fusilli in boiling salted water according to package directions until al dente. Drain and return to the pot. Add the lentil sauce and toss well to combine. Serve at once.

Linguine with Artichoke-Marinara Sauce

**MAKES 4 TO 6 MAIN-DISH
OR 8 PASTA-COURSE SERVINGS**

Ready in just about fifteen minutes, this yummy pasta dish is often the rush-hour special in my house.

> 1 tablespoon extra-virgin olive oil
> 3 large cloves garlic, finely chopped
> 2 cups marinara sauce
> ½ cup water
> 1 tablespoon tomato paste
> ⅛ teaspoon crushed red pepper flakes, or to taste
> Salt and freshly ground black pepper, to taste
> 1 (14-ounce) can quartered artichoke hearts, drained and chopped
> 12 ounces linguine, cooked according to package directions until al dente, drained

In a medium saucepan, heat the oil over medium heat. Add the garlic and cook, stirring constantly, until very lightly browned, 1 to 2 minutes, taking care not to burn. Stir in the marinara sauce, water, tomato paste, red pepper flakes, salt, and black pepper; bring to a boil over a medium-high heat. Reduce the heat to low and simmer, uncovered, 10 minutes, stirring occasionally. Stir in the artichokes and simmer, covered, 2 minutes. Serve hot, over linguine.

PER SERVING
Calories 487 ▪ Protein 17g ▪ Total Fat 9g ▪ Sat. Fat 1g ▪
Cholesterol 0mg ▪ Carbohydrate 89g ▪
Dietary Fiber 8g ▪ Sodium 919mg

Linguine with Bread Crumbs and Lemon

**MAKES 3 TO 4 MAIN-DISH
OR 6 PASTA-COURSE SERVINGS**

This delicious dish's completion can be hastened by toasting the bread crumbs a couple days in advance. If you like lemons as much as I do, use the greater amount of juice.

> 1 slice day-old Italian bread (about 1¼ ounces), torn into bite-size pieces
> 2 tablespoons extra-virgin olive oil
> 6 large cloves garlic, finely chopped
> 8 ounces linguine
> ¼ cup chopped fresh flat-leaf parsley
> 1 to 2 tablespoons fresh lemon juice
> ½ teaspoon salt, preferably the coarse variety
> ¼ teaspoon freshly ground black pepper

Preheat the oven to 250F (120C).

Place the bread in a food processor fitted with a knife blade; pulse a few times until coarse crumbs measure about ⅔ cup. Transfer to a light-colored baking sheet. Bake 20 minutes, or until lightly browned, stirring halfway through cooking time. Transfer to a small bowl and set aside.

In a large nonstick skillet, heat 1½ tablespoons of the oil over medium heat. Add the garlic and cook, stirring constantly, 30 to 60 seconds, or until sizzling and fragrant. Remove the skillet from the heat and add the reserved bread crumbs, tossing well to thoroughly coat.

Meanwhile, cook the pasta in a large pot of boiling salted water according to package directions until al dente. Drain and transfer to a large bowl. Add the remaining oil, parsley, lemon juice, salt, and pepper; toss well to combine. Add the bread crumb mixture, tossing well to thoroughly coat. Serve at once.

PER SERVING

Calories 405 ■ Protein 11g ■ Total Fat 11g ■ Sat. Fat 2g ■
Cholesterol 0mg ■ Carbohydrate 65g ■
Dietary Fiber 3g ■ Sodium 434mg

Linguine with Broccoli Sauce and Garlic

MAKES 4 TO 5 MAIN-DISH
OR 6 TO 8 PASTA-COURSE SERVINGS

You can chop the garlic if you like, but I prefer slices because they are more mellow in flavor and add texture to this delicious pasta dish from Sicily. Rapini (broccoli rabe) or cauliflower can be substituted for the broccoli.

3 cups fresh or frozen broccoli florets

12 ounces linguine

2 tablespoons extra-virgin olive oil

4 to 6 large cloves garlic, thinly sliced

¼ teaspoon crushed red pepper flakes, or to taste

1 cup low-sodium vegetable broth

¼ cup chopped fresh flat-leaf parsley

½ teaspoon salt, preferably the coarse variety

Freshly ground black pepper, to taste

Bring a large stockpot filled with salted water to a boil over high heat. Add the broccoli and cook un-

til the broccoli is bright green, 2 minutes. Remove the broccoli with a slotted spoon (do not drain water from stockpot). Place the broccoli in a colander and rinse with cold water. Drain and coarsely chop.

Return the water to a boil in the stockpot. Add the pasta and cook according to package directions until al dente. Drain.

Meanwhile, in a large deep-sided nonstick skillet with a lid, heat the oil over medium heat. Add the garlic and cook, stirring constantly, until lightly browned but not burned, 1 to 2 minutes. Add the broccoli and red pepper flakes; cook, stirring, 2 minutes. Add the broth and bring to a boil over medium-high heat. Reduce the heat and simmer, covered, 2 minutes, or until the broccoli is tender. Add the pasta, parsley, salt, and pepper to skillet, tossing well to combine. Serve at once.

PER SERVING

Calories 409 ■ Protein 16g ■ Total Fat 8g ■ Sat. Fat 1g ■
Cholesterol 0mg ■ Carbohydrate 68g ■
Dietary Fiber 5g ■ Sodium 382mg

Gemelli with Asparagus and Pine Nuts

**MAKES 4 TO 5 MAIN-DISH
OR 8 PASTA-COURSE SERVINGS**

Gemelli is short braided pasta, ideal for tossing with inch-long asparagus, but any tubular variety—penne is a good choice—will work in this appealing spring-time recipe.

¼ cup pine nuts

2 tablespoons extra-virgin olive oil

½ pound thin asparagus, trimmed, cut
    diagonally into 1-inch pieces

1 clove garlic, finely chopped

12 ounces gemelli or other short tubular pasta

2 tablespoons fresh lemon juice

½ teaspoon coarse salt

¼ teaspoon lemon-pepper seasoning

Heat a medium nonstick skillet over medium heat. Add the pine nuts and cook, stirring constantly, until fragrant and lightly browned, about 3 minutes. Immediately remove from skillet and transfer to a small bowl; set aside.

Return the skillet to medium heat and add the oil. Add the asparagus and garlic and cook, stirring often, until the asparagus is slightly tender, 4 to 5 minutes.

Meanwhile, cook the pasta in a large pot of boiling salted water according to package directions until al dente. Drain and return to the pot. Add the asparagus and garlic mixture, reserved pine nuts, lemon juice, salt, and lemon-pepper seasoning; toss gently to combine. Serve at once.

PER SERVING
Calories 437 ■ Protein 14g ■ Total Fat 13g ■ Sat. Fat 2g ■
Cholesterol 0mg ■ Carbohydrate 67g ■
Dietary Fiber 3g ■ Sodium 263mg

Linguine with Caper and Green Olive Marinara Sauce

**MAKES 4 TO 6 MAIN-DISH
OR 8 PASTA-COURSE SERVINGS**

This tangy pasta dish is a good choice for a quick and delicious weeknight supper. If you are watching your salt intake, rinse the olives and capers before cooking.

1 tablespoon extra-virgin olive oil

2 large cloves garlic, thinly sliced

¼ teaspoon crushed red pepper flakes, or to
    taste

2 cups marinara sauce

½ cup pitted green olives, drained and roughly
    chopped

½ cup coarsely chopped fresh flat-leaf parsley

¼ cup capers, drained and roughly chopped

¼ teaspoon dried grated lemon peel

12 ounces linguine

In a large deep-sided nonstick skillet, heat the oil over medium heat. Add the garlic and red pepper flakes and cook, stirring constantly, until fragrant, about 1 minute. Add the marinara sauce, olives, parsley, capers, and lemon peel; bring to a brisk simmer over medium-high heat. Reduce the heat and simmer gently, uncovered, until slightly thickened, about 15 minutes, stirring occasionally.

Meanwhile, cook the linguine in a large pot of

boiling salted water according to package directions until al dente. Drain and add the linguine to the sauce, tossing well to thoroughly coat. Serve at once.

PER SERVING

Calories 456 ■ Protein 13g ■ Total Fat 11g ■ Sat. Fat 2g ■
Cholesterol 0mg ■ Carbohydrate 78g ■
Dietary Fiber 2g ■ Sodium 1,018mg

Linguine with Garden Bolognese

MAKES 6 MAIN-DISH OR 8 PASTA-COURSE SERVINGS

Though traditional Bolognese sauce contains beef, many health-conscious modern Italian cooks use meaty and flavorful sun-dried tomatoes instead.

12 ounces linguine, cooked according to package directions until al dente, drained
Garden Bolognese Sauce (below)

Place the linguine in a large bowl. Add the sauce and toss well to combine. Serve at once.

PER SERVING

Calories 430 ■ Protein 12g ■ Total Fat 12g ■ Sat. Fat 2g ■
Cholesterol 0mg ■ Carbohydrate 71g ■
Dietary Fiber 8g ■ Sodium 717mg

Garden Bolognese Sauce

MAKES 6 SERVINGS

Toss this vegetarian version of the famous sauce with any pasta or serve on a bed of rice or polenta.

2 tablespoons extra-virgin olive oil
1 medium onion (about 6 ounces), chopped
1 medium zucchini (about 6 ounces), chopped
1 medium green or red bell pepper (about 6 ounces), chopped
4 ounces cultivated white button mushrooms, sliced
2 large cloves garlic, finely chopped
1 (26-ounce) jar pasta sauce, preferably the tomato-basil variety
¼ cup dry red wine
½ cup dry-packed sun-dried tomato halves, cut into thin strips with kitchen shears, soaked in warm water to cover for 15 minutes, drained
Salt and freshly ground black pepper, to taste
3 tablespoons finely chopped fresh basil

In a medium stockpot, heat the oil over medium heat. Add the onion, zucchini, bell pepper, mushrooms, and garlic. Cook, stirring often, until the vegetables are softened, about 5 minutes. Stir in the pasta sauce, wine, sun-dried tomatoes, salt, and pepper; bring to a boil over medium-high heat. Reduce heat to medium-low and simmer, uncovered, stirring often, until thickened, about 20 minutes. Stir in the basil and serve hot.

PER SERVING

Calories 220 ■ Protein 4g ■ Total Fat 11g ■ Sat. Fat 2g ■
Cholesterol 0mg ■ Carbohydrate 28g ■
Dietary Fiber 6g ■ Sodium 713mg

Linguine with Garlicky Tomato Sauce

MAKES 4 TO 6 MAIN-DISH
OR 8 PASTA-COURSE SERVINGS

For garlic lovers, this spicy pasta dish's heat can be controlled by reducing the amount of crushed red pepper flakes to just a pinch, or eliminating them entirely.

2½ tablespoons extra-virgin olive oil

6 large cloves garlic, finely chopped

1 (28-ounce) can plum tomatoes, juices included

1 teaspoon dried oregano

½ teaspoon coarse salt

⅛ teaspoon crushed red pepper flakes, or to taste

Freshly ground black pepper, to taste

12 ounces linguine, cooked according to package directions until al dente, drained

In a large nonstick skillet, heat the oil over medium heat. Add the garlic and cook, stirring constantly, until lightly browned but not burned, 1 to 2 minutes. Add the tomatoes and their juices, oregano, salt, red pepper flakes, and black pepper; bring to a boil over medium-high heat. Reduce the heat and simmer, uncovered, until thickened, about 10 minutes, stirring occasionally and breaking up the tomatoes with a large wooden spoon. Serve hot, over linguine.

PER SERVING
Calories 438 ■ Protein 13g ■ Total Fat 10g ■ Sat. Fat 1g ■
Cholesterol 0mg ■ Carbohydrate 74g ■
Dietary Fiber 4g ■ Sodium 665mg

Linguine with Potatoes, Green Beans, and Spinach-Walnut Pesto

MAKES 4 MAIN-DISH OR 6 PASTA-COURSE SERVINGS

This hearty pasta dish is as healthful as it is delicious.

8 ounces linguine

1 pound medium red-skin potatoes, quartered

¼ pound fresh green beans, trimmed and halved

Spinach-Walnut Pesto (below)

In a large stockpot filled with boiling salted water, cook the linguine and potatoes 6 minutes. Add the green beans; cook until potatoes are tender, 4 to 5 minutes. Drain in a colander and return to the pot. Add the pesto, tossing well to combine. Serve at once.

PER SERVING
Calories 424 ■ Protein 12g ■ Total Fat 15g ■ Sat. Fat 2g ■
Cholesterol 0mg ■ Carbohydrate 63g ■
Dietary Fiber 5g ■ Sodium 510mg

Spinach-Walnut Pesto

MAKES ABOUT 1 CUP

This is a delicious and economical pesto to prepare during the winter months when fresh basil is in short supply.

½ (10-ounce) bag washed spinach leaves

¼ cup loosely packed fresh basil leaves

3 tablespoons walnut pieces

2 large cloves garlic, finely chopped

1 teaspoon coarse salt, or to taste

¼ teaspoon freshly ground black pepper

3 tablespoons extra-virgin olive oil

Place the spinach, basil, walnuts, garlic, salt, and pepper in a food processor fitted with a knife blade; process until finely chopped. Add the oil and process until smooth and well-blended. If not using immediately, store tightly covered in the refrigerator for up to 2 days.

PER SERVING (ABOUT 1 TABLESPOON)

Calories 35 ■ Protein 1g ■ Total Fat 3g ■ Sat. Fat 0g ■
Cholesterol 0mg ■ Carbohydrate 1g ■
Dietary Fiber 0g ■ Sodium 125mg

Linguine with Basil-Walnut Pesto

**MAKES 3 TO 4 MAIN-DISH
OR 6 PASTA-COURSE SERVINGS**

Classic basil pesto is enhanced in this recipe with the freshness of parsley and the richness of walnuts. If Italian flat-leaf parsley is unavailable, the curly-leaf variety can be substituted.

1 cup loosely packed fresh basil leaves

1 cup loosely packed fresh flat-leaf parsley leaves

3 tablespoons low-sodium vegetable broth

2 tablespoons chopped walnuts

2 tablespoons extra-virgin olive oil

2 large cloves garlic, finely chopped

¼ teaspoon coarse salt, or to taste

Freshly ground black pepper, to taste

8 ounces linguine, cooked according to package directions until al dente, drained

Place the basil, parsley, broth, walnuts, oil, garlic, salt, and pepper in a food processor fitted with the knife blade; process until smooth and well combined. Transfer to a large bowl and combine with the pasta, tossing to thoroughly coat. Serve at once.

PER SERVING

Calories 409 ■ Protein 13g ■ Total Fat 13g ■ Sat. Fat 2g ■
Cholesterol 0mg ■ Carbohydrate 60g ■
Dietary Fiber 4g ■ Sodium 206mg

> ### ⚘ COOK'S TIP ⚘
> *When shopping for flat-leaf parsley, be careful not to confuse it with fresh cilantro, a stronger-scented herb with a more acidic taste, which it closely resembles.*

Linguine with Parsley, Garlic, Coarse Salt, and Red Pepper Oil

**MAKES 4 MAIN-DISH
OR 6 TO 8 PASTA-COURSE SERVINGS**

This is one of my favorite quick weeknight pasta suppers. It goes particularly well with the Fresh Tomato and Basil Salad (page 36). For a milder dish, use half the amount of red pepper flakes.

> 2 tablespoons extra-virgin olive oil
> ¼ teaspoon crushed red pepper flakes
> 3 large cloves garlic, finely chopped
> ½ cup chopped fresh flat-leaf parsley
> 1 to 1½ teaspoons coarse salt
> 12 ounces linguine, cooked according to package directions until al dente
> Freshly ground black pepper, to taste

In a large deep-sided nonstick skillet, heat oil over medium heat. Add the red pepper flakes and cook, stirring constantly, 2 minutes. Add the garlic and cook, stirring constantly, until garlic is lightly browned, about 30 seconds. Remove from heat and immediately stir in the parsley and salt. Add the pasta and black pepper; toss well to thoroughly combine. Serve at once.

PER SERVING
Calories 382 ▪ Protein 11g ▪ Total Fat 8g ▪ Sat. Fat 1g ▪
Cholesterol 0mg ▪ Carbohydrate 65g ▪
Dietary Fiber 2g ▪ Sodium 544mg

Linguine with Roasted Pepper, Tomato, and Garlic Sauce

**MAKES 4 MAIN-DISH
OR 6 TO 8 PASTA-COURSE SERVINGS**

Made entirely in the oven, this fragrant roasted sauce couldn't be much easier to prepare—just make sure that the oven rack is set in the center. For a variation, add a coarsely chopped yellow or red onion to the mixture before roasting.

> 1 (14-ounce) can whole tomatoes, coarsely chopped, juice included
> 2 medium green bell peppers (about 6 ounces each), cut into ½-inch-wide strips
> 5 large cloves garlic, crushed
> ¼ cup extra-virgin olive oil
> 1 tablespoon balsamic vinegar
> 1 teaspoon chopped fresh rosemary, or ¼ teaspoon dried
> Salt, preferably the coarse variety, and freshly ground black pepper, to taste
> 9 ounces linguine, preferably fresh, cooked according to package directions until al dente, drained

Preheat the oven to 475F (245C). Lightly oil an 11 × 7-inch baking pan and set aside.

Place the tomatoes and their juices, bell peppers, garlic, oil, vinegar, rosemary, salt, and pepper in a large bowl; toss well to combine. Transfer to the prepared baking pan and roast on the center rack 30 minutes, or until the peppers are nicely browned and beginning to char, stirring halfway through cooking time. Remove from the oven and let stand until the mixture stops sizzling.

Add half of the bell pepper mixture to the linguine and toss well to combine. Puree the remaining half in a food processor fitted with the knife blade, or in a blender. Toss with the linguine and serve at once.

PER SERVING

Calories 405 ▪ Protein 10g ▪ Total Fat 15g ▪ Sat. Fat 2g ▪ Cholesterol 0mg ▪ Carbohydrate 59g ▪ Dietary Fiber 5g ▪ Sodium 218mg

---

Linguine with Yellow Tomato Sauce

MAKES 3 TO 4 MAIN-DISH OR 6 PASTA-COURSE SERVINGS

This golden pasta sauce is sweeter than the red tomato–based varieties. Vine-ripened red tomatoes can replace the golden.

3 tablespoons extra-virgin olive oil

2 large cloves garlic, finely chopped

5 ripe yellow tomatoes (about 4 ounces each), coarsely chopped

¼ cup chopped fresh basil

½ teaspoon salt

¼ teaspoon sugar

Freshly ground black pepper, to taste

⅛ teaspoon crushed red pepper flakes, or to taste

8 ounces linguine, cooked according to package directions until al dente, drained

In a large deep-sided nonstick skillet with a lid, heat the oil over medium heat. Add the garlic and

cook, stirring constantly, until sizzling and fragrant, about 1 minute. Add the tomatoes, basil, salt, sugar, black pepper, and red pepper flakes; bring to a brisk simmer over medium-high heat. Reduce the heat to medium-low and cook, stirring occasionally, until tomatoes break down and a sauce forms, about 15 minutes. Add the pasta to the skillet and toss well to combine. Serve at once.

PER SERVING

Calories 442 ▪ Protein 11g ▪ Total Fat 15g ▪ Sat. Fat 2g ▪ Cholesterol 0mg ▪ Carbohydrate 66g ▪ Dietary Fiber 4g ▪ Sodium 377mg

---

Macaroni with Artichokes and Olives

MAKES 3 TO 4 MAIN-DISH OR 6 PASTA-COURSE OR SIDE SALAD SERVINGS

This versatile recipe from Calabria can be served warm as a main-dish or pasta-course, or chilled as a salad.

½ pound small elbow macaroni

½ cup low-sodium vegetable broth

Salt and freshly ground black pepper, to taste

1 (6-ounce) jar marinated quartered artichoke hearts, drained and chopped, 1 tablespoon marinade reserved

¼ cup pitted kalamata olives, chopped

2 tablespoons drained diced pimiento

1 tablespoon extra-virgin olive oil

In a large stockpot, cook the macaroni in boiling salted water according to package directions until just al dente. Drain and return to the pot. Immediately add the broth, salt, and pepper; toss until most of the liquid has been absorbed by the pasta. Add the remaining ingredients, tossing well to combine. Serve warm or at room temperature. (Or cover and refrigerate up to 3 days and serve chilled or return to room temperature.)

PER SERVING

Calories 412 ▪ Protein 14g ▪ Total Fat 12g ▪ Sat. Fat 2g ▪
Cholesterol 0mg ▪ Carbohydrate 64g ▪
Dietary Fiber 6g ▪ Sodium 245mg

Orecchiette with Broccoli, Chickpeas, and Tomatoes

MAKES 4 MAIN-DISH OR 6 PASTA-COURSE SERVINGS

A specialty pasta from Apulia, orecchiette means "little ears." Medium shells (conchiglie) or bow ties (farfalle) can replace the orecchiette.

1 large head broccoli, trimmed into small
    florets (about 3 cups)
8 ounces orecchiette or other medium-size
    pasta
3 tablespoons extra-virgin olive oil
1 small red onion (about 4 ounces), chopped
4 large cloves garlic, finely chopped
⅛ teaspoon crushed red pepper flakes, or to
    taste
1 (14.5-ounce) can diced canned tomatoes,
    juices included
1 (15-ounce) can chickpeas, rinsed and drained
Salt and freshly ground black pepper, to taste

Bring a large stockpot of salted water to a boil over high heat. Add the broccoli and cook until

just tender, about 5 minutes. Remove with a slotted spoon and set in a colander to further drain. Add the orecchiette to the boiling water and cook according to package directions until al dente. Drain in the colander holding the broccoli.

Meanwhile, in a large deep-sided nonstick skillet, heat the oil over medium heat. Add the onion and cook, stirring, until softened, 3 to 5 minutes. Add the garlic and red pepper flakes and cook, stirring constantly, 2 minutes. Add the tomatoes and their juices, chickpeas, salt, and black pepper; bring to a brisk simmer over medium-high heat. Reduce the heat to low and cook, stirring occasionally, 5 minutes. Add the pasta and broccoli mixture and cook, stirring, until heated through. Serve at once.

PER SERVING

Calories 452 ▪ Protein 16g ▪ Total Fat 13g ▪ Sat. Fat 2g ▪
Cholesterol 0mg ▪ Carbohydrate 70g ▪
Dietary Fiber 5g ▪ Sodium 238mg

Baked Orzo with Olives and Fresh Herbs

MAKES 4 MAIN-DISH OR 6 PASTA-COURSE SERVINGS

This is one of my favorite ways to serve orzo, a tiny rice-shaped pasta also known as rosario in Italy. If you don't have fresh herbs, use about 1 tablespoon of mixed dried herbs and add before baking.

3 tablespoons extra-virgin olive oil
1 medium onion (about 6 ounces), finely chopped
1½ cups orzo
½ cup pitted kalamata or other good-quality
    black olives, coarsely chopped
About 5 cups low-sodium vegetable broth

Salt and freshly ground black pepper, to taste
¼ cup chopped fresh basil, oregano, thyme,
mint, and/or parsley

Preheat the oven to 350F (175C). Lightly oil a 2½-quart baking dish and set aside.

In a medium deep-sided skillet, heat the oil over medium heat. Add the onion and cook, stirring, until softened but not browned, 4 to 5 minutes. Add the orzo and cook, stirring, 2 minutes. Add the olives and 2 cups of the broth; bring to a boil over high heat. Reduce the heat and simmer briskly 3 to 4 minutes, stirring constantly, or until orzo has absorbed most of the broth. Add 2 more cups of the broth and return to a boil over high heat. Remove from the heat and season with salt and pepper; transfer to prepared baking dish. Cover and bake 20 minutes. Stir in the herbs and ½ cup of the broth. Bake, covered, 5 to 10 more minutes, or until the orzo is tender yet firm to the bite, adding more broth if necessary to keep the pasta from drying out. Serve warm.

PER SERVING
Calories 305 ▪ Protein 19g ▪ Total Fat 13g ▪ Sat. Fat 2g ▪
Cholesterol 0mg ▪ Carbohydrate 31g ▪
Dietary Fiber 6g ▪ Sodium 798mg

Wild Mushroom Orzo "Risotto"

MAKES 4 TO 6 MAIN-DISH
OR 8 PASTA-COURSE SERVINGS

This is a delicious pasta variation of a regional risotto from Le Marche. The use of orzo, a tiny rice-shaped pasta, in lieu of traditional arborio rice cuts the cook-ing time by about half. Although cremini are not wild but rather cultivated brown mushrooms, their earthy flavor renders them well suited to this dish.

½ ounce dried porcini mushrooms
1 tablespoon extra-virgin olive oil
2 tablespoons finely chopped onion
2 cloves garlic, finely chopped
1 cup sliced fresh cremini and/or cultivated
**   white button mushrooms**
¾ pound orzo
¼ teaspoon dried sage
4 cups low-sodium vegetable broth
¼ cup chopped fresh flat-leaf parsley
Salt, preferably the coarse variety, and freshly
**   ground black pepper, to taste**

In a small bowl, soak the dried mushrooms in ½ cup hot water for 15 minutes; drain, reserving the soaking liquid. Strain the soaking liquid through a coffee filter or paper towel–lined strainer and reserve. Rinse the mushrooms thoroughly; chop coarsely and set aside.

Meanwhile, heat the oil in a large deep-sided nonstick skillet with a lid over medium heat. Add the onion and garlic and cook, stirring, 1 minute. Add the fresh mushrooms and cook, stirring, until they begin to release their liquid, 3 to 5 minutes. Add the orzo and sage and cook, stirring, 1 minute. Add the broth and bring to a boil over medium-high heat. Reduce the heat to low, cover, and simmer 10 minutes. Add the porcini mushrooms and reserved soaking liquid to the skillet. Cook, stirring constantly, until the liquid is absorbed, 2 to 3 minutes. Remove from the heat and stir in the parsley, salt, and pepper. Serve at once.

PER SERVING
Calories 427 ▪ Protein 23g ▪ Total Fat 5g ▪ Sat. Fat 1g ▪
Cholesterol 0mg ▪ Carbohydrate 73g ▪
Dietary Fiber 7g ▪ Sodium 528mg

Orzo "Risotto" with Roasted Red Pepper–Tomato Sauce

MAKES 6 MAIN-DISH OR 8 PASTA-COURSE SERVINGS

This pretty red and green pasta variation on the standard rice risotto requires considerably less stirring and is delicious to boot.

> 1 (14-ounce) can stewed tomatoes, well drained
>
> 1 (12-ounce) jar roasted red bell peppers, well drained
>
> ½ tablespoon balsamic or red wine vinegar
>
> 1 pound orzo
>
> 4 tablespoons extra-virgin olive oil
>
> 2 cloves garlic, finely chopped
>
> 2½ cups low-sodium vegetable broth
>
> 1 teaspoon dried oregano
>
> ½ teaspoon salt, preferably the coarse variety
>
> Freshly ground black pepper, to taste
>
> ½ cup chopped fresh basil

Bring a large stockpot filled with salted water to a boil over high heat.

In a food processor fitted with the knife blade, or a blender, process the tomatoes, bell peppers, and vinegar until smooth and pureed. Set aside.

Add the orzo to the boiling water and cook for half the time recommended on the package. (The pasta should still be very firm in the center.) Drain in a colander and rinse under cold-running water; drain again. Return to the pot and toss with 2 tablespoons of the oil. (At this point, the pasta can be covered and refrigerated up to 24 hours before proceeding with the recipe.)

In a large deep-sided nonstick skillet, heat the remaining oil over medium-high heat. Add the garlic and cook, stirring constantly, until fragrant and sizzling, 15 to 30 seconds. Add 1½ cups of the broth, oregano, salt, and pepper; let come to a boil. Add the reserved orzo and stir to coat; let come to a brisk simmer. Add the remaining broth and cook, stirring constantly, until all the liquid has been absorbed, about 4 minutes. Add the reserved red bell pepper mixture and reduce the heat to medium. Cook, stirring constantly, until the mixture is creamy but not soupy, 3 to 4 minutes. Remove from heat and stir in the basil. Serve at once.

PER SERVING
Calories 417 ▪ Protein 16g ▪ Total Fat 11g ▪ Sat. Fat 1g ▪
Cholesterol 0mg ▪ Carbohydrate 66g ▪
Dietary Fiber 5g ▪ Sodium 390mg

Penne with Roasted Red Pepper Marinara Sauce

**MAKES 4 TO 6 MAIN-DISH
OR 8 PASTA-COURSE SERVINGS**

This straight-from-the-pantry pasta dish is tasty enough to serve for company.

> 1 (12-ounce) jar roasted red bell peppers, drained and coarsely chopped
>
> ½ tablespoon onion powder
>
> 1 teaspoon sugar
>
> ½ teaspoon garlic powder
>
> ½ teaspoon dried oregano
>
> ⅛ teaspoon crushed red pepper flakes, or to taste
>
> 2 (14.5-ounce) cans diced tomatoes with Italian seasoning, juices included

2 tablespoons extra-virgin olive oil

12 ounces penne or other short tubular pasta, cooked according to package directions until al dente, drained

In a large saucepan, combine all the ingredients except the oil and pasta. Bring to a boil over medium-high heat, stirring occasionally. Reduce the heat and simmer, uncovered, stirring occasionally, until reduced and thickened, about 20 minutes. Stir in the oil and toss with the pasta. Serve at once.

PER SERVING

Calories 450 ▪ Protein 14g ▪ Total Fat 9g ▪ Sat. Fat 1g ▪
Cholesterol 0mg ▪ Carbohydrate 80g ▪
Dietary Fiber 6g ▪ Sodium 461mg

⅛ teaspoon crushed red pepper flakes, or to taste

12 ounces linguine, cooked according to package directions until al dente, drained

Cherry or grape tomatoes, halved, for garnish (optional)

Place all the ingredients except the pasta and tomatoes in a food processor fitted with the knife blade; process until smooth and pureed. Toss with the pasta and serve warm or at room temperature, garnished with the tomatoes (if using).

PER SERVING

Calories 463 ▪ Protein 12g ▪ Total Fat 16g ▪ Sat. Fat 2g ▪
Cholesterol 0mg ▪ Carbohydrate 68g ▪
Dietary Fiber 4g ▪ Sodium 129mg

Pasta alla Verde

MAKES 4 TO 6 MAIN-DISH
OR 8 PASTA-COURSE SERVINGS

This tangy green sauce is one of my favorites—for a hotter variation, process one or two seeded and chopped pepperoncini along with the other ingredients. Though optional, the cherry tomatoes provide a pretty color contrast.

1 cup loosely packed fresh basil leaves

1 cup loosely packed fresh flat-leaf parsley

¼ cup extra-virgin olive oil

4 scallions (white and green parts), cut into 1-inch pieces

2 large cloves garlic, finely chopped

1 tablespoon fresh lemon juice

¼ cup pitted green olives

2 tablespoons drained capers

Penne with Roasted Vegetables and Garlic Puree

**MAKES 4 TO 6 MAIN-DISH
OR 8 PASTA-COURSE SERVINGS**

Roasted vegetables and garlic puree lend a full flavor to this delicious pasta dish. If you don't have a large baking sheet, use two standard-size ones.

1 cup low-sodium vegetable broth

1 head garlic, separated into cloves and peeled

4 cups (2 pints) cherry tomatoes, halved

1 large red bell pepper (about 8 ounces), cut into chunks

2 small zucchini (about 4 ounces each), cut into 1-inch-thick rounds

2 small yellow squash (about 4 ounces each), cut into 1-inch-thick rounds

1 bunch (about 6) scallions (white and green parts), cut into 1-inch pieces

2 tablespoons extra-virgin olive oil

Salt, preferably the coarse variety, and freshly ground black pepper, to taste

12 ounces penne or other short tubular pasta

Preheat the oven to 450F (230C). Lightly oil a large baking sheet with sides and set aside.

In a small saucepan with a lid, combine the broth and garlic; bring to a boil over high heat. Reduce the heat to low and simmer, covered, until the garlic is tender, 15 to 20 minutes. Transfer the mixture to a blender or food processor and puree until smooth.

Meanwhile, in a large bowl, place the tomatoes, bell pepper, zucchini, yellow squash, scal-lions, oil, salt, and pepper; toss well to combine. Transfer to the prepared baking sheet and bake 15 to 20 minutes, or until tender and beginning to brown, stirring and turning half-way through cooking time.

In a large stockpot, cook the pasta in boiling salted water according to package directions until al dente. Drain and return to the pot. Add the roasted vegetables and reserved garlic puree, toss-ing well to combine. Serve at once.

PER SERVING
Calories 489 ▪ Protein 18g ▪ Total Fat 9g ▪ Sat. Fat 1g ▪
Cholesterol 0mg ▪ Carbohydrate 87g ▪
Dietary Fiber 9g ▪ Sodium 166mg

Penne with Wild Mushrooms and Peas

**MAKES 4 TO 6 MAIN-DISH
OR 8 PASTA-COURSE SERVINGS**

Peas provide extra protein and fiber in this earthy pasta supper from Umbria. Cultivated white mush-rooms can replace the wild variety.

2 tablespoons extra-virgin olive oil

1 small onion (about 4 ounces), chopped

½ pound fresh wild or cremini mushrooms, thinly sliced

1 (14.5-ounce) can diced tomatoes with Italian seasoning, juices included

1 cup frozen green peas

Salt and freshly ground black pepper, to taste

Pinch crushed red pepper flakes, or to taste (optional)

12 ounces penne or other short tubular pasta, cooked according to package directions until al dente, drained

2 tablespoons finely chopped fresh flat-leaf parsley

In a large deep-sided nonstick skillet, heat the oil over medium heat. Add the onion and cook, stirring, until softened, 3 to 4 minutes. Add the mushrooms and cook, stirring, 1 minute. Add the tomatoes and their juices, peas, salt, black pepper, and red pepper flakes (if using); bring to a brisk simmer over medium-high heat. Reduce the heat and simmer gently, stirring occasionally, until the mixture forms a somewhat thick sauce, about 10 minutes. Add the pasta and parsley; toss to thoroughly combine. Serve at once.

PER SERVING
Calories 449 ■ Protein 15g ■ Total Fat 9g ■ Sat. Fat 1g ■
Cholesterol 0mg ■ Carbohydrate 78g ■
Dietary Fiber 6g ■ Sodium 269mg

Potato Gnocchi with Pesto and Peas

MAKES 4 MAIN-DISH OR 6 PASTA-COURSE SERVINGS

This is a delicious choice for a quick and easy weeknight supper. Because it tastes so good, it's also a great fall-back dish to serve company when you simply don't have the time to spend hours in the kitchen.

1 (16-ounce) package frozen or vacuum-packed potato gnocchi

1 cup frozen green peas

Ligurian Basil Pesto (right)

In a large stockpot, cook the gnocchi in boiling salted water according to package directions until al dente. Meanwhile, place the peas in a colander set in the sink. When the gnocchi are finished cooking, reserve ⅓ cup of the cooking liquid, and then slowly drain the gnocchi over the peas in the colander. Return the gnocchi and peas to the pot and add the pesto and reserved cooking liquid, tossing well to combine. Serve warm.

PER SERVING
Calories 543 ■ Protein 17g ■ Total Fat 20g ■ Sat. Fat 3g ■
Cholesterol 0mg ■ Carbohydrate 76g ■
Dietary Fiber 6g ■ Sodium 288mg

Ligurian Basil Pesto

MAKES ABOUT ⅔ CUP

Classic Ligurian pesto is always made with fresh basil and often contains a small amount of fresh flat-leaf parsley to create an even greener sauce. Because the following recipe contains no cheese, the key to its success is the use of coarse salt, which nicely mimics Parmesan's salty flavor.

2½ cups loosely packed fresh basil leaves

½ cup loosely packed fresh flat-leaf parsley

4 tablespoons pine nuts

2 large cloves garlic, finely chopped

½ teaspoon coarse salt

¼ cup extra-virgin olive oil

Combine the basil, parsley, nuts, garlic, and salt in a food processor fitted with the knife blade, or in a blender. Process until finely chopped. Add the oil and process until smooth. If not using immediately, store tightly covered in the refrigerator for up to 2 days.

PER SERVING (ABOUT 1 TABLESPOON)
Calories 81 ■ Protein 2g ■ Total Fat 8g ■ Sat. Fat 1g ■
Cholesterol 0mg ■ Carbohydrate 3g ■
Dietary Fiber 2g ■ Sodium 97mg

Rigatoni with Eggplant, Artichokes, and Bell Peppers

MAKES 4 MAIN-DISH OR 6 PASTA-COURSE SERVINGS

While most Sicilian pasta dishes are outstanding, this particular recipe is especially noteworthy because it contains no tomatoes.

1 large eggplant (about 1 pound) unpeeled, cubed

Table salt

4 tablespoons extra-virgin olive oil

1 large onion (about 8 ounces), coarsely chopped

2 large cloves garlic, finely chopped

1 (9-ounce) package frozen quartered artichoke hearts

½ cup low-sodium vegetable broth

Salt, preferably the coarse variety, and freshly ground black pepper, to taste

8 ounces rigatoni or other tubular pasta, cooked according to package directions until al dente, drained

1 (7.25-ounce) jar roasted red bell peppers, drained and coarsely chopped

½ cup pitted kalamata or other good-quality black olives, chopped

Sprinkle the eggplant with table salt and set in a colander to drain 30 minutes. Rinse the eggplant under cold-running water and drain well between paper towels.

In a large nonstick skillet with a lid, heat half of the oil over medium-high heat. Add the eggplant and cook, stirring often, until golden, about 5 min-

utes. Remove the eggplant from the skillet and set aside. Reduce the heat to medium and heat 1 tablespoon of the remaining oil. Add the onion and cook, stirring, until softened, 3 to 5 minutes. Add the garlic and cook, stirring constantly, 1 minute.

Add the artichokes, broth, salt, and black pepper; bring to a boil over medium-high heat, separating the artichokes with a large wooden spoon, if necessary. Reduce the heat, cover, and simmer, stirring a few times, until the artichokes are fork-tender, 10 to 15 minutes. Add the reserved eggplant, cooked pasta, bell peppers, olives, and remaining oil to the pan; cook, uncovered, over medium heat, stirring occasionally, until heated through. Serve at once.

PER SERVING

Calories 441 ■ Protein 13g ■ Total Fat 17g ■ Sat. Fat 2g ■ Cholesterol 0mg ■ Carbohydrate 63g ■ Dietary Fiber 9g ■ Sodium 252mg

Penne with Cannellini Beans and Escarole

MAKES 5 TO 6 MAIN-DISH OR 8 PASTA-COURSE SERVINGS

This is a delicious way to sneak a nutrient-rich yet bitter-tasting green like escarole into a healthy diet. Spinach can be substituted for the escarole.

2 tablespoons extra-virgin olive oil

2 large cloves garlic, finely chopped

1 large head escarole (about 1 pound), washed, drained, and coarsely chopped

1 (15.5 ounce) can cannellini or other white beans, rinsed and drained

1 (14.5-ounce) can diced tomatoes with Italian
seasonings, preferably the petite-cut
variety, juices included

Salt and freshly ground black pepper, to taste

12 ounces penne or other short tubular pasta,
cooked according to package directions
until al dente, drained

In a large deep-sided nonstick skillet, heat the oil over medium heat. Add the garlic and cook, stirring, 1 minute. Add the escarole and toss until beginning to wilt, about 2 minutes. Add the beans, tomatoes and their juices, salt, and pepper; bring to a simmer over medium-high heat, stirring often. Reduce the heat to low and add the pasta, tossing well to combine. Serve at once.

PER SERVING
Calories 411 ■ Protein 17g ■ Total Fat 7g ■ Sat. Fat 1g ■
Cholesterol 0mg ■ Carbohydrate 72g ■
Dietary Fiber 9g ■ Sodium 203mg

Potato Gnocchi with Sun-Dried Tomato–Almond Pesto

MAKES 4 MAIN-DISH OR 6 PASTA-COURSE SERVINGS

This almond-rich pesto is also delicious tossed with any cooked pasta or rice, as well as with steamed green beans and asparagus.

1 (16-ounce) package frozen or vacuum-
packed potato gnocchi

6 tablespoons oil-packed sun-dried tomato
halves, drained, 2 tablespoons marinade
reserved

¼ cup loosely packed basil leaves

2 tablespoons slivered almonds

2 large cloves garlic, finely chopped

¼ teaspoon coarse salt, or to taste

Freshly ground black pepper, to taste

In a large stockpot, cook the gnocchi in boiling salted water according to package directions until al dente. Drain through a sieve over a bowl, reserving ¼ cup cooking liquid. Return the gnocchi to the pot and toss with the reserved marinade.

Meanwhile, place the tomatoes, basil, almonds, garlic, salt, and pepper in a food processor fitted with a knife blade; process until finely chopped. Add to the gnocchi, along with the reserved cooking liquid; toss well to thoroughly combine. Serve at once.

PER SERVING
Calories 438 ■ Protein 13g ■ Total Fat 12g ■ Sat. Fat 2g ■
Cholesterol 0mg ■ Carbohydrate 71g ■
Dietary Fiber 3g ■ Sodium 169mg

Rotelle with Arugula and Sun-Dried Tomatoes

**MAKES 3 TO 4 MAIN-DISH
OR 6 PASTA-COURSE SERVINGS**

Spinach can easily stand in for the arugula.

- **2 tablespoons extra-virgin olive oil**
- **1 small onion (about 4 ounces), chopped**
- **2 large cloves garlic, finely chopped**
- **3 cups chopped arugula**
- **½ cup low-sodium canned vegetable broth**
- **⅓ cup chopped drained marinated sun-dried tomatoes**
- **½ teaspoon dried oregano**
- **¼ teaspoon crushed red pepper flakes, or to taste (optional)**
- **Salt and freshly ground black pepper, to taste**
- **8 ounces rotelle, penne, or other short pasta, cooked according to package directions until al dente, drained**

In a large deep-sided nonstick skillet, heat the oil over medium-high heat. Add the onion and cook, stirring constantly, until softened but not browned, about 3 minutes. Add the garlic and cook, stirring constantly, 30 seconds. Reduce the heat to medium and add the arugula, broth, sun-dried tomatoes, oregano, red pepper flakes (if using), salt, and black pepper; cook, stirring, 3 minutes. Add the pasta and cook, tossing and stirring constantly, until heated through. Serve at once.

PER SERVING
Calories 407 ■ Protein 14g ■ Total Fat 11g ■ Sat. Fat 1g ■
Cholesterol 0mg ■ Carbohydrate 65g ■
Dietary Fiber 4g ■ Sodium 224mg

Spaghetti with Garlic and Hot Peppers

**MAKES 4 TO 6 MAIN-DISH
OR 8 PASTA-COURSE SERVINGS**

You can easily reduce the temperature of this spicy pasta dish from the Abruzzi region by halving the amount of red pepper flakes and using the lesser amount of pepperoncini.

- **¼ cup extra-virgin olive oil**
- **3 large cloves garlic, finely chopped**
- **¼ teaspoon red pepper flakes**
- **¼ cup finely chopped fresh flat-leaf parsley**
- **2 to 3 pepperoncini, seeded and chopped**
- **½ teaspoon coarse salt, plus additional to taste**
- **12 ounces spaghetti, cooked according to package directions until al dente, drained**
- **Freshly ground black pepper, to taste**

In a small skillet, heat the oil over medium-low heat. Add the garlic and red pepper flakes and cook, stirring often, until the garlic is very lightly browned, about 5 minutes, taking care not to burn it. Remove the skillet from the heat and immediately stir in the parsley, pepperoncini, and salt.

Place the hot spaghetti in a large bowl. Add the oil and pepper mixture and toss well to thoroughly coat. Season with salt and black pepper as necessary. Serve at once.

VARIATION: *To make **Macaroni with Garlic, Hot Peppers, and Capers:** Substitute small elbow macaroni for the spaghetti and ¼ cup drained capers for the parsley to make a popular dish from the Basilicata region.*

Rotelle with Fennel and Cherry Tomatoes

MAKES 4 TO 6 MAIN-DISH
OR 8 PASTA-COURSE SERVINGS

This unusual pasta dish is ideal to serve during the colder months when fresh fennel and hothouse cherry tomatoes are available in most major supermarkets. Aniseed can replace the fennel seed.

- 1 medium fennel bulb (about 12 ounces), trimmed, cored, coarsely chopped
- 2 tablespoons feathery fronds reserved and chopped
- 3 scallions (white and green parts), thinly sliced
- 12 ounces rotelle or other spiral pasta
- 1 pint (2 cups) cherry tomatoes, quartered
- ½ cup low-sodium vegetable broth
- 4 tablespoons extra-virgin olive oil
- 1 teaspoon coarse salt
- ¼ teaspoon fennel seed
- Freshly ground black pepper, to taste

Bring a large stockpot filled with salted water to a boil over high heat. Place the coarsely chopped fennel and scallions in a colander set in the sink.

Add the pasta to the boiling water and cook according to package directions until just al dente. Slowly drain the pasta over the fennel and scallions in the colander. Return the hot pasta, fennel, and scallions to the pot and add the tomatoes, broth, oil, salt, fennel seed, and pepper; toss well to combine. Cover and let stand 10 minutes. Uncover, toss again, and serve at once, garnished with the reserved fennel fronds.

Rotelle with Mushrooms and Garlic

MAKES 4 TO 6 MAIN-DISH
OR 8 PASTA-COURSE SERVINGS

This is a terrific dish to serve in the fall or winter with a tossed salad and lots of crusty bread.

- ¼ cup extra-virgin olive oil
- 8 ounces fresh cultivated white button mushrooms, sliced
- 1 medium onion (about 6 ounces), chopped
- 4 large cloves garlic, thinly sliced
- Salt, preferably the coarse variety, and freshly ground black pepper, to taste
- 12 ounces rotelle or other spiral pasta, cooked according to package directions until al dente, drained

In a large deep-sided nonstick skillet, heat the oil over medium-high heat. Add the mushrooms and onion and cook, stirring often, until the mushrooms begin to release their liquid, 3 to 4 minutes. Add the garlic, salt, and pepper; cook, stirring constantly, until the mushrooms and onion are tender, about 2 minutes. Add the pasta and toss until heated through and well combined. Serve at once.

PER SERVING
Calories 469 ■ Protein 13g ■ Total Fat 15g ■ Sat. Fat 2g ■ Cholesterol 0mg ■ Carbohydrate 71g ■ Dietary Fiber 4g ■ Sodium 10mg

Spaghetti with Olive Oil

MAKES 4 TO 6 MAIN-DISH
OR 8 PASTA-COURSE SERVINGS

This quick, simple, and economical pasta dish is surprisingly delicious. A tossed green salad rounds out a satisfying meal.

- ¼ cup extra-virgin olive oil
- 2 large cloves garlic, finely chopped
- 1 teaspoon coarse salt, or to taste
- ¼ teaspoon freshly ground black pepper, or to taste
- 12 ounces spaghetti, cooked according to package directions until al dente, drained

In a small skillet, heat oil over medium-low heat. Add the garlic and cook, stirring often, until very lightly browned, about 5 minutes, taking care not to burn it. Remove skillet from heat and immediately stir in the salt and pepper.

Place the hot cooked spaghetti in a large bowl. Add the oil and garlic mixture and toss well to thoroughly coat. Season with additional salt and pepper as necessary. Serve at once.

PER SERVING
Calories 438 ■ Protein 11g ■ Total Fat 15g ■ Sat. Fat 2g ■ Cholesterol 0mg ■ Carbohydrate 64g ■ Dietary Fiber 2g ■ Sodium 476mg

Sicilian Skillet Pasta Pie

MAKES 4 TO 6 MAIN-DISH
OR 8 PASTA-COURSE SERVINGS

This delightful skillet pasta pie goes conveniently from stovetop to oven to table in well under 1 hour.

- 2 tablespoons extra-virgin olive oil
- 1 large onion (about 8 ounces), halved lengthwise, thinly sliced crosswise
- 1 medium red or green bell pepper (about 6 ounces), sliced into thin strips
- 2 cups (1 pint) cherry or grape tomatoes, quartered or halved, depending on size
- 4 large cloves garlic, finely chopped
- 1 (14.5-ounce) can diced tomatoes, juices included
- ¼ cup dry red wine
- ½ cup chopped pitted kalamata or other good-quality black olives
- 2 tablespoons dry-packed sun-dried tomato bits
- Salt and freshly ground black pepper, to taste
- 10 ounces spaghetti or linguine, cooked according to package directions until just al dente, drained

Preheat the oven to 350F (175C).

In a large ovenproof deep-sided nonstick skillet with a lid, heat the oil over medium heat. Add the onion and bell pepper and cook, stirring, until softened but not browned, about 5 minutes. Add the cherry tomatoes and garlic and cook, stirring, 2 minutes. Add the tomatoes and their juices, wine, olives, sun-dried tomatoes, salt, and pepper; bring to a brisk simmer over medium-high heat. Reduce the heat to medium and simmer briskly, uncovered, 5 minutes, stirring occasionally. Add the pasta, tossing well to combine.

Cover the skillet and bake on center rack 30 minutes. Remove from oven and set oven to broil. Return the skillet to center rack and broil until the top is lightly browned, about 5 minutes. Cut into wedges and serve at once.

PER SERVING

Calories 438 ▪ Protein 13g ▪ Total Fat 11g ▪ Sat. Fat 1g ▪
Cholesterol 0mg ▪ Carbohydrate 73g ▪
Dietary Fiber 7g ▪ Sodium 429mg

Rotelle with Roasted Grape Tomatoes and Basil

**MAKES 3 TO 4 MAIN-DISH
OR 4 TO 6 PASTA-COURSE SERVINGS**

Slow oven-roasting concentrates the flavor of grape tomatoes and imparts a magical flavor to an otherwise simple pasta dish. Cherry tomatoes can be substituted for the grape variety, but their larger size may require additional cooking time.

2 pints (4 cups) grape or cherry tomatoes, halved

2 tablespoons extra-virgin olive oil

1 teaspoon coarse salt, plus additional to taste, if necessary

8 ounces rotelle, fusilli, or other spiral-shaped pasta

½ cup loosely packed fresh basil leaves, torn into small pieces

2 large cloves garlic, finely chopped

Freshly ground black pepper, to taste

Preheat the oven to 250F (120C). Line a large baking sheet with sides with parchment paper.

Arrange the tomatoes, cut sides up, in a single layer on the prepared baking sheet. Drizzle with 1 tablespoon of the oil and sprinkle with the salt. Bake in the center of the oven until the tomatoes are dried around the edges but still moist, about 1½ hours.

Meanwhile, cook the pasta in a large stockpot in boiling salted water according to package directions until al dente. Reserve ½ cup of the cooking liquid, then drain well. Return to the pot and add the tomatoes, reserved cooking liquid, basil, remaining oil, garlic, pepper, and salt, if necessary; toss well to thoroughly combine. Serve warm.

PER SERVING

Calories 427 ▪ Protein 13g ▪ Total Fat 11g ▪ Sat. Fat 2g ▪
Cholesterol 0mg ▪ Carbohydrate 71g ▪
Dietary Fiber 6g ▪ Sodium 659mg

Spaghetti with Red Wine and Rosemary Marinara Sauce

**MAKES 5 TO 6 MAIN-DISH
OR 8 PASTA-COURSE SERVINGS**

Though this scrumptious marinara sauce cooks up in less than thirty minutes, the fragrant smells of red wine and rosemary will perfume your home for hours.

> 2 tablespoons extra-virgin olive oil
> 1 cup chopped onion
> 4 cloves garlic, finely chopped
> 1 (28-ounce) can plum tomatoes, juices
>   included
> 1 (6-ounce) can tomato paste
> ¾ cup dry red wine
> 1 tablespoon sugar
> 2 teaspoons dried basil
> 1 teaspoon dried rosemary
> ½ teaspoon salt, preferably the coarse variety
> ⅛ teaspoon crushed red pepper flakes, or to
>   taste (optional)
> Freshly ground black pepper, to taste
> 12 ounces spaghetti, cooked according to
>   package directions until al dente, drained

In a large deep-sided nonstick skillet, heat the oil over medium heat. Add the onion and garlic and cook, stirring often, 3 minutes. Add the tomatoes and their juices, tomato paste, wine, sugar, basil, rosemary, salt, red pepper flakes (if using), and black pepper; bring to a brisk simmer over medium-high heat. Reduce the heat and simmer, uncovered, until reduced and thickened, about 20 minutes, stirring occasionally and breaking up the

tomatoes with a large wooden spoon. Serve hot, over spaghetti.

PER SERVING
Calories 414 ■ Protein 12g ■ Total Fat 7g ■ Sat. Fat 1g ■
Cholesterol 0mg ■ Carbohydrate 71g ■
Dietary Fiber 6g ■ Sodium 849mg

Spinach and Eggplant Lasagna

MAKES 6 MAIN-DISH SERVINGS

This quick and easy lasagna is even better the next day. Though optional, the chopped fresh basil adds a homemade touch to the jarred pasta sauce.

> 1 medium eggplant (about ¾ pound), cubed
> Table salt
> 3 tablespoons extra-virgin olive oil
> 1 medium onion (about 6 ounces), chopped
> 2 large cloves garlic, finely chopped
> Salt and freshly ground black pepper, to taste
> 1 (26-ounce) jar pasta sauce, preferably a
>   tomato-basil variety
> 2 (8-ounce) cans no-salt-added tomato sauce
> 2 tablespoons finely chopped fresh basil
>   (optional)
> 9 oven-ready lasagna noodles
> 2 (10-ounce) packages frozen chopped
>   spinach, thawed and drained well

Sprinkle the eggplant with table salt and set in a colander to drain for 30 minutes. Rinse the eggplant under cold-running water and drain well between paper towels.

Preheat the oven to 375F (190C). Lightly oil a 13 × 9-inch baking dish and set aside.

In a large nonstick skillet with a lid, heat 2 tablespoons of the oil over medium heat. Add the onion and cook, stirring, until softened, 3 to 5 minutes. Add the garlic and cook, stirring, 1 minute. Add the eggplant, salt, and pepper; toss well to combine. Reduce the heat to medium-low, cover, and cook until the eggplant is just tender, stirring occasionally, about 8 minutes.

In a medium bowl, combine the pasta sauce, tomato sauce, basil (if using), and remaining oil. Spread one-fourth (about 1 cup) of the sauce in the bottom of the prepared dish. Arrange 3 noodles crosswise over sauce, leaving equal space around the noodles so that they don't overlap or touch the sides of the dish. Arrange one-third of the eggplant over the noodles. Arrange one-third of the spinach over the eggplant. Pour another one-fourth of the sauce over the spinach. Repeat twice, beginning with noodles, then eggplant, then spinach, and ending with sauce. Cover tightly with oiled foil (if foil touches the sauce, cover with a sheet of parchment paper or waxed paper first) and bake for 1 hour, or until the eggplant is very tender. Let stand 10 minutes before cutting and serving.

PER SERVING

Calories 325 ▪ Protein 11g ▪ Total Fat 12g ▪ Sat. Fat 2g ▪
Cholesterol 0mg ▪ Carbohydrate 49g ▪
Dietary Fiber 6g ▪ Sodium 869mg

Zucchini Lasagna with Roasted Red Pepper Sauce

MAKES 6 MAIN-DISH SERVINGS

Broiling the vegetables until they just begin to char is the secret to the success of this tasty casserole, which is ideal for dinner parties, as it can be assembled a day ahead of baking

> 6 medium zucchini (about 6 ounces each), cut into ½-inch-thick rounds
>
> 6 medium tomatoes (about 6 ounces each), cut into ¼-inch-thick slices
>
> 3 tablespoons extra-virgin olive oil
>
> Salt, preferably the coarse variety, to taste, plus ½ teaspoon
>
> 2 medium onions (about 6 ounces each), chopped
>
> 6 large cloves garlic, finely chopped
>
> 2 (12-ounce) jars roasted red bell peppers, drained
>
> 2 ounces bread, preferably whole wheat, torn into small pieces
>
> 2 tablespoons balsamic or red wine vinegar
>
> ¼ teaspoon crushed red pepper flakes
>
> ¼ teaspoon freshly ground black pepper
>
> 9 oven-ready lasagna noodles
>
> ½ cup chopped fresh basil

Preheat the oven to broil. Lightly oil a 13 × 9-inch baking dish. Lightly oil 2 baking sheets.

Arrange the zucchini and tomato slices on separate prepared baking sheets. Brush the tops evenly with 1½ tablespoons of the oil. Sprinkle with coarse salt, to taste. Working in two stages, broil 4 to 6 inches from the heat source until the tops are nicely browned and beginning to char, about 8 minutes for the zucchini, about 5 minutes for the tomatoes. (Do not turn the vegetables.) Set aside to cool slightly.

Preheat the oven to 375F (190C).

In a medium nonstick skillet, heat 1 tablespoon of the remaining oil over medium heat. Add the onion and cook, stirring, until softened, about 3 minutes. Add the garlic and cook, stirring, 1 minute. Set aside to cool slightly.

In a food processor fitted with the knife blade,

or in a blender, combine the reserved onion mixture, bell peppers, bread, vinegar, remaining ½ tablespoon oil, ½ teaspoon salt, crushed red pepper flakes, and black pepper; process until smooth and pureed. Set aside.

Arrange 3 lasagna noodles in the bottom of the prepared baking dish. Top with half of the zucchini slices, half of the tomatoes, half of the basil, and about one-third of the red bell pepper sauce. Repeat layers. Finish with a layer of noodles, and then top with the remaining sauce. Cover tightly with oiled foil (if foil touches the sauce, cover with a sheet of parchment paper or waxed paper first) and bake 50 minutes, or until the noodles are tender. Let stand 10 minutes before cutting and serving.

PER SERVING

Calories 302 ■ Protein 10g ■ Total Fat 9g ■ Sat. Fat 1g ■
Cholesterol 0mg ■ Carbohydrate 51g ■
Dietary Fiber 9g ■ Sodium 75mg

Rice and Other Grains

Rice rules in the kitchens of northern Italy, with polenta ranking a close second. It's not that northern Italians shun pasta—indeed, they eat plenty of it, but Italy's alpine and subalpine regions historically have grown more rice and corn than the wheat-producing south. Piedmont and Lombardy supply much of the world with arborio rice, the plump, starchy, short-grain variety that is the basis for the area's creamy risottos. Long-grain rice and, occasionally, brown rice are eaten as well; both are incorporated into baked dishes and casseroles, tossed into salads, and stuffed into vegetables. Originally made with buckwheat and other grains, polenta has been a basic foodstuff of northern Italy since Etruscan times. When Columbus brought corn to Europe and the crop flourished in the northern regions of Italy, the coarsely ground kernels not only replaced the buckwheat in the porridge, but gradually replaced much of the bread and pasta in the diet. It wasn't long before southern Italians began to mockingly label their northern countrymen as *polentoni*, or polenta-eaters. Barley, on the other hand, is a unifying grain, said to be a staple of the Roman gladiators; ancient historical accounts often refer to gladiators as *hordearii*, or barley-men. Used in soups, stews, casseroles, and salads, barley is still regarded as a source of strength and nourishment to the body as well as the soul. Everywhere in Italy mothers feed it to convalescing children, and adults eat it as well. Food traditions die hard, but that, after all, is the fun of it!

Baked Herbed Rice

MAKES 4 MAIN-DISH OR 6 TO 8 SIDE-DISH SERVINGS

Here is a delicious and foolproof way to serve rice.

- **1½ cups long-grain white rice**
- **1 bunch (about 6) scallions (white and green parts), thinly sliced**
- **1 celery stalk, chopped**
- **1 tablespoon extra-virgin olive oil**
- **1 teaspoon dried thyme leaves, crumbled**
- **Salt and freshly ground black pepper, to taste**
- **3 cups low-sodium vegetable broth, heated to boiling**
- **2 tablespoons chopped fresh flat-leaf parsley or basil**

Preheat the oven to 350F (175C). Lightly grease a 2½-quart casserole or baking dish.

Place the rice, scallions, celery, oil, thyme, salt, and pepper in prepared casserole. Quickly add the boiling broth, stirring well to combine. Cover tightly with foil or lid, and bake 30 to 40 minutes, or until the liquid is completely absorbed and the rice is tender. Stir in the parsley and serve at once.

PER SERVING

Calories 222 ■ Protein 9g ■ Total Fat 3g ■ Sat. Fat 0g ■
Cholesterol 0mg ■ Carbohydrate 40g ■
Dietary Fiber 3g ■ Sodium 271mg

Italian-Style Rice Casserole

MAKES 4 TO 6 MAIN-DISH OR 8 SIDE-DISH SERVINGS

This quick, simple, and delicious casserole is ideal for carefree entertaining.

- **3½ cups low-sodium vegetable broth**
- **½ cup dry white wine**
- **1 cup long-grain white rice**
- **16 ounces frozen peas**
- **6 ounces carrots, chopped**
- **1 medium onion (about 6 ounces), chopped**
- **8 gaeta, kalamata, or other good-quality black olives, pitted and chopped**
- **1 (12-ounce) jar roasted red bell peppers, drained and chopped**
- **3 tablespoons extra-virgin olive oil**
- **½ teaspoon dried thyme**
- **¼ teaspoon dried oregano**
- **Salt and freshly ground black pepper, to taste**

Preheat the oven to 300F (150C). Lightly grease a 2½-quart casserole or baking dish.

In a medium stockpot, combine all the ingredients and bring to a boil over high heat; reduce the heat to medium-high and simmer briskly for 5 minutes, stirring a few times. Reduce the heat to low, cover, and simmer 20 minutes, stirring occasionally.

Transfer the mixture to the prepared casserole. Bake, uncovered, 20 to 25 minutes, or until the mixture is creamy and most of the liquid has evaporated, stirring a few times. Serve at once.

PER SERVING

Calories 486 ■ Protein 21g ■ Total Fat 13g ■ Sat. Fat 2g ■
Cholesterol 0mg ■ Carbohydrate 68g ■
Dietary Fiber 13g ■ Sodium 719mg

Lemon–Pine Nut Rice

MAKES 4 MAIN-DISH OR 6 TO 8 SIDE-DISH SERVINGS

This tangy medley of rice, lemon, and pine nuts is a satisfying main course served with a tossed green salad or tasty side dish for almost any Italian-style entrée. While you can steam the rice, cooking the grains pasta-style saves time and can be applied to any variety of rice.

1½ cups long-grain white rice
3 tablespoons extra-virgin olive oil
¼ cup pine nuts
1 medium green or red bell pepper, finely
    chopped
4 scallions, thinly sliced
2 large cloves garlic, finely chopped
6 tablespoons fresh lemon juice
¼ cup finely chopped fresh flat-leaf parsley
Salt, preferably the coarse variety, and freshly
    ground black pepper, to taste

In a large stockpot, bring about 3 quarts salted water to a boil over high heat. Add the rice and boil until tender yet firm to the bite, stirring a few times, 12 to 15 minutes. Drain in a colander and set aside.

Meanwhile, in a large deep-sided nonstick skillet, heat the oil over medium heat. Add the pine nuts and cook, stirring constantly, 2 minutes. Add the bell pepper, scallions, and garlic; cook, stirring often, until the vegetables are fragrant and softened, about 5 minutes. Add the reserved rice and toss well to combine. Remove from the heat and add the lemon juice, parsley, salt, and pepper; toss well to combine. Serve warm.

PER SERVING
Calories 419 ▪ Protein 8g ▪ Total Fat 16g ▪ Sat. Fat 2g ▪
Cholesterol 0mg ▪ Sodium 10mg ▪
Carbohydrate 63g ▪ Dietary Fiber 3g

> ### ⌁ COOK'S TIP ⌁
> The juice of 1 medium lemon equals about 3 tablespoons.

Venetian-Style Rice and Peas

MAKES 4 MAIN-DISH OR 6 TO 8 SIDE-DISH SERVINGS

Risi e bisi is a favorite springtime dish in the Veneto region of northern Italy. Because it's more souplike than a risotto, you may need to add more broth to keep its consistency somewhat loose. Do not substitute regular long-grain white rice here, as the dish will not be nearly as creamy. Serve in bowls with lots of crusty Italian bread to sop up the delicious juices.

5½ to 6 cups low-sodium vegetable broth
2 tablespoons extra-virgin olive oil
½ cup finely chopped onion
1½ cups arborio rice
½ teaspoon salt, plus additional to taste, if
    necessary
2 cups frozen green peas, thawed
1 tablespoon finely chopped fresh parsley
Freshly ground black pepper, to taste

Bring the broth to a simmer in a large pot. In a large deep-sided nonstick skillet, heat the oil over medium heat. Add the onion and cook, stirring, until softened but not browned, 2 to 3 minutes. Add the rice and cook, stirring, 2 minutes.

Stir in 3½ cups of the simmering broth and the salt; bring to a brisk simmer over medium-high heat. Reduce the heat to medium-low and simmer until most of the liquid has been absorbed, about 10 minutes, stirring occasionally and adjusting heat as necessary to maintain a gentle simmer. Stir in 1 more cup of the broth and the peas; simmer until most of the liquid has been absorbed, about 10 minutes, stirring occasionally and adjusting heat as necessary to maintain a gentle simmer. Stir in 1 more cup of the broth and simmer until rice is cooked al dente and mixture is creamy but rather souplike, about 5 minutes, stirring occasionally and adjusting heat as necessary to maintain a gentle simmer. If necessary, add another ½ cup of broth and continue to simmer, stirring occasionally, until desired consistency is achieved. Remove from heat and stir in the parsley and pepper. Serve at once.

PER SERVING

Calories 442 ▪ Protein 24g ▪ Total Fat 7g ▪ Sat. Fat 1g ▪
Cholesterol 0mg ▪ Carbohydrate 69g ▪
Dietary Fiber 8g ▪ Sodium 1,072mg

Baked Risotto with Spring Vegetables

MAKES 4 MAIN-DISH OR 6 SIDE-DISH SERVINGS

Baking the risotto eliminates the almost-constant stirring required in traditional stovetop recipes. Feel free to substitute any of your favorite precooked veggies for the asparagus, peas, and carrots. Short-grain brown rice can replace the arborio rice, but increase the baking time accordingly.

2 tablespoons extra-virgin olive oil
1 small onion (about 4 ounces), finely chopped
1 cup arborio rice

3 cloves garlic, finely chopped
½ cup dry white wine
3½ cups low-sodium vegetable broth
½ teaspoon salt
¼ teaspoon lemon-pepper seasoning
½ pound fresh asparagus, trimmed, cut into 2-inch pieces, and steamed until crisp-tender
1 cup frozen baby peas, cooked according to package directions and drained
6 ounces baby carrots, halved lengthwise and steamed until crisp-tender
4 scallions (white and green parts), thinly sliced
¼ cup chopped fresh flat-leaf parsley

Preheat the oven to 425F (220C).

In a large deep-sided oven-proof skillet with a lid, heat the oil over medium heat. Add the onion and cook, stirring, until softened but not browned, about 2 to 3 minutes. Add the rice and garlic and cook, stirring, 2 minutes. Add the wine and cook, stirring, until almost completely absorbed. Add the broth, salt, and lemon-pepper seasoning; bring to a boil over high heat. Cover the skillet and transfer to the oven.

Bake 45 to 50 minutes, or until the rice is just tender. Stir in the asparagus, peas, carrots, scallions, and parsley. Serve at once.

PER SERVING

Calories 363 ▪ Protein 17g ▪ Total Fat 7g ▪ Sat. Fat 1g ▪
Cholesterol 0mg ▪ Carbohydrate 53g ▪
Dietary Fiber 7g ▪ Sodium 813mg

Microwave Risotto with Saffron

MAKES 3 MAIN-DISH OR 4 TO 6 SIDE-DISH SERVINGS

The use of the microwave not only speeds up the cooking time of traditional risotto, but virtually eliminates the constant stirring. The following recipe is based on a 1,000-watt microwave oven, so you might need to vary the cooking time accordingly.

> 2 tablespoons extra-virgin olive oil
> 2 tablespoons finely chopped onion
> 1 cup arborio rice
> ⅓ cup dry white wine
> ½ teaspoon salt, plus additional as necessary
> ¼ teaspoon freshly ground black pepper, plus
>   additional as necessary
> 1 pinch saffron
> 3 cups low-sodium vegetable broth, plus
>   additional as necessary

In a 4-cup microwave-safe casserole with a lid, combine the oil and onion. Microwave, covered, on High 3 minutes. Remove the cover and continue cooking uncovered. Stir in the rice, wine, salt, pepper, and saffron. Cook 2 minutes on High. Stir in 1 cup of the broth and cook on High 5 minutes. Stir in 1 cup of the broth and cook on High for 10 minutes, stirring halfway through cooking time. Stir in ½ cup of the broth and cook on High 4 minutes. Stir in remaining ½ cup of broth and cook on High 2 minutes. The rice should be tender yet still chewy and slightly creamy. If runny, cover and let stand until excess liquids are absorbed. If rice is too hard, add additional broth in ½-cup increments and cook on High in 2-minute intervals until desired consistency is achieved. Season with additional salt and pepper as necessary. Serve at once.

PER SERVING

Calories 356 ■ Protein 12g ■ Total Fat 9g ■ Sat. Fat 1g ■
Cholesterol 0mg ■ Carbohydrate 51g ■
Dietary Fiber 2g ■ Sodium 713mg

VARIATION: *To make* **Microwave Risotto with Truffles***: Omit the saffron and add 1¾ ounces finely chopped preserved black truffles and 1 teaspoon white or black truffle oil when you stir in the first ½ cup of broth and cook on High for 4 minutes. Proceed as otherwise directed in the recipe.*

Risotto with Peas and Basil

MAKES 4 MAIN-DISH OR 6 SIDE-DISH SERVINGS

This popular risotto can be made with freshly shelled peas, if available. If you don't have a large deep-sided nonstick skillet, use a wide heavy-bottomed pan but reduce the heat to medium-low when you begin to add the liquids. The risotto will be done about 25 to 30 minutes after the first addition of broth.

> 4 to 5 cups low-sodium vegetable broth
> 2 tablespoons extra-virgin olive oil
> ¼ cup finely chopped onion
> 1½ cups arborio rice
> ½ cup dry white wine
> 2 cups frozen green peas, thawed
> Salt and freshly ground black pepper, to taste
> ¼ cup finely chopped fresh basil

Bring the broth to a simmer in a large pot. In a large deep-sided nonstick skillet, heat the oil over medium heat. Add the onion and cook, stirring, until softened but not browned, about 2 to 3 minutes. Add the rice and cook, stirring, 2 minutes.

Add the wine and cook, stirring constantly, until almost all the wine has been absorbed. Add ½ cup of the simmering broth and cook, stirring constantly, until almost all the liquid has been absorbed. Continue adding the simmering broth by ½ cup, cooking and stirring after each addition until it is almost completely absorbed and the rice begins to soften, about 15 minutes after the first addition of broth. Add the peas, salt, and pepper and another ½ cup of broth, stirring constantly until almost all the liquid has been absorbed. Add remaining broth by ½ cup as needed, continuing to stir constantly until the mixture is creamy, the rice is tender yet firm to the bite, and almost all the liquid has been absorbed. Remove from the heat and stir in the basil. Serve at once.

PER SERVING

Calories 439 ▪ Protein 20g ▪ Total Fat 7g ▪ Sat. Fat 1g ▪
Cholesterol 0mg ▪ Carbohydrate 68g ▪
Dietary Fiber 7g ▪ Sodium 612mg

Risotto with Radicchio

MAKES 4 MAIN-DISH OR 6 SIDE-DISH SERVINGS

This unusual risotto recipe from the Veneto region is special enough to serve company, yet easy enough to serve for a quick weeknight supper. If you don't have a large deep-sided nonstick skillet, use a wide heavy-bottomed pan but reduce the heat to medium-low when you begin to add the liquids. The risotto will be done about 25 to 30 minutes after the first addition of broth.

4 to 5 cups low-sodium vegetable broth
2 tablespoons extra-virgin olive oil
¼ cup finely chopped onion
1½ cups arborio rice
½ cup dry white wine
1 medium head radicchio (about 6 ounces), chopped
½ teaspoon salt
¼ teaspoon freshly ground black pepper
2 tablespoons finely chopped fresh flat-leaf parsley (optional)

Bring the broth to a simmer in a large pot. In a large deep-sided nonstick skillet, heat the oil over medium heat. Add the onion and cook, stirring, until just softened, about 2 to 3 minutes. Add the rice and cook, stirring, 2 minutes.

Add the wine and cook, stirring constantly, until almost all the wine has been absorbed. Add ½ cup of the simmering broth and cook, stirring constantly, until almost all the liquid has been absorbed. Continue adding the simmering broth by ½ cup, cooking and stirring after each addition until it is almost completely absorbed and the rice begins to soften, about 15 minutes after the first addition of broth. Add the radicchio, salt, pepper, and another ½ cup of broth, stirring constantly until almost all the liquid has been absorbed. Add remaining broth by the ½ cupful as needed, continuing to stir constantly until the mixture is creamy, the rice is tender yet firm to the bite, and almost all the liquid has been absorbed. Remove from the heat and stir in the parsley (if using). Serve at once.

PER SERVING

Calories 393 ▪ Protein 17g ▪ Total Fat 7g ▪ Sat. Fat 1g ▪
Cholesterol 0mg ▪ Carbohydrate 60g ▪
Dietary Fiber 4g ▪ Sodium 807mg

Roasted Asparagus Risotto

MAKES 4 MAIN-DISH OR 6 SIDE-DISH SERVINGS

Roasting the asparagus lends this popular Venetian risotto a smoky appeal. If you don't have a large deep-sided nonstick skillet, use a wide heavy-bottomed pan but reduce the heat to medium-low when you begin to add the liquids. The risotto will be done about 25 to 30 minutes after the first addition of broth.

¾ **pound medium asparagus, trimmed**
2½ **tablespoons extra-virgin olive oil**
¼ **teaspoon coarse salt**
Freshly ground black pepper, to taste
¼ **cup finely chopped red onion**
1½ **cups arborio rice**
½ **cup dry white wine**
4 to 5 cups low-sodium vegetable broth,
　　heated to a simmer
Table salt, to taste

Preheat the oven to 425F (220C). Lightly oil a baking sheet with sides.

Place the asparagus on the prepared baking sheet and toss with ½ tablespoon of the oil, coarse salt, and pepper. Spread in a single layer. Roast 10 minutes, or until just tender and slightly browned, turning once. Remove from the oven and let cool slightly. Cut into 2-inch pieces and set aside.

In a large deep-sided nonstick skillet, heat the remaining oil over medium heat. Add the onion and cook, stirring, until softened but not browned, about 2 to 3 minutes. Add the rice and cook, stirring, 2 minutes.

Add the wine and cook, stirring constantly, until almost all the wine has been absorbed. Add ½

cup of the simmering broth and cook, stirring constantly, until almost all the liquid has been absorbed. Continue adding the simmering broth by ½ cup, cooking and stirring after each addition until it is almost completely absorbed and the rice begins to soften, about 15 minutes after the first addition of broth. Add the reserved asparagus, salt, and pepper and another ½ cup of the broth, stirring constantly until almost all the liquid has been absorbed. Add remaining broth by ½ cup as needed, continuing to stir constantly until the mixture is creamy, the rice is tender yet firm to the bite, and almost all the liquid has been absorbed. Remove from the heat and serve at once.

PER SERVING

Calories 409 ■ Protein 17g ■ Total Fat 9g ■ Sat. Fat 1g ■
Cholesterol 0mg ■ Carbohydrate 60g ■
Dietary Fiber 4g ■ Sodium 533mg

Roasted Beet Risotto

MAKES 4 MAIN-DISH OR 6 SIDE-DISH SERVINGS

I love roasted beets, and make this luscious red risotto often—sometimes with diced canned beets in lieu of the fresh when pressed for time. If you don't have a large deep-sided nonstick skillet, use a wide heavy-bottomed pan but reduce the heat to medium-low when you begin to add the liquids. The risotto will be done about 25 to 30 minutes after the first addition of broth.

3 to 4 medium beets, washed
4 to 5 cups low-sodium vegetable broth
2 tablespoons extra-virgin olive oil
¼ **cup finely chopped onion**
1½ **cups arborio rice**

2 large cloves garlic, finely chopped

½ cup dry white wine

½ teaspoon salt

¼ teaspoon freshly ground black pepper

2 tablespoons chopped fresh flat-leaf parsley

Preheat the oven to 375F (190C).

Wrap the beets in aluminum foil and place in a baking pan. Roast 45 to 50 minutes, or until tender. Remove from oven and unwrap. Set aside to cool slightly. Peel off skins and cut into cubes. Set aside.

Bring the broth to a simmer in a large pot. In a large deep-sided nonstick skillet, heat the oil over medium heat. Add the onion and cook, stirring, until softened but not browned, about 2 to 3 minutes. Add the rice and garlic and cook, stirring, 2 minutes.

Add the wine and cook, stirring constantly, until almost all the wine has been absorbed. Add ½ cup of the simmering broth and cook, stirring constantly, until almost all the liquid has been absorbed. Continue adding the simmering broth by ½ cup, cooking and stirring after each addition until it is almost completely absorbed and the rice begins to soften, about 15 minutes after the first addition of broth. Add the reserved beets, salt, and pepper and another ½ cup of the broth, stirring constantly until almost all the liquid has been absorbed. Add remaining broth by ½ cup as needed, continuing to stir constantly until the mixture is creamy, the rice is tender yet firm to the bite, and almost all the liquid has been absorbed. Remove from the heat and stir in the parsley. Serve at once.

PER SERVING

Calories 413 ■ Protein 17g ■ Total Fat 7g ■ Sat. Fat 1g ■
Cholesterol 0mg ■ Carbohydrate 65g ■
Dietary Fiber 5g ■ Sodium 847mg

Risotto with Zucchini and Sun-Dried Tomatoes

MAKES 4 MAIN-DISH OR 6 SIDE-DISH SERVINGS

Flecked with green and red, this creamy Tuscan-style risotto is as colorful as it is delicious. If you don't have a large deep-sided nonstick skillet, use a wide heavy-bottomed pan but reduce the heat to medium-low when you begin to add the liquids. The risotto will be done 25 to 30 minutes after the first addition of broth.

4 to 5 cups low-sodium vegetable broth

2 tablespoons extra-virgin olive oil

¼ cup finely chopped onion

1½ cups arborio rice

½ cup dry white wine

½ large zucchini (about 4 ounces), finely diced

½ cup dry-packed sun-dried tomato halves, cut into thin strips with kitchen shears, soaked in warm water to cover for 15 minutes, drained

1 teaspoon dried thyme leaves

Salt and freshly ground black pepper, to taste

2 tablespoons chopped fresh basil (optional)

Bring the broth to a simmer in a large pot. In a large deep-skillet nonstick skillet, heat the oil over medium heat. Add the onion and cook, stirring, until softened but not browned, about 2 to 3 minutes. Add the rice and cook, stirring, 2 minutes.

Add the wine and cook, stirring constantly, until almost all the wine has been absorbed. Add ½ cup of the simmering broth and cook, stirring constantly, until almost all the liquid has been absorbed. Continue adding the simmering broth by

½ cup, cooking and stirring after each addition until it is almost completely absorbed and the rice begins to soften, about 15 minutes after the first addition of broth. Add the zucchini, sun-dried tomatoes, thyme, salt, and pepper and another ½ cup of broth, stirring constantly until almost all the liquid has been absorbed. Add remaining broth by ½ cup as needed, continuing to stir constantly until the mixture is creamy, the rice is tender yet firm to the bite, and almost all the liquid has been absorbed. Remove from the heat and stir in the basil (if using). Serve at once.

PER SERVING

Calories 405 ▪ Protein 17g ▪ Total Fat 7g ▪ Sat. Fat 1g ▪
Cholesterol 0mg ▪ Carbohydrate 63g ▪
Dietary Fiber 5g ▪ Sodium 674mg

Other Grains

Italian Barley

MAKES 3 MAIN-DISH OR 4 TO 6 SIDE-DISH SERVINGS

This filling grain dish can serve as a meal on its own, or side dish for almost any entrée.

> 1 tablespoon extra-virgin olive oil
> ½ cup chopped onion
> ½ cup chopped green bell pepper
> 1 large clove garlic, finely chopped
> 1 (16-ounce) can stewed tomatoes, juices included
> 2 cups low-sodium vegetable broth or water
> ½ teaspoon dried oregano
> ½ teaspoon dried basil
> Salt and freshly ground black pepper, to taste
> ¾ cup pearled barley

In a medium deep-sided skillet with a lid, heat the oil over medium heat. Add the onion, bell pepper, and garlic; cook, stirring, until softened, about 3 minutes. Add the tomatoes and their juices, broth, oregano, basil, salt, and pepper; bring to a boil over high heat.

Stir in the barley, reduce the heat to low, cover, and simmer, stirring occasionally, until the barley is tender and liquids are mostly absorbed, 50 minutes to 1 hour. The mixture should be slightly soupy. If too soupy, cook uncovered over medium heat, stirring often, until some of the liquids have evaporated. Serve warm.

Lemon-Thyme Polenta with Roasted Vegetables

MAKES 6 SERVINGS

You can use regular thyme instead of the lemon variety, although the polenta won't have the same citruslike fragrance.

3¾ cups low-sodium vegetable broth

1 cup polenta or coarse-ground yellow
    cornmeal

3½ tablespoons extra-virgin olive oil

4 large cloves garlic, finely chopped

4 teaspoons chopped fresh lemon thyme

½ teaspoon salt, plus additional to taste

¼ teaspoon freshly ground pepper, plus
    additional to taste

¼ cup balsamic vinegar

¼ cup oil-packed sun-dried tomatoes, drained
    and very finely chopped or pureed

5 Italian or Japanese eggplants (about 4
    ounces each), cut into 1-inch cubes

3 medium zucchini (about 6 ounces), cut into
    1-inch thick slices

2 medium red onions (about 6 ounces each),
    cut into eighths

8 small red potatoes, quartered

1 large red bell pepper (about 8 ounces), cut
    into 1-inch pieces

Lightly oil a 9 × 5-inch loaf pan and set aside.

In a large stockpot, bring 3½ cups of the broth to a boil over high heat. Slowly add the polenta, stirring constantly with a long-handled wooden spoon. Reduce the heat to low and stir in 1 tablespoon of the oil, half of the garlic, half of the thyme, salt, and pepper. Cover and cook, stirring occasionally, until polenta is tender, about 15 minutes. Remove from the heat and let stand, covered, 5 minutes. Spread the polenta mixture in the bottom of the prepared pan. Let stand until firm, about 20 minutes. Unmold onto an ungreased baking sheet; cut into 12 slices. Brush the tops evenly with ½ tablespoon of the oil and set aside.

Meanwhile, preheat the oven to 400F (205C). In a large bowl, combine the remaining broth, remaining oil, the vinegar, sun-dried tomatoes, and the remaining garlic and thyme. Add the eggplant, zucchini, onions, potatoes, and bell pepper. Season with salt and pepper and toss well to combine. Let marinate about 15 minutes at room temperature.

Transfer the vegetables to a large baking sheet with sides. Bake 30 minutes, or until tender and lightly browned, stirring and turning halfway through cooking time. Remove from oven and cover with foil to keep warm. Set the oven to broil.

Broil the polenta slices 6 to 8 inches from heat source until lightly browned. Place 2 polenta slices on each of 6 serving plates; top evenly with the vegetables and accumulated cooking juices. Serve at once.

Polenta Pie with Spinach

MAKES 6 TO 8 SERVINGS

This is an excellent company dish as it can be assembled 24 hours before baking. You can also prepare it using well-drained, cooked chopped broccoli.

4 tablespoons plus 1 teaspoon extra-virgin olive oil
1 large onion (about 8 ounces), finely chopped
4 large cloves garlic, finely chopped
2 (10-ounce) packages frozen chopped spinach, cooked according to package directions, squeezed as dry as possible between layers of paper towels
¼ cup finely chopped fresh basil (optional)
Salt and freshly ground black pepper, to taste
3 cups water
3 cups low-sodium vegetable broth
2 cups polenta or coarse-ground yellow cornmeal
Fresh basil leaves, for garnish (optional)
2 cups favorite pasta sauce, or All-Purpose Tomato Sauce (page 131; optional), heated

Preheat the oven to 375F (190C). Lightly oil a 10-inch ceramic pie or quiche dish; set aside.

In a large nonstick skillet, heat 2 tablespoons of the oil over medium heat. Add the onion and cook, stirring, until softened but not browned, about 3 minutes. Add half of the garlic and cook, stirring, 1 minute. Add the spinach, chopped basil (if using), salt, and pepper; stir until thoroughly combined. Remove from heat and set aside.

In a large stockpot, bring the water and broth to a boil over high heat. Slowly add the polenta, stirring constantly with a long-handled wooden spoon. Reduce the heat to low and stir in 2 tablespoons of the remaining oil, remaining garlic, and salt. Cover and cook, stirring occasionally, until the polenta is tender, about 15 minutes. Remove from the heat and let stand, covered, 5 minutes.

Immediately spoon half the polenta into the prepared pie plate, pressing down with the back of a large spoon to form a smooth surface. Spoon the spinach filling over top, spreading to within a ½ inch of the outside rim of the polenta. Carefully spoon the remaining polenta over the filling, using your fingers to evenly spread and the back of a large spoon to form a smooth surface. Brush the top evenly with the remaining oil.

Cover with foil and bake 30 minutes. Remove the foil and bake 15 minutes, or until the top is lightly browned. Remove from the oven and let rest 15 minutes. Cut into wedges and serve at once, garnished with the basil leaves (if using), and accompanied by the pasta sauce (if using).

PER SERVING
Calories 420 ▪ Protein 15g ▪ Total Fat 15g ▪ Sat. Fat 2g ▪
Cholesterol 0mg ▪ Carbohydrate 60g ▪
Dietary Fiber 14g ▪ Sodium 741mg

Vegetables, Beans, and Other Legumes

Vegetables and legumes take center stage in most Italian homes. Each season, in every region throughout Italy, fresh vegetables shine in main courses and side dishes, and are enthusiastically incorporated into a myriad of *antipasti*, soups, stews, salads, pasta, risotto, and other grain dishes. Many experts attribute the particular healthfulness of the Italian variation of the Mediterranean diet as much to its focus on vegetables as to its reliance on olive oil.

Broccoli, spinach, tomatoes, and countless other vegetables, individually and collectively, have been associated with lower rates of heart disease, cancer, and other illnesses.

Loaded with iron, protein, and fiber, the lowly bean is held in high esteem, as well—borlotti beans, cannellini beans, chickpeas, and kidney beans, in combination with other vegetables or served solo with some good olive oil, are culinary delights.

The same applies to nuts of all varieties, particularly almonds, pine nuts, and walnuts. Maybe part of the reason the Mediterranean diet is so effective for Italians is because they think of vegetables as being better than medicine. Italians not only love what they eat, but are confident that what they eat is healthy—perhaps the power of positive thinking explains it all.

Grilled Asparagus Spears

MAKES 4 SERVINGS

The grill and a little olive oil, balsamic vinegar, and coarse salt give asparagus terrific flavor in this easy recipe. While a stovetop grilling pan can accommodate asparagus of medium thickness, only use thick, mature vegetables if using a charcoal or gas grill.

1 pound large asparagus, trimmed
1 tablespoon extra-virgin olive oil
½ teaspoon coarse salt
Freshly ground black pepper, to taste
½ tablespoon balsamic vinegar

Prepare a medium-hot charcoal grill or gas grill. Position the grill rack 4 to 6 inches from heat source. Or, place a stovetop grilling pan with grids over medium-high heat.

Meanwhile, soak the asparagus 5 minutes in water to cover in a large bowl. Drain well and transfer to a baking sheet with sides. Using a spatula, toss with the oil, salt, and pepper until evenly coated. Transfer to grill rack or pan and grill until just tender and lightly browned, about 5 minutes, turning frequently. Return to the baking sheet and toss with the vinegar. Serve warm or at room temperature.

PER SERVING
Calories 44 ■ Protein 1g ■ Total Fat 4g ■ Sat. Fat 1g ■
Cholesterol 0mg ■ Carbohydrate 3g ■
Dietary Fiber 1g ■ Sodium 236mg

Asparagus with Tomato Vinaigrette

MAKES 4 SERVINGS

Serve this versatile recipe as an appetizing antipasto, elegant first course, or tasty side dish.

1 pound medium asparagus, trimmed
3 tablespoons extra-virgin olive oil
2 tablespoons red wine vinegar
2 medium plum tomatoes (about 2 ounces each), finely chopped
2 scallions (white and green parts), finely chopped
1 tablespoon finely chopped fresh flat-leaf parsley
Salt and freshly ground black pepper, to taste

Bring a large stockpot filled with salted water to a boil over high heat. Prepare an ice-water bath and set aside.

Add the asparagus to boiling water and cook until just tender, about 5 minutes, depending on thickness. Drain and transfer to ice-water bath for 5 minutes. Drain well and transfer to shallow serving platter or long serving dish.

Meanwhile, in a small bowl, whisk together the oil and vinegar. Stir in the tomatoes, scallions, parsley, salt, and pepper. Add to the asparagus, tossing gently to combine. Serve at room temperature. (Alternatively, cover and refrigerate a minimum of 3 hours, or overnight, and serve chilled or return to room temperature.)

Sautéed Asparagus with Garlic

MAKES 4 SERVINGS

This Northern Italian side dish is delicious served over a bed of rice or orzo pasta.

- **3 tablespoons extra-virgin olive oil**
- **3 large cloves garlic, finely chopped**
- **1 pound medium asparagus, trimmed**
- **1 teaspoon coarse salt, or to taste**
- **¼ teaspoon freshly ground black pepper**

In a large nonstick skillet, heat the oil over medium heat. Add the garlic and cook, stirring, 30 seconds. Add the asparagus, salt, and pepper; cook, turning often, until asparagus is lightly browned and just tender, about 10 minutes. Serve at once.

Sautéed Artichokes with Tomatoes

MAKES 4 TO 6 SERVINGS

If you can't find young artichokes, select medium-size ones and cut into quarters after trimming.

- **3 tablespoons fresh lemon juice**
- **1 pound small young artichokes**
- **¼ cup extra-virgin olive oil**
- **4 large cloves garlic, finely chopped**
- **1 (16-ounce) can plum tomatoes, juices included**
- **½ teaspoon dried oregano**
- **½ cup dry white wine**
- **Salt and freshly ground black pepper, to taste**
- **Country-style Italian bread, for dipping into juices (optional)**

Fill a medium bowl with water and add the lemon juice. Set aside. With a sharp, serrated knife, cut about ½ inch off the top of each artichoke. Pull off and discard the tough, dark green outer leaves to expose the pale green inner hearts. Trim the dark stem end of each artichoke. Cut each artichoke in half. With a small spoon or your fingers, scrape out any prickly inner leaves. As you work, drop the artichokes into the lemon water to prevent browning.

In a large nonstick skillet, heat the oil over medium heat. Add the garlic and cook, stirring constantly, until softened but not browned, 1 to 2 minutes. Add the tomatoes and their juices, and oregano. Cook about 5 minutes, stirring and mashing the tomatoes with a large wooden spoon until well blended.

Meanwhile, drain the artichokes. Add to the skillet, along with the wine, salt, and pepper; bring to a brisk simmer over medium-high heat. Reduce the heat to medium-low and cook, partially covered, until the artichokes are tender, stirring occasionally, about 10 minutes. Serve warm or at room temperature, accompanied with bread (if using).

PER SERVING

Calories 191 ■ Protein 3g ■ Total Fat 14g ■ Sat. Fat 2g ■ Cholesterol 0mg ■ Carbohydrate 12g ■ Dietary Fiber 4g ■ Sodium 286mg

Sautéed Artichokes and Mushrooms with Lemon-Mint Pesto

MAKES 4 TO 5 SERVINGS

Frozen quartered artichokes make quick work of this delicious side dish.

> 1 tablespoon extra-virgin olive oil
> 6 ounces cultivated white button mushrooms, thinly sliced
> 1 large clove garlic, finely chopped
> 1 (12-ounce) package frozen quartered artichoke hearts, thawed
> ½ cup low-sodium vegetable broth
> Salt and freshly ground black pepper, to taste
> Lemon-Mint Pesto (opposite)

In a large nonstick skillet with a lid, heat the oil over medium heat. Add the mushrooms and cook, stirring, until just beginning to give off their liq-

uid, about 4 minutes. Add the garlic and cook, stirring, 1 minute. Add the artichokes, broth, salt, and pepper; bring to a boil over medium-high heat. Reduce the heat, cover, and simmer, stirring a few times, until the artichokes are fork-tender, about 10 minutes. Uncover and cook over medium heat until liquid is reduced by half, stirring occasionally. Remove from heat and stir in the Lemon-Mint Pesto. Serve warm.

PER SERVING

Calories 162 ■ Protein 6g ■ Total Fat 11g ■ Sat. Fat 2g ■ Cholesterol 0mg ■ Carbohydrate 14g ■ Dietary Fiber 7g ■ Sodium 259mg

Lemon-Mint Pesto

MAKES ABOUT ⅓ CUP

This tangy pesto is also delightful as a topping for grilled eggplant or zucchini.

> 2 cups loosely packed fresh mint leaves
> 2 large cloves garlic, finely chopped
> ¼ teaspoon coarse salt, or more to taste
> ¼ teaspoon lemon-pepper seasoning
> 2 tablespoons extra-virgin olive oil
> 1 teaspoon fresh lemon juice, or to taste

Combine the mint, garlic, salt, and lemon-pepper seasoning in a food processor fitted with the knife blade, or in a blender. Process until finely chopped. Add the oil and lemon juice; process until smooth. If not using immediately, store tightly covered in the refrigerator up to 2 days.

PER SERVING (ABOUT 4 TEASPOONS)

Calories 82 ■ Protein 2g ■ Total Fat 7g ■ Sat. Fat 1g ■ Cholesterol 0mg ■ Carbohydrate 5g ■ Dietary Fiber 3g ■ Sodium 153mg

Tuscan Beans with Tomatoes and Sage

**MAKES 3 TO 4 MAIN-DISH SERVINGS
OR 6 TO 8 SIDE-DISH OR APPETIZER SERVINGS**

You can serve this versatile Tuscan specialty as a side dish or as a meal in itself accompanied by lots of crusty bread and a green salad. It's also wonderful on a bed of polenta or smeared on toasted Italian or French bread. A fresh rosemary sprig can replace the sage.

**¼ cup extra-virgin olive oil
3 cloves garlic, finely chopped
2 (15-ounce) cans cannellini or other white
    beans, rinsed and drained
1 cup low-sodium vegetable broth
1 (14-ounce) can stewed tomatoes, chopped,
    juices included
4 fresh sage leaves
Salt and freshly ground black pepper, to taste**

In a medium stockpot, heat the oil over medium heat. Add the garlic and cook, stirring constantly, until just beginning to brown, about 2 minutes. Add the beans, broth, tomatoes and their juices, sage, salt, and pepper; bring to a brisk simmer over medium-high heat, stirring occasionally and breaking up the tomatoes with a wooden spoon. Reduce the heat to medium-low and simmer, uncovered, stirring occasionally, until thickened, about 20 minutes. Serve warm.

PER SERVING
Calories 236 ▪ Protein 11g ▪ Total Fat 10g ▪ Sat. Fat 1g ▪
Cholesterol 0mg ▪ Carbohydrate 28g ▪
Dietary Fiber 9g ▪ Sodium 260mg

Roasted Beets and Arugula

MAKES 4 SERVINGS

The sweetness of roasted beets is a pleasant contrast to peppery arugula in the following recipe.

**4 medium beets, unpeeled
2 scallions (white and green parts), thinly sliced
2 tablespoons extra-virgin olive oil
½ tablespoon red wine vinegar
Salt and freshly ground black pepper, to taste
4 cups arugula or spinach, torn into bite-size
    pieces**

Preheat the oven to 375F (190C).

Wrap the beets in aluminum foil and place in a shallow baking pan or sheet. Roast for 45 to 50 minutes, or until tender. Remove from the oven and unwrap. Set aside to cool slightly. Peel off the skins and cut into cubes.

Transfer warm beets to a serving bowl and toss with the scallions, oil, vinegar, salt, and pepper.

To serve, divide the greens among 4 serving plates. Top with equal portions of the beet mixture and serve at once.

PER SERVING
Calories 103 ▪ Protein 2g ▪ Total Fat 7g ▪ Sat. Fat 1g ▪
Cholesterol 0mg ▪ Carbohydrate 9g ▪
Dietary Fiber 3g ▪ Sodium 71mg

Stewed Bell Peppers and Tomatoes

MAKES 4 TO 6 SERVINGS

This is wonderful served warm over polenta or spread over plain focaccia once it thickens and cools to room temperature.

3 tablespoons extra-virgin olive oil
2 large onions (about 8 ounces each), cut in half lengthwise and thinly sliced crosswise
4 large bell peppers (about 8 ounces each), preferably 2 green and 2 red, cut into 1-inch wide strips
1 (14-ounce) can stewed tomatoes, juices included
Salt and freshly ground black pepper, to taste

In a large deep-sided nonstick skillet, heat the oil over medium heat. Add the onions and cook, stirring, until just softened, about 3 minutes. Add the bell peppers and cook, stirring, until just softened, about 3 minutes. Add the tomatoes and their juices, salt, and pepper; bring to a brisk simmer over medium-high heat. Reduce the heat and simmer gently, uncovered, until the vegetables are soft but not mushy, 25 to 30 minutes, stirring occasionally. Serve warm or at room temperature.

PER SERVING
Calories 209 ■ Protein 4g ■ Total Fat 11g ■ Sat. Fat 2g ■
Cholesterol 0mg ■ Carbohydrate 28g ■
Dietary Fiber 6g ■ Sodium 259mg

Fresh Broccoli with Garlic and Lemon

MAKES 4 SERVINGS

Select bright green broccoli with tight buds for this tasty dish.

3 tablespoons extra-virgin olive oil
3 large cloves garlic, finely chopped
1 tablespoon fresh lemon juice
1 pound fresh broccoli florets
½ teaspoon coarse salt
¼ teaspoon freshly ground black pepper

In a small nonstick skillet, heat the oil over medium-low heat. Add the garlic and cook, stirring often, until softened and fragrant but not browned, 3 to 5 minutes. Remove the skillet from the heat and stir in the lemon juice.

Meanwhile, place the broccoli in a steaming basket set over boiling water; cover and steam over medium heat until broccoli is crisp-tender and bright green, 3 to 5 minutes. Drain and transfer to a large serving bowl. Add the oil and garlic mixture, salt, and pepper; toss well to combine. Serve warm.

PER SERVING
Calories 127 ■ Protein 4g ■ Total Fat 11g ■ Sat. Fat 1g ■
Cholesterol 0mg ■ Carbohydrate 7g ■
Dietary Fiber 4g ■ Sodium 255mg

Fresh Broccoli Marinara

MAKES 4 SERVINGS

This is a quick and delicious way to enjoy an important cruciferous vegetable.

- **2 tablespoons extra-virgin olive oil**
- **2 large cloves garlic, finely chopped**
- **1 (14.5-ounce) can diced tomatoes with Italian seasonings, juices included**
- **1 pound fresh broccoli florets**
- **Salt and freshly ground black pepper, to taste**

In a large nonstick skillet with a lid, heat the oil over medium heat. Add the garlic and cook, stirring constantly, 1 minute. Add the tomatoes and their juices and bring to a brisk simmer over medium-high heat. Reduce the heat and simmer gently, uncovered, until the liquids are reduced by about one-half, stirring occasionally. Place the broccoli on top of the tomatoes, and season with salt and pepper. Bring to a brisk simmer over medium-high heat. Cover and cook over medium-low heat until the broccoli is tender yet still bright green, about 8 to 10 minutes. Toss well to combine with the sauce and serve warm or just above room temperature.

PER SERVING

Calories 115 ▪ Protein 5g ▪ Total Fat 7g ▪ Sat. Fat 1g ▪
Cholesterol 0mg ▪ Carbohydrate 11g ▪
Dietary Fiber 5g ▪ Sodium 238mg

Italian-Style Kabobs with Brussels Sprouts and Potatoes

MAKES 4 LARGE OR 6 SMALL SERVINGS

Even confirmed Brussels sprouts naysayers enjoy these tasty kabobs. If desired, remove skewers after broiling and transfer the vegetables to a large serving bowl, tossing well to combine.

- **8 small new red potatoes (about ½ pound), halved or quartered, depending on size**
- **8 fresh or frozen Brussels sprouts**
- **1 large green or red bell pepper (about 8 ounces), quartered and cut in half crosswise**
- **½ large red onion (about 4 ounces), quartered and cut in half crosswise**
- **⅓ cup dairy-free Italian-style salad dressing**
- **Salt, preferably the coarse variety, and freshly ground black pepper, to taste**

Preheat the oven to broil.

In a medium saucepan, combine the potatoes and Brussels sprouts; add enough water to cover by 1 inch. Bring to a boil over high heat. Reduce the heat to medium, partially cover, and cook until the Brussels sprouts and potatoes are just tender, 10 minutes. Drain well and let cool slightly.

Alternately thread the potatoes, Brussels sprouts, bell peppers, and onion on each of 4 metal skewers. Place on an ungreased baking sheet and brush with half of the salad dressing, then season with salt and pepper. Broil 6 to 8 inches from heat source until browned and tender, turning occasionally and basting with the remaining dressing, about 8 minutes. Serve warm or at room temperature.

PER SERVING

Calories 224 ▪ Protein 8g ▪ Total Fat 10g ▪ Sat. Fat 2g ▪ Cholesterol 0mg ▪ Carbohydrate 31g ▪ Dietary Fiber 9g ▪ Sodium 202mg

Butternut Squash Puree

MAKES 6 SERVINGS

Serve this tasty winter squash dish as you would mashed potatoes. If the butternut variety is unavailable, use a sweet variety of cooking pumpkin instead. To turn it into a soup, reheat the puree in a stockpot with additional broth or water to achieve the desired consistency.

- 3 tablespoons extra-virgin olive oil
- 1 large onion (about 8 ounces), finely chopped
- 1 large butternut squash (about 3 pounds), peeled, seeded, and cubed
- 2 cups low-sodium vegetable broth, plus additional broth or water as necessary
- ½ teaspoon salt
- ¼ teaspoon freshly ground black pepper
- Chopped fresh chives, for garnish (optional)

In a large deep-sided nonstick skillet, heat the oil over medium heat. Add the onion and cook, stirring, until softened but not browned, about 5 minutes. Add the squash, 2 cups broth, salt, and pepper; bring to a boil over high heat. Reduce the heat to medium and cook, partially covered, until squash is tender, 15 to 20 minutes, stirring occasionally and adding additional broth or water as necessary to keep squash from drying out.

Working in batches, transfer the squash mixture to a food processor fitted with the knife blade, or to a blender. Process until smooth and pureed. Serve warm, garnished with the chives (if using).

PER SERVING

Calories 180 ▪ Protein 6g ▪ Total Fat 7g ▪ Sat. Fat 1g ▪ Cholesterol 0mg ▪ Carbohydrate 27g ▪ Dietary Fiber 5g ▪ Sodium 359mg

Basil Carrots

MAKES 4 SERVINGS

Just about any herb can replace the basil in this tasty carrot dish—chopped fresh mint is an especially refreshing variation.

- 1 pound baby carrots
- ½ cup low-sodium vegetable broth
- 1 tablespoon extra-virgin olive oil
- 1 tablespoon finely chopped fresh basil leaves, or 1 teaspoon dried basil leaves
- Salt, preferably the coarse variety, and freshly ground black pepper, to taste

Place the carrots and enough salted water to cover in a large deep-sided skillet with a lid. Bring to a boil over high heat. Reduce the heat to medium, cover, and simmer briskly until just crisp-tender, about 5 minutes, depending on thickness. Drain in a colander and set aside.

Add the broth to the skillet and reduce to about ¼ cup over medium-high heat. Return the carrots to the skillet and add the oil, basil, salt, and pepper; cook, tossing and stirring constantly, until the carrots have absorbed most of the broth. Serve at once.

PER SERVING

Calories 80 ▪ Protein 2g ▪ Total Fat 4g ▪ Sat. Fat 1g ▪
Cholesterol 0mg ▪ Carbohydrate 10g ▪
Dietary Fiber 3g ▪ Sodium 105mg

Roasted Carrots with Rosemary and Sage

MAKES 4 TO 6 SERVINGS

The perfect Thanksgiving side dish, these fragrant carrots can conveniently be roasted alongside your Tofurky roast at 300F (150C) by adjusting the cooking time to about 1 hour.

1 (16-ounce) bag washed baby carrots
¼ teaspoon dried rosemary
¼ teaspoon salt
⅛ teaspoon ground sage
Freshly ground black pepper, to taste
2 tablespoons extra-virgin olive oil

Preheat oven to 350F (175C). Lightly grease a baking sheet with a rim.

Place the carrots on the baking sheet and sprinkle evenly with the rosemary, salt, sage, and pepper, then drizzle with the oil. Using a wide spatula, toss to thoroughly coat. Arrange in a single layer and roast about 40 minutes, or until lightly browned and tender, stirring and turning occasionally. Serve warm.

PER SERVING

Calories 103 ▪ Protein 1g ▪ Total Fat 7g ▪ Sat. Fat 1g ▪
Cholesterol 0mg ▪ Carbohydrate 9g ▪
Dietary Fiber 3g ▪ Sodium 173mg

Italian-Style Carrots with Oregano and Parsley

MAKES 4 TO 6 SERVINGS

Served at room temperature, these carrots also make a tasty antipasto for up to 6.

1 pound carrots, peeled, cut into 2-inch chunks
¼ cup white wine vinegar
1 tablespoon extra-virgin olive oil
1 tablespoon chopped fresh oregano, or 1 teaspoon dried oregano
1 tablespoon finely chopped fresh flat-leaf parsley
1 large clove garlic, finely chopped
¼ teaspoon coarse salt, or to taste
Freshly ground black pepper, to taste

In a large saucepan, combine the carrots, vinegar, and enough salted water to cover. Bring to a boil over high heat. Reduce heat to medium-high and cook until carrots are tender, 15 to 20 minutes. Drain the carrots and transfer to a bowl; immediately toss with remaining ingredients. Let stand about 5 minutes to allow the flavors to blend. Serve warm or at room temperature.

PER SERVING

Calories 77 ▪ Protein 1g ▪ Total Fat 4g ▪ Sat. Fat 1g ▪
Cholesterol 0mg ▪ Carbohydrate 12g ▪
Dietary Fiber 3g ▪ Sodium 154mg

Fennel Gratin

MAKES 4 TO 6 SERVINGS

A white bulbous vegetable with stalks bearing bright green feathery fronds, fennel grows wild throughout much of Italy. Faintly redolent of licorice, it's delicious raw for dipping and in salads, or cooked in soups and gratins.

> 3 fennel bulbs (about 12 ounces each), trimmed, cored, and cut crosswise into ⅜-inch-thick slices, ¼ cup feathery fronds reserved and finely chopped
> ¼ cup water
> 4 ounces packaged crostini (Italian crackers; see Cook's Tip, page 108), ground into fine crumbs, or ½ cup unseasoned dry bread crumbs
> Juice of 1 large lemon (about 4 tablespoons)
> 2 tablespoons rinsed and drained capers
> 2 tablespoons extra-virgin olive oil
> Salt and freshly ground black pepper, to taste
> 1½ cups low-sodium vegetable broth, reduced over high heat to ½ cup
> Pitted black olives (optional)

Preheat the oven to 375F (190C). Lightly oil an 8½- or 9-inch pie plate or gratin and set aside.

In a large nonstick skillet with a tight-fitting lid, combine the sliced fennel and the water. Bring to a boil over high heat. Reduce the heat to medium, cover, and steam until the fennel is crisp-tender, 3 to 4 minutes. Remove the skillet from the heat and set aside briefly to cool (do not discard liquids).

In a small bowl, place the crostini crumbs, lemon juice, capers, and oil. Season with salt and pepper, and stir well to combine.

Transfer the fennel and cooking liquids to the prepared baking dish. With your fingers, distribute the crostini crumb mixture evenly over the fennel; pour the broth over top. Bake, uncovered, 25 to 30 minutes, or until the top is lightly browned. Sprinkle with the reserved chopped fennel fronds and garnish with the olives (if using). Serve at once.

PER SERVING
Calories 193 ■ Protein 8g ■ Total Fat 8g ■ Sat. Fat 1g ■ Cholesterol 0mg ■ Carbohydrate 25g ■ Dietary Fiber 7g ■ Sodium 418mg

> **⅋ COOK'S TIP ⅋**
> *While fennel is regularly stocked in most major supermarkets throughout the fall and winter, it is often mislabeled anise—an annual herb grown mainly for its similar licorice-flavored seeds.*

Green Beans with Tomatoes and Garlic

MAKES 4 TO 6 SERVINGS

These green beans literally melt in your mouth, so don't be put off by the long cooking time—they are well worth the wait.

> 2 tablespoons extra-virgin olive oil
> 1½ pounds fresh green beans, trimmed
> 1 large tomato (about 8 ounces), seeded and chopped
> 2 large cloves garlic, finely chopped

½ teaspoon dried oregano

1 teaspoon salt, or to taste

Freshly ground black pepper, to taste

Low-sodium vegetable broth or water, as
necessary

In a large nonstick skillet with a lid, heat the oil over medium-high heat. Add the beans and cook, stirring and tossing often, just until softened, about 5 minutes. Reduce the heat to medium-low and add the tomato, garlic, oregano, salt, and pepper, stirring well to combine. Cover and cook until beans are very tender, about 1 hour, stirring occasionally, adding broth or water as necessary to keep mixture from drying out. Serve warm.

PER SERVING

Calories 126 ■ Protein 4g ■ Total Fat 7g ■ Sat. Fat 1g ■
Cholesterol 0mg ■ Carbohydrate 15g ■
Dietary Fiber 6g ■ Sodium 548mg

Green Beans with Walnut Sauce

MAKES 6 SERVINGS

Green beans are a vegetable with a definite affinity for nuts. Dressed in a toasted walnut sauce is a grand way to present them on special occasions.

¼ cup chopped walnuts

½ cup packed flat-leaf parsley

1 tablespoon extra-virgin olive oil

½ tablespoon tomato paste

2 large cloves garlic, finely chopped

½ teaspoon coarse salt, or to taste

1¾ pounds green beans, trimmed to yield 1½
pounds

¼ cup low-sodium vegetable broth (optional)

Place the walnuts, parsley, oil, tomato paste, garlic, and salt in a food processor fitted with the knife blade, or in a blender. Process until a smooth paste is formed. Set aside.

Meanwhile, bring a large stockpot filled with salted water to a boil over high heat. Add the beans and cook until tender but still slightly crisp, about 7 minutes. If not using the optional broth, reserve ¼ cup of the cooking liquid, then drain the beans well. Transfer to a serving bowl. Add the walnut sauce and either the broth or reserved cooking liquid, tossing well to combine. Serve warm.

**PER SERVING (WITH THE OPTIONAL
VEGETABLE BROTH)**

Calories 96 ■ Protein 4g ■ Total Fat 5g ■ Sat. Fat 1g ■
Cholesterol 0mg ■ Carbohydrate 10g ■
Dietary Fiber 5g ■ Sodium 47mg

VARIATION: *Substitute toasted hazelnuts for the walnuts.*

Green Beans with Wild Mushrooms and Tomato

MAKES 4 SERVINGS

This delicious side dish is also wonderful tossed with pasta or served over rice.

1 pound fresh green beans, trimmed

2 tablespoons extra-virgin olive oil

½ cup chopped onion

4 ounces fresh wild, cremini, and/or cultivated white mushrooms, sliced

1 medium tomato (about 6 ounces), seeded and chopped

Salt and freshly ground black pepper, to taste

Bring a large stockpot filled with salted water to a boil over high heat. Add the green beans and boil until crisp-tender, 3 to 5 minutes. Drain.

In a large deep-sided nonstick skillet, heat the oil over medium heat. Add the onion and cook, stirring, until softened, about 3 minutes. Add the mushrooms and tomato and cook, stirring often, until mushrooms are tender and have released their liquid, about 5 minutes. Add the green beans, salt, and pepper; toss until heated through. Serve warm.

PER SERVING
Calories 118 ▪ Protein 3g ▪ Total Fat 7g ▪ Sat. Fat 1g ▪
Cholesterol 0mg ▪ Carbohydrate 13g ▪
Dietary Fiber 5g ▪ Sodium 12mg

Grilled Leeks with Herbed Vinaigrette

MAKES 6 SERVINGS

Use this tasty herbed vinaigrette to dress up any number of grilled or steamed vegetables.

6 large leeks (about 8 ounces each), trimmed and washed

5½ tablespoons extra-virgin olive oil

1½ tablespoons white-wine vinegar

2 teaspoons Dijon mustard

Salt and freshly ground black pepper, to taste

2 to 3 tablespoons finely chopped assorted fresh herbs, such as chives, parsley, mint, basil, and tarragon

2 tablespoons chopped pimiento

2 tablespoons finely chopped kalamata or other good-quality black olives

Prepare a medium-hot charcoal grill or gas grill. Position the grill rack 4 to 6 inches from heat source. Or, place a stovetop grilling pan with grids over medium-high heat.

Bring a large stockpot filled with salted water to a boil over high heat. Split each leek lengthwise to within 1½ inches of the root end. Using kitchen string, tie the leeks in 3 bundles of 2 leeks each and boil until just tender, about 5 minutes. Drain and refresh under cold-running water. Remove and discard the strings. Cut the leeks apart at the root ends and drain them on paper towels. (At this point, the leeks may be refrigerated, covered, up to 1 day before proceeding with the recipe.)

In a small bowl, whisk together 4 tablespoons

of the oil, vinegar, mustard, salt, and pepper; stir in the herbs, pimiento, and olives. Set aside.

Brush the leeks with the remaining 1½ tablespoons oil. Working in batches, if necessary, grill until lightly browned, 3 to 4 minutes per side. As they cook, transfer the leeks to a baking sheet with sides and keep warm. When all the leeks are finished cooking, drizzle with the vinaigrette and, using a wide spatula, turn to evenly coat. Serve warm or at room temperature.

PER SERVING
Calories 177 ■ Protein 2g ■ Total Fat 13g ■ Sat. Fat 2g ■ Cholesterol 0mg ■ Carbohydrate 15g ■ Dietary Fiber 2g ■ Sodium 71mg

Oven-Braised Leeks

MAKES 6 SERVINGS

Highly valued aromatics in soups, leeks deserve a recipe of their own. Among all the members of the onion family, the leek provides the most iron and, next to scallions, the greatest amount of vitamin A. Served over lettuce, these plump, tender leeks make a fine first course. They are also a fine addition to a cold buffet table.

2 cups low-sodium vegetable broth

1 stalk celery, chopped

Juice of 1 medium lemon (about 3 tablespoons)

1 teaspoon whole black peppercorns

1 teaspoon whole coriander seed

¼ teaspoon dried oregano

3 pounds (6 large or 12 small) leeks, trimmed and washed

Salt and freshly ground black pepper, to taste

2 tablespoons extra-virgin olive oil

Preheat the oven to 375F (190C). In a small saucepan, bring the broth, celery, lemon juice, peppercorns, coriander, and oregano to a boil over high heat. Reduce the heat to medium and simmer briskly 10 minutes. Set aside.

Arrange the leeks in a gratin or shallow baking dish just large enough to hold them without touching in a single layer. Season with salt and pepper, then drizzle with the olive oil, turning the leeks to coat. Pour the broth mixture over the leeks, cover tightly with foil, and bake 25 to 30 minutes for large leeks, or 12 to 15 minutes for the small, or until the leeks are just softened.

Remove the foil and bake 10 to 20 minutes, or until the leeks are lightly browned and tender when pierced through the center with the tip of a sharp knife depending on size, turning the leeks a few times with tongs. Remove from the oven and, using tongs, transfer the leeks to a shallow serving bowl.

Return the cooking liquid to the saucepan and reduce over high heat until about ½ cup liquid remains. Strain over the leeks. Let cool to room temperature before serving. (Alternatively, cover and refrigerate a minimum of 1 hour, or up to 2 days, and serve chilled.)

PER SERVING
Calories 121 ■ Protein 5g ■ Total Fat 5g ■ Sat. Fat 1g ■ Cholesterol 0mg ■ Carbohydrate 16g ■ Dietary Fiber 3g ■ Sodium 198mg

Baked Onions

MAKES 4 SERVINGS

Full of fiber and vitamin C, vitamin B$_6$, potassium, and other key nutrients, onions are good for you—this recipe gives you a delicious excuse to eat a whole one with supper.

> **4 large yellow or red onions (about 8 ounces each), peeled**
> **2 tablespoons extra-virgin olive oil**
> **¼ cup seasoned Italian-style dry bread crumbs**
> **Salt, preferably the coarse variety, and freshly ground black pepper, to taste**

Preheat the oven to 350F (175C).

Cut each onion down to the root end into 8 wedges, taking care not to cut through the root so that onion stays intact. Place each onion on a piece of aluminum foil. Rub the insides of each onion with ½ tablespoon of the oil. Draw the foil up the sides of each onion and sprinkle each with 1 tablespoon of the bread crumbs. Sprinkle with salt and pepper. Twist the foil to seal and bake 45 minutes, or until the onions are soft but not falling apart. Carefully unwrap and let onions cool a few minutes before serving.

PER SERVING
Calories 173 ▪ Protein 4g ▪ Total Fat 7g ▪ Sat. Fat 1g ▪
Cholesterol 0mg ▪ Carbohydrate 25g ▪
Dietary Fiber 4g ▪ Sodium 206mg

Grilled Red Onions with Balsamic Vinegar and Rosemary

MAKES 6 SERVINGS

These onions are delicious as a side dish or topping for veggie burgers.

> **2 tablespoons balsamic vinegar**
> **1½ teaspoons chopped fresh rosemary leaves or ½ teaspoon dried**
> **1¾ pounds red onions (about 3 large), cut crosswise into ½-inch-thick slices**
> **1½ tablespoons extra-virgin olive oil, heated (see Cook's Tip, opposite page)**
> **Salt, preferably the coarse variety, and freshly ground black pepper, to taste**
> **¼ cup finely chopped fresh flat-leaf parsley**

Prepare a medium-hot charcoal grill or gas grill. Position the grill rack 4 to 6 inches from heat source. Or, place a stovetop grilling pan with grids over medium-high heat.

In a small saucepan, heat the vinegar and rosemary over low heat until hot (do not let mixture boil). Remove pan from heat and let mixture stand, covered, 20 minutes.

Brush the onion slices on both sides with the warm oil and season with salt and pepper. Grill in batches until lightly charred, 4 to 6 minutes on each side. As onions finish cooking, transfer to a large bowl, separating rings. While still hot, toss with vinegar mixture and parsley, and season with salt and pepper. Serve warm or at room temperature.

PER SERVING

Calories 82 ■ Protein 2g ■ Total Fat 4g ■ Sat. Fat 1g ■
Cholesterol 0mg ■ Carbohydrate 12g ■
Dietary Fiber 3g ■ Sodium 5mg

> ✃ **COOK'S TIP** ✃
>
> *Heating thins the olive oil, making it easier to brush evenly over the onions.*

Baked Potatoes with Bay Leaves

MAKES 4 SERVINGS

Bay leaves are among the most valued of aromatics in Mediterranean cooking, particularly Italian cuisine.

4 large russet potatoes (about 8 ounces each), scrubbed
4 teaspoons extra-virgin olive oil
Salt, preferably the coarse variety, and freshly ground black pepper, to taste
4 medium bay leaves

Preheat the oven to 400F (205C).

Cut each potato in half lengthwise. Rub each half with ½ teaspoon of the oil, then sprinkle with salt and pepper. Place a bay leaf in the center of one of the halves. Press the halves back together and wrap in a single layer of aluminum foil. Repeat with the remaining potatoes.

Transfer the potatoes to the oven and bake about 1 hour, or until tender through the center. Serve hot.

PER SERVING

Calories 180 ■ Protein 4g ■ Total Fat 5g ■ Sat. Fat 1g ■
Cholesterol 0mg ■ Carbohydrate 32g ■
Dietary Fiber 3g ■ Sodium 11mg

Italian-Style Baked "French Fried" Potatoes

MAKES 4 SERVINGS

Dried rosemary or oregano can be added along with the garlic salt, but if adding the herbs, omit the paprika.

2 large russet potatoes (about 8 ounces each), scrubbed, cut into ½-inch-thick slices
1 tablespoon extra-virgin olive oil
½ tablespoon fresh lemon juice
Garlic salt, to taste
Sweet paprika, to taste

Preheat the oven to 450F (230C). Soak the potatoes in ice water to cover 15 minutes. Lightly grease a large baking sheet with sides and set aside.

Drain the potatoes well and dry between paper towels. Place on the prepared baking sheet and drizzle with the oil and lemon juice, then sprinkle lightly with the garlic salt. Using a wide spatula, toss to evenly coat. Spread out in a single layer and bake 30 minutes, or until golden brown, turning once halfway through cooking time. Sprinkle lightly with paprika and serve at once.

PER SERVING

Calories 98 ■ Protein 2g ■ Total Fat 4g ■ Sat. Fat 1g ■
Cholesterol 0mg ■ Carbohydrate 16g ■
Dietary Fiber 1g ■ Sodium 5mg

Potato Tortino

MAKES 6 SERVINGS

This delicious potato casserole is wonderful served with Fresh Broccoli Marinara (page 99) or as a side dish to the Panini with Grilled Eggplant, Roasted Peppers, and Spinach-Pesto Sauce (page 143) or the Grilled Portobello Mushroom Sandwiches with Lemon-Basil Pesto (page 144).

2 ounces packaged crostini (Italian crackers; see Cook's Tip, opposite page), ground into fine crumbs, or ¼ cup unseasoned dry bread crumbs
2 pounds small waxy potatoes, left whole
4 tablespoons extra-virgin olive oil
1 large onion (about 8 ounces), cut in half lengthwise, thinly sliced crosswise
Salt and freshly ground black pepper, to taste
¼ cup low-sodium vegetable broth

Preheat the oven to 400F (205C). Lightly grease a 10-inch ceramic pie or quiche dish and sprinkle with half of the crostini crumbs; set aside.

In a large saucepan or medium stockpot, place the potatoes in enough salted water to cover by 2 inches. Bring to a boil over high heat. Reduce the heat slightly and boil until just tender, 10 minutes. Drain well and let cool slightly. When cool enough to handle, cut the potatoes into ¼-inch-thick slices.

Meanwhile, heat 3 tablespoons of the oil in a large nonstick skillet over medium heat. Add the onion and cook, stirring, until translucent and just beginning to brown, about 8 minutes, sea-

soning with salt and pepper the last few minutes of cooking.

Arrange one-third of the potatoes in the bottom of the prepared dish, then top with one-half of the onion. Repeat layers, ending with potatoes. Pour the broth evenly over all. Sprinkle evenly with the remaining crostini crumbs, then drizzle evenly with the remaining oil. Bake 25 to 30 minutes, or until golden brown. Let stand a few minutes before serving. Serve warm.

PER SERVING

Calories 204 ■ Protein 4g ■ Total Fat 10g ■ Sat. Fat 1g ■ Cholesterol 0mg ■ Carbohydrate 27g ■ Dietary Fiber 3g ■ Sodium 68mg

> ### ❧ COOK'S TIP ❧
> *If you are using packaged crostini (also labeled as Italian crackers), Trader Joe's carries a tasty dairy-free brand imported from Italy.*

Mashed Rosemary Potatoes with Olive Oil and Garlic

MAKES 6 TO 8 SERVINGS

This is the mashed version of roasted rosemary potatoes, and, I think, an equally tasty one. Though optional, the chives lend it even more flavor and pretty flecks of green.

3 pounds russet potatoes, peeled and cut into chunks
8 to 12 large cloves garlic, peeled
1 cup low-sodium vegetable broth, plus additional as necessary

1 teaspoon dried rosemary

3 tablespoons extra-virgin olive oil

2 to 4 tablespoons chopped fresh chives or the green parts of scallions (optional)

¾ teaspoon coarse salt, or to taste

Freshly ground black pepper, to taste

In a medium stockpot, place the potatoes in enough salted water to cover by a few inches. Bring to a boil over high heat. Add the garlic, reduce the heat to medium-high, and cook until potatoes are very tender, about 25 minutes. Drain well in a colander.

Meanwhile, in a small saucepan, boil the broth over high heat until reduced to ½ cup. Remove from heat and add the rosemary. Cover and let steep about 10 minutes.

Transfer the potatoes and garlic to a large bowl (or return to stockpot) and mash briefly with a potato masher or fork. Add the broth mixture and remaining ingredients, mashing until not quite smooth, and adding additional broth for a softer consistency. Serve at once.

PER SERVING

Calories 208 ■ Protein 6g ■ Total Fat 7g ■ Sat. Fat 1g ■
Cholesterol 0mg ■ Carbohydrate 32g ■
Dietary Fiber 3g ■ Sodium 332mg

Venetian-Style Sautéed Potatoes and Onions

MAKES 4 SERVINGS

Parboiling the potatoes eliminates much of the stirring required in traditional recipes for this classic Venetian dish.

1 pound medium boiling potatoes, halved or quartered, depending on size

2 tablespoons extra-virgin olive oil

1 large onion (about 8 ounces), cut in half lengthwise, thinly sliced crosswise

About 1 cup low-sodium vegetable broth

Garlic salt, to taste

Freshly ground black pepper, to taste

In a large saucepan or medium stockpot, place the potatoes in enough salted water to cover by 2 inches. Bring to a boil over high heat. Reduce the heat slightly and boil until just tender, 10 to 15 minutes. Drain well and let cool slightly. When cool enough to handle, cut into bite-size pieces.

In a large nonstick skillet, heat the oil over medium heat. Add the onion and cook, stirring, until translucent and just beginning to brown, about 8 minutes. Add the potatoes, and half of the broth. Season with garlic salt; cook, stirring often, until potatoes are fork-tender and mixture is creamy, about 15 minutes, adding broth as necessary to prevent mixture from drying out. Season with additional garlic salt, if necessary, and pepper. Serve warm.

PER SERVING

Calories 161 ■ Protein 5g ■ Total Fat 7g ■ Sat. Fat 1g ■
Cholesterol 0mg ■ Carbohydrate 21g ■
Dietary Fiber 3g ■ Sodium 403mg

Sautéed Spinach with Garlic

MAKES 4 SERVINGS

Here's a delicious way to give frozen spinach a fresh lift.

- **1 (1-pound) package frozen chopped spinach, cooked according to package directions and drained**
- **2 tablespoons extra-virgin olive oil**
- **2 large cloves garlic, finely chopped**
- **½ teaspoon salt, preferably the coarse variety, or to taste**
- **Freshly ground black pepper, to taste**

Place the spinach between paper towels and press down to extract the excess water, changing the paper towels as often as necessary.

In a medium nonstick skillet, heat the oil over medium heat. Add the garlic and cook, stirring constantly, until softened but not browned, about 2 minutes. Add the spinach, salt, and pepper; cook, stirring frequently, until heated through, about 5 minutes. Serve hot.

PER SERVING
Calories 89 ■ Protein 3g ■ Total Fat 7g ■ Sat. Fat 1g ■
Cholesterol 0mg ■ Carbohydrate 5g ■
Dietary Fiber 3g ■ Sodium 319mg

Wilted Spinach with Garlic and Pine Nuts

MAKES 4 SERVINGS

This recipe also makes an excellent filling for broiled or grilled portobello mushrooms.

- **1 tablespoon pine nuts**
- **1½ tablespoons extra-virgin olive oil**
- **2 large cloves garlic, finely chopped**
- **1 teaspoon fresh lemon juice**
- **1 (10-ounce) bag washed fresh spinach leaves**
- **Salt, preferably the coarse variety, and freshly ground black pepper, to taste**

Heat a large nonstick skillet over medium heat. Add the pine nuts and cook, stirring constantly, until lightly toasted and fragrant, about 3 minutes, taking care not to burn. Immediately remove from skillet and set aside.

Add the oil to the skillet and heat over medium heat. Add the garlic and lemon juice and cook, stirring constantly, 1 minute. Add the spinach and increase the heat to medium-high. Cook, tossing constantly, until the spinach is just wilted, about 3 minutes. Remove from the heat and add the pine nuts, salt, and pepper; toss well to combine. Serve at once.

PER SERVING
Calories 76 ■ Protein 3g ■ Total Fat 7g ■ Sat. Fat 1g ■
Cholesterol 0mg ■ Carbohydrate 4g ■
Dietary Fiber 2g ■ Sodium 56mg

Broiled Summer Squash with Cinnamon

MAKES 6 SERVINGS

Cinnamon often appears in savory dishes throughout Italy. Combined with sugar, it transforms ordinary summer squash into something special.

2 tablespoons light brown sugar

½ teaspoon ground cinnamon

4 medium summer squash (about 6 ounces each), preferably 2 green and 2 yellow, cut into ½-inch-thick rounds

2 tablespoons extra-virgin olive oil

Salt, to taste

Preheat the oven to broil. Position the oven rack 6 to 8 inches from heat source. Lightly oil a large baking sheet.

In a small bowl, combine the sugar and cinnamon. Arrange the squash in a single layer on the prepared baking sheet and brush with half of the oil. Sprinkle with half of the sugar mixture. Place under the broiler and broil until lightly browned, about 5 minutes. Remove the baking sheet from the oven and turn the squash over. Brush with the remaining oil, then sprinkle with remaining sugar mixture. Return to the broiler and broil until lightly browned, about 5 minutes. Season with salt. Serve at once.

PER SERVING

Calories 73 ▪ Protein 1g ▪ Total Fat 5g ▪ Sat. Fat 1g ▪ Cholesterol 0mg ▪ Carbohydrate 8g ▪ Dietary Fiber 1g ▪ Sodium 5mg

Baked Tomatoes Florentine Style

MAKES 4 SERVINGS

The term *Florentine* seems to be synonymous with spinach in cooking, particularly in Tuscan cuisine, which glorifies the iron-rich green. Like most Tuscan dishes, this baked tomato recipe is a delicious exercise in healthfulness and simplicity.

4 large ripe yet firm tomatoes (about 8 ounces each)

Salt, to taste

½ pound fresh spinach, washed, stemmed, and chopped, or ½ (10-ounce) bag fresh washed spinach leaves, chopped

1 tablespoon plus 2 teaspoons extra-virgin olive oil

1 shallot, finely chopped

1 cup soft white bread crumbs

⅛ teaspoon freshly grated nutmeg

Freshly ground black pepper, to taste

1 to 2 cups hot water or vegetable broth

Preheat the oven to 350F (175C). Cut a thin slice off the top of each tomato and discard. Seed each tomato and lightly salt the insides. Turn the seeded tomatoes upside down on several layers of paper towels and drain about 20 minutes.

Meanwhile, bring about 6 cups of water to a boil in a kettle or saucepan. Place the spinach in a colander. Slowly pour the boiling water over the spinach, turning the spinach with a wooden spoon until wilted. Press the spinach down in the colander with the back of the spoon to extract most of the liquid. Set aside.

In a medium nonstick skillet, heat the 1 tablespoon oil over medium heat. Add the shallot and cook, stirring often, until softened but not browned, about 2 minutes. Add the spinach and increase the heat to high; cook, stirring constantly, until all of the liquids released from the spinach have evaporated, 1 to 2 minutes. Remove from heat and add the bread crumbs, nutmeg, salt, and pepper; stir well to combine.

Fill tomatoes evenly with spinach mixture. Arrange upright in a shallow baking dish just large enough to comfortably accommodate their size. Brush the tops and sides of each tomato with ½ teaspoon of the remaining oil. Pour enough warm water around the tomatoes to measure ½ inch deep. Bake, uncovered, 20 to 25 minutes, or until tops are lightly browned. Serve at once.

PER SERVING

Calories 136 ▪ Protein 4g ▪ Total Fat 7g ▪ Sat. Fat 1g ▪
Cholesterol 0mg ▪ Carbohydrate 17g ▪
Dietary Fiber 4g ▪ Sodium 105mg

Italian Stewed Tomatoes

MAKES 4 SERVINGS

In Italy, stewed tomatoes are a popular vegetable side dish. These are nice over rice or polenta.

    6 large tomatoes (about 8 ounces each),
        peeled, seeded, and cut into small pieces
    ¼ cup chopped celery
    2 tablespoons chopped onion
    1 tablespoon chopped green bell pepper
    ½ teaspoon dried basil or oregano

    1 tablespoon sugar
    ½ teaspoon salt
    Freshly ground black pepper, to taste

In a large saucepan or medium stockpot, combine all the ingredients. Cover and cook over medium heat until the tomatoes are softened but not mushy, about 10 minutes, stirring occasionally. Serve warm or at room temperature. (Alternatively, cover and refrigerate up to 3 days and return to room temperature, or gently reheat, before serving.)

PER SERVING

Calories 81 ▪ Protein 3g ▪ Total Fat 1g ▪ Sat. Fat 0g ▪
Cholesterol 0mg ▪ Carbohydrate 18g ▪
Dietary Fiber 4g ▪ Sodium 301mg

Tomatoes with Arugula

MAKES 4 TO 6 SERVINGS

This simple yet delicious side dish or salad is popular in northern Italy during the summer months.

    6 medium vine-ripened tomatoes (about 6
        ounces each), cut into ½-inch-thick slices
    2 tablespoons finely chopped arugula or
        spinach
    3 tablespoons extra-virgin olive oil
    ½ teaspoon coarse salt, or to taste
    Freshly ground black pepper, to taste

In a large bowl, toss all the ingredients together gently yet thoroughly to combine. Let stand about 15 minutes at room temperature to allow the flavors to blend. Toss again and serve at room temperature. (Alternatively, cover and refrigerate a minimum of 3 hours or overnight and serve chilled.)

Chilled Stuffed Plum Tomatoes with Parsley and Bread Crumbs

MAKES 6 SERVINGS

These simple stuffed plum tomatoes become an impressive appetizer or first course served on a bed of lettuce leaves.

12 large plum tomatoes (about 3 ounces each)
Table salt
3 slices white or whole wheat bread (3 ounces), toasted, crusts removed
3 tablespoons red wine vinegar
½ cup finely chopped fresh flat-leaf parsley
2 tablespoons extra-virgin olive oil
½ teaspoon coarse salt
Freshly ground black pepper, to taste
Lettuce leaves (optional)

Working horizontally, slice off the upper eighth of each tomato and discard. Using a spoon or your fingers, hollow out each tomato, discarding seeds and juices. Sprinkle the insides lightly with the table salt and turn upside down to drain on paper towels about 10 minutes.

Sprinkle each slice of toast with 1 tablespoon vinegar. Crumble the bread into a small bowl and add the parsley, oil, coarse salt, and pepper, stirring until thoroughly combined. Place the drained tomato halves, hollowed-sides up, in a shallow container large enough to hold them in a single layer. Fill with equal portions of the parsley mixture. Cover and refrigerate a minimum of 3 hours, or overnight. Serve chilled, on a bed of lettuce leaves (if using).

Sicilian-Style Roasted Stuffed Tomatoes

MAKES 6 SERVINGS

Serve these delicious stuffed tomatoes as an antipasto, side dish, or first course.

6 medium tomatoes (about 6 ounces each)
Table salt
2 tablespoons extra-virgin olive oil
2 tablespoons finely chopped onion
¼ cup finely chopped parsley
2 large cloves garlic, finely chopped
1 cup lightly toasted fresh white bread crumbs (see Cook's Tip, page 114)
3 tablespoons capers, drained
1 teaspoon coarse salt
½ teaspoon dried oregano
Freshly ground black pepper, to taste

Preheat oven to 350F (175C). Lightly oil a shallow baking dish just large enough to hold the tomatoes in a single layer.

Cut a slice from the top of each tomato. Gently squeeze out the seeds from each tomato, leaving the pulp in place. Lightly salt the insides of each tomato and place them upside down to drain on paper towels about 20 minutes.

Meanwhile, in a medium nonstick skillet over medium heat, heat 1 tablespoon of the oil. Add the onion and cook, stirring, until just softened, about 2 minutes. Add the parsley and garlic and cook, stirring constantly, 1 minute. Remove the skillet from the heat and add the bread crumbs, capers, coarse salt, oregano, and pepper; toss well to combine.

Fill the tomatoes loosely with equal portions of the bread crumb mixture. Arrange the stuffed tomatoes in a single layer in the prepared pan. Drizzle the tops evenly with the remaining 1 tablespoon olive oil. Bake about 30 minutes, or until the tomatoes are soft but not falling apart and the tops are lightly browned. Serve warm or at room temperature.

PER SERVING

Calories 150 ▪ Protein 4g ▪ Total Fat 6g ▪ Sat. Fat 1g ▪
Cholesterol 0mg ▪ Carbohydrate 21g ▪
Dietary Fiber 3g ▪ Sodium 523mg

> ### ❧ COOK'S TIP ❧
> *To toast bread crumbs, preheat the oven to 250F (120C). Place the bread crumbs on a light-colored baking sheet. Bake on the center rack 20 minutes, or until lightly browned, stirring halfway through cooking time.*

Mashed Turnips with Pears

MAKES 4 TO 6 SERVINGS

The addition of the fruit takes the edge off of the bitter turnip flavor in this surprisingly tasty alternative to standard mashed potatoes. An apple can replace the pear.

1½ pounds small turnips, peeled and quartered
4 large cloves garlic, peeled
1 ripe pear (about 6 ounces), peeled, cored, and chopped
1½ tablespoons extra-virgin olive oil
½ teaspoon coarse salt
Freshly ground black pepper, to taste

Place the turnips and garlic cloves in a steaming basket set over boiling water; cover and steam over medium heat until the turnips are fork-tender, about 15 minutes. Drain and transfer the turnips and garlic to a food processor fitted with the knife blade, or to a blender. Add the pear, oil, salt, and pepper; process until smooth but still slightly chunky. Serve at once.

PER SERVING

Calories 120 ▪ Protein 2g ▪ Total Fat 5g ▪ Sat. Fat 1g ▪
Cholesterol 0mg ▪ Carbohydrate 18g ▪
Dietary Fiber 4g ▪ Sodium 350mg

Mixed Vegetables with Capers and Olive Oil

MAKES 4 TO 6 SIDE-DISH OR 8 APPETIZER SERVINGS

Serve these tasty mixed vegetables warm as a side dish or chilled as a terrific make-ahead antipasto.

1 medium boiling potato (about 4 ounces), peeled and cut into bite-size chunks
2 medium carrots (about 6 ounces), peeled and cut crosswise into ¾-inch-thick slices

1 medium zucchini (about 6 ounces), cut
  crosswise into ¾-inch-thick slices
¼ pound fresh green beans, trimmed
2 tablespoons extra-virgin olive oil
1 tablespoon capers, drained
1 tablespoon finely chopped fresh flat-leaf
  parsley
Salt, preferably the coarse variety, and freshly
  ground black pepper, to taste

Bring a medium stockpot filled with salted water to a boil over high heat. Add the potato and carrots and reduce heat to medium-high; cook, partially covered, 10 minutes. Add the zucchini and cook, partially covered, 2 minutes. Add the green beans and cook, partially covered, 3 minutes, or until all the vegetables are tender yet still somewhat firm. Drain well and transfer to a shallow serving bowl.

While still quite warm, add the remaining ingredients, tossing well to thoroughly combine. Serve slightly warm or at room temperature. (Alternatively, cover and refrigerate a minimum of 3 hours, or up to 1 day, and served chilled or return to room temperature.)

PER SERVING
Calories 124 ■ Protein 2g ■ Total Fat 7g ■ Sat. Fat 1g ■
Cholesterol 0mg ■ Carbohydrate 15g ■
Dietary Fiber 4g ■ Sodium 51mg

Marinated Lemon Zucchini

MAKES 4 TO 6 SERVINGS

This is one of my favorite ways to eat zucchini. For a tasty variation, use fresh basil in lieu of the parsley.

Juice of 2 medium lemons (6 tablespoons)
2 tablespoons extra-virgin olive oil
2 tablespoons finely chopped fresh flat-leaf
  parsley
1 large clove garlic, finely chopped
½ teaspoon coarse salt
¼ teaspoon freshly ground black pepper
4 medium zucchini (about 6 ounces each), cut
  into ½-inch-thick rounds

In a large bowl, whisk together the lemon juice, oil, parsley, garlic, salt, and pepper. Add the zucchini and toss well to thoroughly combine. Cover and refrigerate a minimum of 8 hours, or overnight, stirring and turning a few times.

Preheat the oven to broil. Position the oven rack 4 to 6 inches from heat source. Lightly oil a large baking sheet.

Remove the zucchini from the marinade (reserve marinade, if desired) and arrange in a single layer on the prepared baking sheet. Broil until lightly browned, about 3 minutes each side. Serve at once, dressed with the reserved marinade (if using).

PER SERVING
Calories 90 ■ Protein 2g ■ Total Fat 7g ■ Sat. Fat 1g ■
Cholesterol 0mg ■ Carbohydrate 7g ■
Dietary Fiber 2g ■ Sodium 241mg

Sautéed Zucchini with Scallions

MAKES 4 SERVINGS

This easy sauté showcases the versatility of zucchini.

2 tablespoons extra-virgin olive oil

1 bunch (about 6) scallions (white and green parts), thinly sliced

4 medium zucchini (about 6 ounces each), trimmed, cut lengthwise into quarters, then sliced crosswise into ½-inch-thick pieces

Salt and freshly ground black pepper, to taste

In a large nonstick skillet, heat the oil over medium heat. Add the scallions and cook, stirring, until just softened, 2 to 3 minutes. Add the zucchini, salt, and pepper; cook, stirring often, until the zucchini is tender, about 10 minutes. Serve at once.

PER SERVING
Calories 93 ▪ Protein 3g ▪ Total Fat 7g ▪ Sat. Fat 1g ▪
Cholesterol 0mg ▪ Carbohydrate 7g ▪
Dietary Fiber 3g ▪ Sodium 10mg

Zucchini Stuffed with Olives and Tomatoes

MAKES 4 TO 8 SERVINGS

You can prepare small Italian eggplants in this manner as well.

4 small zucchini (about 6 ounces each), halved lengthwise

4 teaspoons extra-virgin olive oil

1 large onion (about 8 ounces), finely chopped

2 cloves garlic, finely chopped

1 medium tomato (about 6 ounces), peeled, seeded, and coarsely chopped

½ cup dry plain bread crumbs

½ cup kalamata or other good-quality black olives, pitted and chopped

2 teaspoons finely chopped fresh flat-leaf parsley

1 teaspoon finely chopped fresh basil

1 teaspoon fresh thyme leaves, or ¼ teaspoon dried thyme

Salt and freshly ground black pepper, to taste

About ½ cup low-sodium vegetable broth

Preheat the oven to 425F (220C). Scoop out the insides from each zucchini half, leaving a ⅜-inch-thick shell. Coarsely chop the insides and set aside.

In a large nonstick skillet, heat the oil over medium heat. Add the onion and garlic and cook, stirring frequently, until the vegetables are softened, about 5 minutes. Add the tomato and chopped zucchini and cook, stirring occasionally, until the zucchini is tender and most of the liquids have evaporated, 15 to 20 minutes.

Remove the skillet from the heat and add the bread crumbs, olives, parsley, basil, thyme, salt, and pepper. Let cool a few minutes.

Stuff the zucchini shells with the cooled filling. Arrange in a shallow baking dish just large enough to accommodate their size; pour in enough vegetable broth to cover the bottom of the casserole. Bake 20 to 25 minutes, or until the tops are lightly browned and shells are tender when pierced with the tip of a sharp knife. Serve warm or at room temperature.

PER SERVING

Calories 177 ■ Protein 6g ■ Total Fat 8g ■ Sat. Fat 1g ■
Cholesterol 0mg ■ Carbohydrate 23g ■
Dietary Fiber 5g ■ Sodium 339mg

Vegetable Main Dishes

Grilled Artichoke Kabobs with Brown Rice

MAKES 6 SERVINGS

These delectable kabobs are wonderful served on a bed of orzo as well. If you can't find young artichokes, select medium-size ones and cut into quarters after trimming, then steam a few minutes before grilling.

> 6 tablespoons fresh lemon juice (the juice from 2 medium lemons)
> 4 tablespoons extra-virgin olive oil
> 18 small young artichokes
> ¼ teaspoon crumbled dried thyme leaves
> Salt, preferably the coarse variety, and freshly ground black pepper, to taste
> 4½ cups hot cooked brown rice

Soak 6 wooden skewers in water 15 minutes. Prepare a medium charcoal grill or gas grill. Position the grill rack 6 to 8 inches from heat source. Or, place a stovetop grilling pan with grids over medium heat.

In a small bowl, combine 2 tablespoons of the lemon juice and 2 tablespoons of the olive oil; set aside.

Fill a medium bowl with water and 2 tablespoons of the lemon juice. Set aside. With a sharp, serrated knife, cut about ½ inch off the top of each artichoke. Pull off and discard the tough, dark green outer leaves to expose the pale green inner hearts. Trim the dark stem end of each artichoke. If the artichokes are larger than about 1½ inches in diameter, cut in half lengthwise. With a small spoon or your fingers, scrape out any prickly inner leaves. As you work, drop the artichokes into the lemon water to prevent browning.

Drain the artichokes and transfer to a large bowl; add the remaining lemon juice, oil, thyme, salt, and pepper, tossing well to thoroughly combine.

Thread artichokes evenly onto skewers and grill until tender and lightly browned, turning often, about 15 minutes. To serve, divide the rice among each of 6 serving plates and top with an artichoke kabob. Season with salt and pepper, and drizzle evenly with the reserved lemon juice and oil mixture. Serve at once.

PER SERVING

Calories 324 ▪ Protein 8g ▪ Total Fat 10g ▪ Sat. Fat 1g ▪
Cholesterol 0mg ▪ Carbohydrate 54g ▪
Dietary Fiber 8g ▪ Sodium 123mg

Braised Sweet and Sour Cabbage with Kidney Beans

MAKES 4 MAIN-DISH OR 6 SIDE-DISH SERVINGS

This is a delicious way to prepare a healthful and inexpensive vegetable that is often overlooked. In Italy, it's typically served over rice or polenta as a hearty main course. Chilled, it also makes a refreshing side dish or salad.

2 tablespoons extra-virgin olive oil
2 medium onions (6 ounces each), chopped
1 small head green cabbage (about 1 pound), cored and shredded
1 cup low-sodium vegetable broth

1 (15-ounce) can red kidney beans, rinsed and drained
¼ cup red wine vinegar
2 tablespoons sugar
Salt and freshly ground black pepper, to taste

In a large deep-sided skillet with a lid, heat the oil over medium-low heat. Add the onion and cook, stirring occasionally, until very tender and light golden, about 30 minutes. Add the cabbage and broth; bring to a boil over high heat. Reduce the heat, cover, and simmer, stirring occasionally, until the cabbage is tender, about 15 minutes.

Uncover and increase the heat to high; cook, stirring often, until most of the liquids have evaporated, about 2 minutes. Add the beans, vinegar, sugar, salt, and pepper; cook over high heat, stirring often, until most of the liquids have evaporated, about 2 minutes. Serve warm. (Alternatively, let cool to room temperature before covering and refrigerating a minimum of 2 hours, and serve chilled.)

PER SERVING

Calories 239 ▪ Protein 11g ▪ Total Fat 8g ▪ Sat. Fat 1g ▪
Cholesterol 0mg ▪ Carbohydrate 35g ▪
Dietary Fiber 8g ▪ Sodium 153mg

Stuffed Artichokes with Sun-Dried Tomatoes and Basil

MAKES 4 MAIN-DISH SERVINGS
OR 8 FIRST-COURSE OR SIDE-DISH SERVINGS

This dish is ideally prepared in early fall when the artichokes have grown huge and the basil is still thriving. Served atop a ladle-full of your favorite pasta sauce and garnished with a sprig of fresh basil, this entrée is as elegant as it is delicious. The stuffing is also an excellent filling for baked or broiled mushrooms, particularly giant portobellos.

2 large lemons

8 large artichokes (about 12 ounces each)

¼ cup extra-virgin olive oil

2 large onions (about 8 ounces each), finely chopped

½ cup dry-packed sun-dried tomato halves, snipped into bits with kitchen shears or scissors

4 large cloves garlic, finely chopped

½ cup finely chopped fresh flat-leaf parsley

¼ cup finely chopped fresh basil

Salt and freshly ground black pepper, to taste

3 cups fresh bread crumbs, including crust, from day-old Italian or French bread (about 4 ounces)

Pasta sauce (optional)

Fill a large bowl with water and add the juice from one of the lemons. Cut off the stem of each artichoke flush to the base so that the artichoke can stand upright. Cut about 2 inches from the top. Bend back and pull off the tough, dark green outer leaves to expose the pale green leaves. Trim the edges of the base, if necessary. Drop each artichoke into water as you finish.

Fill a Dutch oven large enough to accommodate a 9-inch steaming basket with about 1 inch of water. Slice remaining lemon into thin rounds and place in pot. Drain artichokes in a colander and rinse briefly under running water. Arrange the artichokes, upside down, in steaming basket and place in pot. Bring to a boil over high heat. Cover tightly, reduce the heat to medium, and steam until artichoke bottoms are just tender, 20 minutes. Remove steaming basket and let artichokes cool slightly. Strain the cooking liquid into a glass measuring container and reserve.

Preheat the oven to 400F (205C). In a large nonstick skillet, heat the oil over medium heat. Add the onions and cook, stirring frequently, 2 minutes. Add sun-dried tomatoes, garlic, and 6 tablespoons of the reserved cooking liquid. Cook, stirring often, until onions and tomatoes are softened, about 3 minutes. Remove from heat and stir in the parsley, basil, salt, and pepper. Add the bread crumbs, stirring well to combine. Add ½ cup of the reserved cooking liquid, stirring well to combine. With a wooden spoon, push stuffing into 8 equal mounds. Set aside.

With your fingers, spread open the center of each cooled artichoke; twist out the inner purple-tinged leaves. Remove the hairy fibers in center by scraping them out with a melon baller or sharp grapefruit spoon. Fill the center of each artichoke with an equal portion of stuffing, pushing the leaves gently apart to accommodate filling. (At this point, artichokes can be covered and refrigerated up to 6 hours before proceeding.)

Return the stuffed artichokes to the Dutch oven and spoon 1 tablespoon of the reserved cooking liquid over each. Bake, covered, 20 minutes, or until artichokes are very tender when pierced near the base with the tip of a sharp knife. Spoon another 1 tablespoon of the reserved cooking liquid over each and cook, uncovered, until tops are lightly browned and crusty, 5 to 10 minutes.

Transfer to a large heated serving platter or divide evenly among 4 individual serving plates. Serve warm, accompanied with pasta sauce (if using). Or, serve at room temperature, without sauce. (Artichokes can be covered and refrigerated up to 24 hours before bringing to room temperature, or reheating in a low oven, and serving.)

PER SERVING

Calories 448 ▪ Protein 18g ▪ Total Fat 16g ▪ Sat. Fat 2g ▪ Cholesterol 0mg ▪ Carbohydrate 71g ▪ Dietary Fiber 25g ▪ Sodium 676mg

Stuffed Cabbage
with Brown Rice

MAKES 4 MAIN-DISH OR 8 SIDE-DISH SERVINGS

While you can use long-grain white rice, I prefer the nuttier, chewier texture of the whole-grain brown variety in this homey dish. If you are short on time, prepared pasta sauce can be used in lieu of the All-Purpose Tomato Sauce.

8 large, whole, outside cabbage leaves
1 tablespoon extra-virgin olive oil
¼ cup chopped onion
2 tablespoons chopped green bell pepper
2 large cloves garlic, finely chopped
2 cups slightly undercooked brown rice
2 tablespoons chopped, drained, oil-packed
    sun-dried tomatoes
2 tablespoons tomato paste mixed with 1
    tablespoon water and pinch sugar
½ teaspoon dried oregano
½ teaspoon dried thyme
Salt and freshly ground black pepper, to taste
1 cup low-sodium vegetable broth
½ recipe All-Purpose Tomato Sauce (page 131)

Preheat the oven to 425F (220C). Lightly oil a 13 × 9-inch baking dish and set aside.

Partially fill a large stockpot with water and bring to a boil over high heat. Add the cabbage leaves and boil until slightly tender, about 1 minute. Remove with tongs and drain well.

In a medium nonstick skillet, heat the oil over medium heat. Add the onion and bell pepper and cook, stirring, until softened, about 3 minutes. Add the garlic and cook, stirring, 1 minute. Remove the skillet from the heat and add the rice, sun-dried tomatoes, tomato paste mixture, oregano, thyme, salt, and pepper; toss well to thoroughly combine.

Place one-eighth of the rice mixture on the stem end of each cabbage leaf and roll up, tucking the sides in as you go. Transfer, seam sides down, to the prepared baking dish.

Pour the broth over the cabbage rolls. Cover tightly with foil and bake 20 to 25 minutes, or until the cabbage is tender and the filling is hot through the center. Transfer the rolls to a serving platter and drizzle evenly with the All-Purpose Tomato Sauce. Serve at once.

PER SERVING
Calories 229 ▪ Protein 8g ▪ Total Fat 7g ▪ Sat. Fat 1g ▪
Cholesterol 0mg ▪ Carbohydrate 36g ▪
Dietary Fiber 6g ▪ Sodium 459mg

Cranberry Beans
with Rosemary

MAKES 6 MAIN-DISH OR 8 TO 10 SIDE-DISH SERVINGS

This versatile Venetian bean recipe is excellent on its own or spread over polenta or plain focaccia. While the finished dish should be rather pastelike, not soupy, you can easily turn it into a soup by adding vegetable broth to achieve the desired consistency. Add some cooked pasta, and it becomes *pasta e fagioli*. Cannellini beans can replace the cranberry beans.

3 tablespoons extra-virgin olive oil
2 large cloves garlic, peeled
1 pound cranberry beans (borlotti), soaked
    overnight in cold water to cover, and drained

6 to 8 cups water

2 sprigs fresh rosemary

2 teaspoons salt

Freshly ground black pepper, to taste

In a medium stockpot, heat the oil over medium heat. Add the garlic and cook, stirring constantly, 30 seconds. Add the beans and enough water to cover them, the rosemary, and salt; bring to a boil over high heat. Reduce the heat, cover, and simmer, stirring occasionally, until the beans are tender, 1 to 1½ hours. Remove the lid, season with pepper, and simmer about 30 minutes, or until the beans are very tender and the consistency of refried beans, stirring occasionally and adding water if necessary to prevent the beans from becoming too dry. Remove and discard the rosemary. Serve warm.

PER SERVING

Calories 314 ∎ Protein 18g ∎ Total Fat 7g ∎ Sat. Fat 1g ∎ Cholesterol 0mg ∎ Carbohydrate 46g ∎ Dietary Fiber 12g ∎ Sodium 723mg

Cannellini Beans with Grilled Radicchio

MAKES 6 SERVINGS

If you are short on time, improvise with two 15.5-ounce cans cannellini or other white beans, rinsed and drained, heated with the tomatoes, oil, garlic, and other seasonings—the resulting dish will still be delicious.

1½ cups dried cannellini beans, soaked overnight in water to cover and drained

4½ cups water

1 (14.5-ounce) can diced tomatoes, juices included

4 tablespoons extra-virgin olive oil

2 cloves garlic, peeled, left whole, crushed

3 fresh sage leaves

1 sprig fresh rosemary

1 large bay leaf

Salt, preferably the coarse variety, and freshly ground black pepper, to taste

6 small heads radicchio (about 4 ounces each), halved

In a medium stockpot, combine the beans, water, tomatoes and their juices, 2 tablespoons of the oil, garlic, sage, rosemary, bay leaf, salt, and pepper; bring to a boil over high heat. Reduce heat, cover, and simmer, stirring occasionally, until the beans are tender, 1 to 1½ hours. If the mixture seems too souplike, cook, uncovered, over medium heat, stirring often, until reduced to the consistency of baked beans. Remove and discard the sage, rosemary, and bay leaf.

Preheat the oven to broil. Lightly grease a baking sheet.

Place the radicchio on the prepared baking sheet and brush evenly on all sides with the remaining 2 tablespoons oil, then sprinkle with salt and pepper. Broil 4 to 6 inches from heating element until lightly browned, about 4 to 5 minutes each side.

To serve, place 2 radicchio halves on each of 6 plates and top with equal portions of beans. Serve at once.

PER SERVING

Calories 293 ∎ Protein 14g ∎ Total Fat 10g ∎ Sat. Fat. 1g ∎ Cholesterol 0mg ∎ Carbohydrate 40g ∎ Dietary Fiber 9g ∎ Sodium 177mg

Eggplant Cutlets with Tomato Sauce and Olives

MAKES 4 SERVINGS

Beefy center-cut eggplant slices are satisfying substitutes for the traditional veal or chicken cutlets.

> **4 (¾-inch-thick) center-cut eggplant rounds, cut crosswise from a large (about 1 pound) eggplant, sprinkled with salt and set in a colander to drain 30 minutes**
> **Freshly ground black pepper, to taste**
> **¼ cup extra-virgin olive oil**
> **1 large clove garlic, peeled**
> **1 recipe All-Purpose Tomato Sauce (page 131), or favorite pasta sauce**
> **¼ cup chopped pitted kalamata or other good-quality olives**

Rinse the eggplant slices under cold-running water and drain well between paper towels. Season on both sides with pepper.

In a large nonstick skillet, heat the oil over medium heat. Add the garlic and cook, stirring, until fragrant but not browned, about 2 minutes. Remove and discard the garlic. Add the eggplant and cook until nicely browned, about 4 minutes on each side. Transfer to a serving platter or individual serving plates and top with equal portions of the tomato sauce. Sprinkle evenly with the olives and serve at once.

PER SERVING
Calories 252 ■ Protein 3g ■ Total Fat 22g ■ Sat. Fat 2g ■ Cholesterol 0mg ■ Carbohydrate 15g ■ Dietary Fiber 4g ■ Sodium 725mg

Italian-Style Lentils

MAKES 6 MAIN-DISH OR 8 TO 10 SIDE-DISH SERVINGS

In Italy, lentils are traditionally eaten on New Year's Eve for good luck. Fortunately, you can enjoy this iron-rich, protein-packed dish any time of the year for good health.

> **1 pound lentils, picked over and rinsed**
> **2 medium onions (about 6 ounces each), 1 quartered, 1 finely chopped**
> **2 medium carrots (about 4 ounces each), 1 quartered, 1 finely chopped**
> **2 stalks celery, 1 quartered, 1 finely chopped**
> **1 large bay leaf**
> **Salt, to taste**
> **3 tablespoons extra-virgin olive oil**
> **¼ cup tomato sauce**
> **2 to 3 fresh large sage leaves, torn into pieces**
> **Freshly ground black pepper, to taste**

In a medium stockpot, combine the lentils, quartered onion, quartered carrot, quartered celery, bay leaf, and salt; add enough water to cover. Bring to a boil over medium-high heat. Reduce the heat, partially cover, and simmer gently, stirring occasionally, until the lentils are tender but not mushy, about 45 minutes, depending on the age of the lentils. When the lentils are done, if most of the water has not been absorbed, simmer, uncovered, stirring often, until most of the liquid has evaporated. Remove and discard the quartered onion, carrot, celery, and bay leaf.

Meanwhile, in a large deep-sided nonstick skillet, heat the oil over medium heat. Add the chopped onion, chopped carrot, and chopped celery; cook, stirring often, until softened, about 5 minutes. Add the tomato sauce and sage and let come to a simmer. Reduce the heat to low and cook, stirring occasionally, 10 minutes. Add the lentils, salt, and pepper and cook, stirring often, 5 minutes. Serve warm.

PER SERVING
Calories 357 ■ Protein 23g ■ Total Fat 8g ■ Sat. Fat 1g ■
Cholesterol 0mg ■ Carbohydrate 53g ■
Dietary Fiber 25g ■ Sodium 94mg

Stuffed Peppers with Arborio Rice and Basil

MAKES 4 SERVINGS

This is a terrific dinner party dish, as the assembled stuffed peppers can be stored, covered, in the refrigerator overnight before baking. The use of arborio rice ensures that the grains will not harden in the refrigerator like regular long-grain white rice tends to do.

2½ tablespoons extra-virgin olive oil
1 medium onion (about 6 ounces), finely chopped
3 large cloves garlic, finely chopped
1½ pounds ripe tomatoes, peeled, seeded, and chopped
¼ cup low-sodium vegetable broth
Salt and freshly ground black pepper, to taste
1 cup arborio rice, slightly undercooked according to package directions
½ cup finely chopped fresh basil
¼ cup chopped pitted black kalamata olives
4 large red or green bell peppers (8 to 10 ounces each)
2 cups favorite pasta sauce, or All-Purpose Tomato Sauce (page 131) (optional), heated

Preheat the oven to 400F (205C).

In a large nonstick skillet, heat 2 tablespoons of the oil over medium heat. Add the onion and cook, stirring, until softened but not browned, 3 to 5 minutes. Add the garlic and cook, stirring, 1 minute. Add the tomatoes, broth, salt, and pepper; bring to a boil over medium-high heat. Reduce the heat to medium and simmer briskly, stirring frequently to prevent scorching, until the mixture has thickened and most of the liquids have evaporated, 15 to 20 minutes.

Remove the skillet from the heat and add the rice, basil, and olives, stirring well to thoroughly combine. Season with additional salt and pepper as necessary. Set aside.

Cut a lid off the stem end of each pepper and reserve. Remove the seeds and white membranes from each pepper shell. Brush the outsides of the lids and shells with the remaining ½ tablespoon of oil. Stuff each pepper shell lightly (do not pack) with equal amounts of the rice mixture and top with the corresponding lid (lids will not close).

Place the stuffed peppers upright in a baking dish just large enough to accommodate their size. Add enough water to the dish to measure ½ inch. Cover tightly with foil and bake for 50 minutes to 1 hour, or until the peppers are tender when pierced with the tip of a sharp knife. Remove the foil and bake 5 minutes, or until the lids just begin to blister. Serve at once, accompanied by the heated pasta sauce (if using).

PER SERVING
Calories 360 ■ Protein 8g ■ Total Fat 11g ■ Sat. Fat 1g ■
Cholesterol 0mg ■ Carbohydrate 61g ■
Dietary Fiber 6g ■ Sodium 147mg

Braised Romaine and Kidney Beans

MAKES 3 TO 4 MAIN-DISH

OR 5 TO 6 SIDE-DISH SERVINGS

This is delicious served over rice or orzo. Escarole or curly endive can be substituted for the romaine lettuce.

> 2 tablespoons extra-virgin olive oil
>
> 1 small onion (about 4 ounces), chopped
>
> 2 large cloves garlic, finely chopped
>
> 1 large head Romaine lettuce, washed, separated into leaves, cut crosswise into 1-inch-thick strips
>
> 2 (15-ounce) cans kidney beans, rinsed and drained
>
> Salt and freshly ground black pepper, to taste

In a large nonstick skillet with a lid, heat the oil over medium heat. Add the onion and cook, stirring, until softened but not browned, about 3 minutes. Add the garlic and cook, stirring, 1 minute. Add the lettuce and reduce the heat to medium-low. Cover and cook, stirring a few times, until the lettuce is wilted and tender, about 10 minutes. Uncover and stir in the beans, salt, and pepper. Increase the heat to medium-high and cook, stirring frequently, until most of the liquid has evaporated and beans are heated through, about 5 minutes. Serve at once.

PER SERVING

Calories 364 ▪ Protein 20g ▪ Total Fat 11g ▪ Sat. Fat 1g ▪ Cholesterol 0mg ▪ Carbohydrate 51g ▪ Dietary Fiber 16g ▪ Sodium 26mg

Tomatoes Stuffed with Orzo and Mint

MAKES 4 MAIN-DISH OR 8 SIDE-DISH SERVINGS

This delicious regional dish from Calabria is a good choice for entertaining, as the assembled stuffed tomatoes can be held at room temperature a few hours before baking. The cooked stuffed tomatoes can be held at room temperature a few hours before serving.

> 8 large ripe yet firm tomatoes (8 to 10 ounces each)
>
> Salt
>
> 1 cup orzo
>
> ¼ cup plus 4 teaspoons extra-virgin olive oil
>
> ¼ cup coarsely chopped fresh mint leaves
>
> 3 large cloves garlic, finely chopped
>
> Salt, preferably the coarse variety, and freshly ground black pepper, to taste
>
> 8 whole fresh mint leaves (optional)

Cut a slice from the top of each tomato about ½ inch thick and reserve. Gently squeeze out the seeds from each tomato. Using a small, sharp knife or a melon batter, scoop out the pulp and reserve, discarding any white core. Lightly salt the inside of each tomato shell. Turn the shells upside down on several layers of paper towels and drain 30 minutes.

Meanwhile, cook the orzo in boiling salted water according to package directions until not quite done al dente. Drain well.

Chop the reserved tomato pulp and place in a medium bowl. Add the orzo, the ¼ cup oil, chopped mint, garlic, salt, and pepper; stir well to combine. Let set 20 minutes at room temperature to allow the flavors to blend.

Preheat the oven to 350F (175C). Lightly oil a shallow baking dish just large enough to comfortably accommodate the tomatoes in a single layer. Set aside.

Sprinkle the insides of the drained tomatoes with a little pepper. Fill the tomatoes evenly with the orzo mixture (do not pack down). Cover with the reserved tops. Arrange upright in the prepared dish. Brush ½ teaspoon of the oil over the tops and sides of each tomato. Bake the tomatoes, uncovered, 25 minutes. Remove the lids and bake 5 to 10 minutes, or until the tomatoes are soft but not falling apart and the tops are lightly browned.

Let the tomatoes cool slightly and serve warm, or serve at room temperature. Garnish with the optional mint leaves (if using).

PER SERVING

Calories 330 ▪ Protein 7g ▪ Total Fat 20g ▪ Sat. Fat 3g ▪ Cholesterol 0mg ▪ Carbohydrate 36g ▪ Dietary Fiber 6g ▪ Sodium 41mg

Baked Mixed Vegetable Casserole

MAKES 4 TO 6 SERVINGS

From Apulia, this peasant-style vegetable casserole, called *tiella*, is delicious with a tossed green salad and lots of crusty Italian bread.

1 pound small boiling potatoes, scrubbed
4 tablespoons extra-virgin olive oil
2 large onions (about 8 ounces each), thinly sliced
1 pound zucchini, preferably a mixture of green and yellow, thinly sliced
6 cloves garlic, finely chopped
Salt and freshly ground black pepper, to taste
½ cup loosely packed fresh basil, chopped
1 (14.5-ounce) can diced tomatoes with Italian seasonings, juices included
½ cup fresh bread crumbs, preferably whole wheat

Preheat the oven to 400F (205C). Lightly oil an 11 × 7-inch casserole and set aside.

Place the potatoes in a large saucepan or medium stockpot with enough salted water to cover; bring to a boil over high heat. Reduce the heat slightly and boil 10 minutes. Drain and let cool. Cut into thin slices and set aside.

Meanwhile, in a large nonstick skillet, heat 3 tablespoons of the oil over medium heat. Add the onions and cook, stirring, until softened, about 5 minutes. Add the zucchini and garlic and cook, stirring, 5 minutes. Remove from the heat and season with salt and pepper.

Place half of the onion-zucchini mixture in the bottom of the prepared casserole. Top with the potato slices and sprinkle with half of the basil. Cover with the remaining onion-zucchini mixture. Top with the tomatoes and their juices. Sprinkle with the remaining basil, followed by the bread crumbs. Drizzle with the remaining 1 tablespoon oil. Bake, covered, 30 minutes. Uncover and bake 10 minutes, or until the top is lightly browned. Serve warm.

PER SERVING

Calories 329 ▪ Protein 7g ▪ Total Fat 15 ▪ Sat. Fat 2g ▪ Cholesterol 0mg ▪ Carbohydrate 44g ▪ Dietary Fiber 7g ▪ Sodium 348mg

Spaghetti Squash with Garden Bolognese Sauce

MAKES 5 TO 6 MAIN-DISH OR 8 SIDE-DISH SERVINGS

Like its namesake, spaghetti squash is naturally bland and lends itself well to most pasta sauces. While the Garden Bolognese Sauce (page 61) is one of my favorites, try tossing it with any of the pasta sauces throughout this cookbook.

1 (4-pound) spaghetti squash
1 recipe Garden Bolognese Sauce (page 61)

Preheat the oven to 375F (190C). Prick squash in several places with a large fork. Place on an ungreased baking sheet and bake 1 hour, or until softened and easily pierced through the center, turning over halfway through cooking time.

Cool slightly. Using an oven mitt to hold the squash, cut in half, and while still hot, scoop out the seeds. Using a fork, twist out flesh, transferring to a large bowl. If necessary, separate any thick strands of flesh into thinner strands with your fingers. Add the sauce, tossing well to thoroughly coat. Serve at once.

PER SERVING
Calories 384 ▪ Protein 7g ▪ Total Fat 15g ▪ Sat. Fat 2g ▪
Cholesterol 0mg ▪ Carbohydrate 59g ▪
Dietary Fiber 11g ▪ Sodium 917mg

Winter Vegetable Stew

MAKES 4 MAIN-DISH SERVINGS

This homey winter stew is wonderful with lots of crusty Italian bread and a green salad.

¼ cup extra-virgin olive oil
1 large onion (about 8 ounces), chopped
1 stalk celery, chopped
1 large clove garlic, finely chopped
1 (16-ounce) can whole tomatoes, chopped, juices included
½ teaspoon dried oregano
½ teaspoon dried thyme leaves
½ teaspoon sugar
Salt and freshly ground black pepper, to taste
1 head cabbage (about 2 pounds), tough outer leaves removed, quartered, cored, and cut into ½-inch-thick slices
1½ pounds medium boiling potatoes, peeled and cut into bite-size chunks
2 medium carrots (about 4 ounces each), cut into ½-inch-thick rounds

In a large stockpot, heat the oil over medium heat. Add the onion and celery and cook, stirring, until softened, about 3 minutes. Add the garlic and cook, stirring, 1 minute. Add the tomatoes and their juices, oregano, thyme, sugar, salt, and pepper; bring to a brisk simmer over medium-high heat, stirring often.

Add the cabbage, potatoes, and carrots and simmer, tossing and stirring, until the cabbage begins to wilt. Reduce the heat, cover, and simmer gently, stirring occasionally, until the vegetables are tender, about 45 minutes. Serve hot.

Zucchini Roll-Ups

**MAKES 3 TO 4 MAIN-DISH
OR 6 TO 8 SIDE-DISH SERVINGS**

Involtini, or roll-ups, are typically made with thin slices of beef or veal and are called *braciole* in some parts of Italy. These vegetarian versions are lighter and, as a result, ideal for summer.

- 3 large long zucchini (about 8 ounces each), trimmed
- 1 cup cooked white or brown rice
- 1 (7.25-ounce) jar roasted red bell peppers, drained and chopped
- 3 scallions (white and green parts), finely chopped
- 2 tablespoons finely chopped fresh basil leaves
- 2 tablespoons extra-virgin olive oil
- 1 large clove garlic, finely chopped
- Salt and freshly ground black pepper, to taste
- 1 medium plum tomato (about 3 ounces), chopped
- About 2 cups favorite pasta sauce, or All-Purpose Tomato Sauce (page 131), heated

Preheat the oven to 400F (205C). Lightly grease a baking sheet with sides.

Bring a large saucepan or medium stockpot filled with salted water to a boil over high heat. Add the zucchini and boil 5 minutes. Drain and let cool. Stand each zucchini upright. Using a vegetable peeler, remove and discard skin from either side. Slice lengthwise into ⅜-inch-thick strips. (You will have about 6 to 8 slices per zucchini.)

In a medium bowl, combine the rice, bell peppers, scallions, basil, 1 tablespoon of the oil, garlic, salt, and black pepper. Spoon equal portions (about 1 tablespoon) along each zucchini strip. Carefully roll up and fasten with wooden picks.

Arrange the roll-ups on the prepared baking sheet and distribute the chopped tomato evenly over the top. Drizzle evenly with the remaining 1 tablespoon oil. Bake 10 minutes, or until heated through. Ladle equal portions of pasta sauce on serving plates and top with equal portions of the roll-ups. Serve at once.

Pizza, Breads, Sandwiches, and Other Lighter Fare

An Italian meal seldom begins without bread. Indeed, Italians eat about a half pound of it a day, in the form of *pane* (bread), *panini* (rolls), pizza, *focaccia*, *calzoni*, *stromboli*, and stuffed breads. Certainly the best known abroad of these is pizza, arguably Italy's national dish, and quite possibly the most popular food on the planet. But is pizza healthy? When it's made with the right ingredients, it's one of the healthiest foods you can eat, essentially a meal in itself, with plenty of protein, vitamins, carbohydrates, and only moderate quantities of sodium and cholesterol. Unfortunately, the popularization of pizza in America has compromised its healthfulness in the form of excess cheese and meats. Fortunately, the classic Neapolitan pizza is alive and well in southern Italy, unadorned save for a smear of tomato sauce, a drizzle of olive oil, a sprinkling of herbs, and perhaps one or two tasty toppings such as mushrooms, onions, or olives. While cheese is used on some pizzas, it's used sparingly, so as not to smother the other ingredients. With the exception of the Pesto Pizza, the pizza recipes in this chapter were selected because they are distinctly better without cheese. But if you must use cheese, a vegan substitute is not recommended as they typically don't melt well. In any case, *goda* (enjoy)!

Pizza and Focaccia

Quick Puff Pastry Broccoli Pizza

MAKES 4 TO 6 MAIN-DISH
OR 8 TO 12 APPETIZER SERVINGS

This rectangular pizza is perfect for a quick weeknight supper for 4 to 6, or snack for 8. For delicious party appetizers, cut the pizza into 12 pieces.

½ (about 17-ounce) package frozen puff pastry
    sheets (1 sheet), thawed according to
    manufacturer's directions
All-purpose flour for dusting
2 tablespoons extra-virgin olive oil
1 medium onion (about 6 ounces), cut in half
    lengthwise and thinly sliced crosswise
1½ cups small broccoli florets
Salt, preferably the coarse variety, and freshly
    ground black pepper, to taste
¾ cup prepared pizza sauce, or All-Purpose
    Tomato Sauce (page 131)
Dried oregano, to taste

Preheat the oven to 400F (205C).

Unfold the pastry on a lightly floured surface. Roll into a 14 × 10-inch rectangle and place on an ungreased baking sheet. Fold over the edge about ½ inch to form a rim. Prick everything but the rim of the pastry thoroughly with a fork. Bake on the center rack 10 minutes.

Meanwhile, in a large nonstick skillet, heat half of the oil over medium heat. Add the onion and cook, stirring occasionally, until just softened, about 3 minutes. Add the broccoli, salt, and pepper; cook, stirring occasionally, until the broccoli is softened,

about 5 minutes. Remove from heat and let cool slightly.

Spread pizza sauce over pastry crust to rim. Top with the vegetable mixture. Sprinkle with the oregano, salt, and pepper, and then drizzle with the remaining oil. Bake 5 minutes, or until heated through. Serve at once.

PER SERVING
Calories 409 ▪ Protein 7g ▪ Total Fat 25g ▪ Sat. Fat 5g ▪
Cholesterol 0mg ▪ Carbohydrate 44g ▪
Dietary Fiber 6g ▪ Sodium 502mg

Eggplant Pizza

MAKES 8 SERVINGS

This heart-healthy pizza is a satisfying light meal served with a mixed green salad. If you are short on time, use commercially prepared pizza sauce in lieu of the All-Purpose Tomato Sauce.

¾ pound unpeeled eggplant, cut into ⅛-inch-
    thick slices
Table salt
Cornmeal for dusting (optional)
1 recipe Quick-Rising Pizza Dough (page 130),
    or Semolina Pizza Dough (page 130)
All-purpose flour for dusting
¾ cup All-Purpose Tomato Sauce (page 131), at
    room temperature
2 tablespoons extra-virgin olive oil
½ teaspoon dried oregano
Salt, preferably the coarse variety, and freshly
    ground black pepper, to taste

Preheat the oven to 400F (205C). Lightly oil a large baking sheet and set aside. Place the eggplant in a colander in the sink and sprinkle liberally with table salt; let sit for 30 minutes. Rinse thoroughly and pat dry with paper towels.

Arrange the eggplant slices in a single layer on the prepared baking sheet. Bake 6 to 8 minutes, or until tender and lightly browned, turning halfway through cooking. Remove from the oven and let cool.

Increase the oven temperature to 500F (260C). Set a rack on the lowest position. Sprinkle a 12- to 14-inch pizza pan with cornmeal, or lightly oil; set aside.

Turn the dough out onto a lightly floured work surface. Roll and stretch into a 12- to 14-inch circle. Transfer the dough to the prepared pan. Spread the tomato sauce evenly over the top to within ½ inch of the edge of the dough. Arrange the eggplant slices evenly over the sauce, overlapping if necessary; brush evenly with the oil, then sprinkle evenly with the oregano, salt, and pepper. Bake for 12 to 15 minutes, or until the bottom is crisp and the edge of the crust is beginning to brown. Cut into wedges and serve at once.

PER SERVING

Calories 183 ▪ Protein 5g ▪ Total Fat 6g ▪ Sat. Fat 1g ▪
Cholesterol 0mg ▪ Carbohydrate 29g ▪
Dietary Fiber 3g ▪ Sodium 350mg

Quick-Rising Pizza Dough

MAKES 1 (14-INCH) PIZZA CRUST

Unlike standard yeast, the rapid-rise variety does not need to be dissolved separately in liquid and requires a 10-minute resting period instead of the typical 1½- to 2-hour rise.

2 to 2⅓ cups all-purpose white flour, preferably unbleached, plus additional as necessary
1 (¼-ounce) package (about 1 tablespoon) quick-acting or rapid-rise yeast
1 teaspoon salt
½ teaspoon sugar
¾ cup plus 2 tablespoons very warm water (120F to 130F; 50C to 55C)
2 teaspoons extra-virgin olive oil

In a large bowl, combine 1½ cups of the flour, the yeast, salt, and sugar. With a wooden spoon, stir in the warm water and oil. Stir vigorously until well mixed. Gradually add enough of the remaining flour to make a firm, soft dough. Turn out onto a lightly floured work surface and knead for about 8 minutes, or until smooth and elastic. Shape the dough into a ball. Cover with plastic wrap and let rest for 10 minutes. The dough is ready to be shaped and rolled as directed in recipe.

PER SERVING (⅛ RECIPE)

Calories 130 ▪ Protein 4g ▪ Total Fat 2g ▪ Sat. Fat 0g ▪
Cholesterol 0mg ▪ Carbohydrate 25g ▪
Dietary Fiber 1g ▪ Sodium 268mg

Semolina Pizza Dough

MAKES 1 (14-INCH) PIZZA CRUST

Milled from hard durum wheat, semolina flour makes a chewy pizza crust with a slightly nutty flavor. It can be found in health food stores and Italian specialty markets. If desired, all-purpose white flour can be used in lieu of the semolina.

2½ teaspoons extra-virgin olive oil

⅛ teaspoon sugar

1 cup warm water (105F to 115F; 40C to 45C)

1 (¼-ounce) package active dry yeast (about 1 tablespoon)

1¼ teaspoons salt

1 cup semolina flour

1¼ to 1½ cups all-purpose white flour, preferably unbleached, plus additional as necessary

Grease a large bowl with 1 teaspoon of the oil and set aside. In another large bowl, dissolve the sugar in the warm water. Sprinkle in the yeast and let sit until foamy, about 5 minutes. Stir in the remaining oil and salt. With a wooden spoon, gradually stir in the semolina flour and enough of the all-purpose flour to make a firm, soft dough.

Turn out onto a lightly floured work surface and knead until the dough is smooth and elastic, about 8 minutes, adding additional all-purpose flour as needed to prevent sticking. Gather the dough into a ball and place in prepared bowl, turning to coat in the oil. Cover with plastic wrap and let rise at room temperature until doubled in bulk, 1½ to 2 hours. Turn the dough out onto a lightly floured work surface and knead briefly to release any air pockets. Shape the dough into a ball. The dough is ready to be shaped and rolled as directed in recipe.

PER SERVING (⅛ RECIPE)
Calories 150 ▪ Protein 5g ▪ Total Fat 2g ▪ Sat. Fat 0g ▪
Cholesterol 0mg ▪ Carbohydrate 28g ▪
Dietary Fiber 2g ▪ Sodium 335mg

All-Purpose Tomato Sauce

MAKES ABOUT 2¼ CUPS

Use this multipurpose tomato sauce on pasta and vegetables, as well as pizza.

1 tablespoon extra-virgin olive oil

3 large cloves garlic, finely chopped

1 (28-ounce) can plum tomatoes, chopped, juices included, or 2 pounds ripe plum tomatoes, peeled and chopped, accumulated juices included

2 tablespoons tomato paste

½ teaspoon dried oregano

¼ teaspoon dried thyme leaves

Salt and freshly ground black pepper, to taste

In a large deep-sided nonstick skillet, heat the oil over medium heat. Add the garlic and cook, stirring often, until lightly browned but not burnt, about 2 minutes. Add the tomatoes and their juices, tomato paste, oregano, thyme, salt, and pepper; bring to a brisk simmer over high heat. Reduce the heat and simmer, uncovered, stirring occasionally, until reduced to about 2¼ cups, about 20 minutes for fresh tomatoes, or 30 minutes for canned tomatoes. Use as directed in recipe. (Completely cooled sauce can be refrigerated, covered, up to 3 days.)

PER SERVING (PER ¼ CUP)
Calories 36 ▪ Protein 1g ▪ Total Fat 2g ▪ Sat. Fat 0g ▪
Cholesterol 0mg ▪ Carbohydrate 5g ▪
Dietary Fiber 1g ▪ Sodium 217mg

Pizza with Peppers and Onions

MAKES 6 SERVINGS

This is yummy pizza—the absence of cheese really allows the palate to appreciate the inherent sweetness of the bell peppers and onions.

3 tablespoons extra-virgin olive oil

1 extra-large yellow onion (about 10 ounces), thinly sliced

3 medium bell peppers (about 6 ounces each), preferably 1 green, 1 red, and 1 yellow, cut into ½-inch-thick slices

1 (10-ounce) can refrigerated pizza dough (see Cook's Tip, right)

1 (14.5-ounce) can diced canned tomatoes, drained

½ teaspoon dried oregano

½ teaspoon coarse salt

Freshly ground black pepper, to taste

Preheat the oven to 350F (175C). Lightly oil a standard-size baking sheet and set aside.

In a large nonstick skillet, heat 2 tablespoons of the oil over medium heat. Add the onion and cook, stirring, until just softened, about 3 minutes. Add the bell peppers and cook, stirring, until just softened, about 3 minutes.

Unroll the pizza dough onto prepared baking sheet and press to fit. Brush ½ tablespoon of the remaining oil evenly over the dough. Spread the tomatoes evenly over the dough, and then top with the bell pepper-and-onion mixture. Drizzle evenly with the remaining ½ tablespoon oil. Sprinkle with the oregano, coarse salt, and black pepper. Bake in the center of the oven 15 minutes, or until very lightly browned. Transfer to bottom rack and bake 5 minutes, or until the edges are nicely browned. Cut into wedges and serve warm.

PER SERVING
Calories 214 ▪ Protein 5g ▪ Total Fat 8g ▪ Sat. Fat 1g ▪ Cholesterol 0mg ▪ Carbohydrate 32g ▪ Dietary Fiber 3g ▪ Sodium 307mg

> ## ❧ COOK'S TIP ❧
> *Refrigerated 10-ounce cans of pizza dough can be found alongside the canned biscuits in the refrigerated section of most supermarkets. Fresh or frozen 16-ounce bags of pizza dough, also available in most stores, can be used as well, but you will need to thaw the dough first, if necessary, and work a bit harder to stretch and fit it into the baking sheet. Also, the pizza will have a thicker crust and may take an extra 5 minutes or so to brown.*

Pesto Pizza

MAKES 8 SERVINGS

Though pesto sauce typically contains cheese, you'll never miss it in this scrumptious yet heart-healthy pizza, a perfect appetizer for parties, as it holds up well at room temperature.

Cornmeal for dusting (optional)

¾ cup loosely packed fresh basil leaves

3 tablespoons extra-virgin olive oil

1 large clove garlic, finely chopped

½ teaspoon coarse salt

Freshly ground black pepper, to taste

1 recipe Quick-Rising Pizza Dough (page 130),
   or Semolina Pizza Dough (page 130)

All-purpose flour for dusting

4 medium plum tomatoes (about 2 ounces
   each), thinly sliced

Table salt, to taste

Preheat the oven to 500F (260C). Set a rack on the lowest position. Sprinkle a 12- to 14-inch pizza pan with cornmeal (if using) or lightly oil; set aside.

In a food processor fitted with the knife blade, or in a blender, combine the basil, 2 tablespoons of the oil, garlic, coarse salt, and pepper; process until smooth.

Turn the dough out onto a lightly floured work surface. Roll and stretch into a 12- to 14-inch circle. Transfer the dough to the prepared pan. Spread the pesto sauce evenly over the top to within ½ inch of the edge of the dough. Arrange the tomato slices evenly over the sauce; drizzle evenly with the remaining 1 tablespoon oil, and then sprinkle lightly with table salt and pepper. Bake for 12 to 15 minutes, or until the bottom is crisp and the edge of the crust is beginning to brown. Cut into wedges and serve at once.

PER SERVING

Calories 185 ■ Protein 5g ■ Total Fat 7g ■ Sat. Fat 1g ■
Cholesterol 0mg ■ Carbohydrate 27g ■
Dietary Fiber 2g ■ Sodium 388mg

Pizza Primavera

MAKES 8 SERVINGS

While "primavera" means "springtime" in Italian, in culinary terms it translates as fresh vegetables. Feel free to substitute your favorites in the following recipe.

Cornmeal for dusting (optional)

1 recipe Quick-Rising Pizza Dough (page 130)
   or Semolina Pizza Dough (page 130)

All-purpose flour for dusting

2½ tablespoons garlic-flavored olive oil

4 medium plum tomatoes (about 2 ounces
   each), thinly sliced

4 ounces cultivated white mushrooms, thinly
   sliced

1 small onion (about 4 ounces), cut in half
   lengthwise and very thinly sliced crosswise

1 small zucchini (about 4 ounces), cut in half
   lengthwise and thinly sliced crosswise

4 ounces thin asparagus, trimmed and cut into
   2-inch lengths

2 tablespoons chopped fresh basil

Coarse salt and freshly ground black pepper, to
   taste

Preheat the oven to 500F (260C). Set a rack on the lowest position. Sprinkle a 12- to 14-inch pizza pan with cornmeal (if using) or lightly oil; set aside.

Turn the dough out onto a lightly floured work surface. Roll and stretch into a 12- to 14-inch circle. Transfer the dough to the prepared pan. Spread ½ tablespoon of the oil evenly over the top to within ½ inch of the edge of the dough. Arrange the tomatoes, mushrooms, onion, zucchini, and asparagus evenly over the top; drizzle evenly with the remaining 2 tablespoons oil, then sprinkle evenly with the basil, salt, and pepper. Bake for 12 to 15 minutes, or until the bottom is crisp and the edge of the crust is beginning to brown. Cut into wedges and serve at once.

PER SERVING

Calories 192 ■ Protein 5g ■ Total Fat 6g ■ Sat. Fat 1g ■
Cholesterol 0mg ■ Carbohydrate 30g ■
Dietary Fiber 3g ■ Sodium 273mg

Frying-Pan Pizza with Sun-dried Tomatoes, Olives, and Onions

MAKES 4 TO 6 SERVINGS

Made with scone dough, this unusual yet delicious pizza crust mixes up quickly and requires no rising time. You can use it as a base for your favorite toppings.

2 cups self-rising flour, plus extra for dusting

1 tablespoon chopped fresh oregano, parsley, rosemary, basil, and/or thyme, or 1 teaspoon dried

Freshly ground black pepper, to taste

4 tablespoons extra-virgin olive oil

6 to 8 tablespoons water, plus additional as necessary

5 to 6 tablespoons pizza sauce, or All-Purpose Tomato Sauce (page 131)

3 tablespoons chopped fresh basil leaves (optional)

½ small onion (about 2 ounces), very thinly sliced

Dried oregano

Salt, to taste

3 tablespoons chopped, drained oil-packed sun-dried tomatoes, 1 tablespoon marinade reserved

6 to 8 pitted kalamata or other good-quality black olives, halved

Preheat the oven to broil.

In a large bowl, combine the flour, fresh herbs, and pepper. Make a well in the center and pour in 2 tablespoons of the olive oil, followed by 6 tablespoons water. Mix until a soft (not sticky) dough forms, adding more water as necessary to achieve the proper consistency. Turn out onto a lightly floured work surface and knead lightly. Roll out to a circle large enough to fit the bottom of a 10-inch nonstick skillet (you can use a larger skillet for easier removal).

Heat 1 tablespoon of the remaining oil in the skillet over medium heat. Place the dough in the skillet and cook until the bottom is lightly browned, about 5 to 8 minutes. Slide the dough, browned side down, onto a pizza pan or large baking sheet. Heat the remaining olive oil in the skillet. Place the dough, browned side up, back in the skillet and cook the underside for 5 minutes, or until lightly browned.

Meanwhile, spread the pizza sauce to within ½ inch of the edge of the dough. Sprinkle evenly with 2 tablespoons of the basil (if using). Arrange the onion over the top. Sprinkle lightly with the dried oregano, salt, and pepper, then drizzle evenly with the reserved sun-dried tomato marinade.

Transfer the pizza back to the pizza pan and broil 6 to 8 inches from the heating element until the onion is softened and just beginning to brown, rotating pan a few times to evenly cook, about 3 minutes. Remove from the heat and top evenly with the sun-dried tomatoes and olives. Place on the center rack and broil until tomatoes and olives are just heated through, about 1 minute, taking care not to burn. Sprinkle with the remaining basil (if using) and serve at once.

PER SERVING

Calories 408 ▪ Protein 7g ▪ Total Fat 20g ▪ Sat. Fat 3g ▪ Cholesterol 0mg ▪ Carbohydrate 51g ▪ Dietary Fiber 3g ▪ Sodium 988mg

Wild Mushroom Pizza with Caramelized Onions

MAKES 8 SERVINGS

Serve this earthy pizza with a spinach salad for a satisfying fall or winter meal.

Cornmeal for dusting (optional)
3 tablespoons extra-virgin olive oil
1 medium onion (about 6 ounces), cut in half lengthwise and thinly sliced crosswise
¾ pound fresh wild, cremini, and/or cultivated mushrooms, sliced
2 large cloves garlic, finely chopped
4 teaspoons chopped fresh sage, or 1 teaspoon dry rubbed
Salt, preferably the coarse variety, and freshly ground black pepper, to taste
1 recipe Quick-Rising Pizza Dough (page 130), or Semolina Pizza Dough (page 130)
All-purpose flour for dusting

Preheat the oven to 500F (260C). Set a rack on the lowest position. Sprinkle a 12- to 14-inch pizza pan with cornmeal (if using) or lightly oil; set aside.

In a medium nonstick skillet, heat the oil over medium heat. Add the onion and cook, stirring, until softened and translucent, about 5 minutes. Add the mushrooms and cook, stirring, until mushrooms begin to release their liquid, about 5 minutes, adding the garlic the last minute or so of cooking. Remove from the heat and toss with the sage, salt, and pepper. Let cool.

Turn the dough out onto a lightly floured work surface. Roll and stretch into a 12- to 14-inch circle. Transfer the dough to the prepared pan. Arrange the mushroom-onion mixture evenly over the top to within ½ inch of the edge of the dough. Bake for 12 to 15 minutes, or until the bottom is crisp and the edge of the crust is beginning to brown. Cut into wedges and serve at once.

PER SERVING
Calories 193 ▪ Protein 5g ▪ Total Fat 7g ▪ Sat. Fat 1g ▪
Cholesterol 0mg ▪ Carbohydrate 29g ▪
Dietary Fiber 2g ▪ Sodium 270mg

Focaccia with Artichoke and Green Olive Paste

MAKES 8 MAIN-DISH OR 16 APPETIZER SERVINGS

Use the versatile artichoke and green olive paste as a bruschetta or crostini topping, or toss with hot cooked pasta. For a richer variation, substitute good-quality black olives for the green variety, if desired.

> 1 (6-ounce) jar marinated quartered artichoke
>   hearts, drained
> 1 cup pitted green olives, preferably stuffed
>   with pimiento
> 3 tablespoons extra-virgin olive oil
> ½ teaspoon dried thyme leaves
> Salt, preferably the coarse variety, and freshly
>   ground black pepper, to taste
> 1 loaf plain focaccia (about 16 ounces)

In a food processor fitted with the knife blade, process the artichokes, olives, oil, and thyme until a soft paste forms. Season with salt and pepper. Spread evenly over the focaccia. Cut into 8 squares and serve within 1 hour.

PER SERVING
Calories 228 ▪ Protein 6g ▪ Total Fat 9g ▪ Sat. Fat 1g ▪
Cholesterol 0mg ▪ Carbohydrate 32g ▪
Dietary Fiber 3g ▪ Sodium 495mg

Potato Focaccia

MAKES 4 TO 6 MAIN-DISH OR 8 APPETIZER SERVINGS

Taking advantage of quick-acting yeast, the following recipe is simple enough for even first-time focaccia bakers to make with ease. Fresh or dried thyme leaves can replace the rosemary, if desired.

> 1 recipe Quick-Rise Focaccia Dough
>   (opposite page)
> 1 medium russet potato (about 6 ounces),
>   peeled, cut in half lengthwise, and thinly
>   sliced crosswise
> 1 small onion (about 4 ounces), very thinly
>   sliced and separated into rings
> 2 tablespoons extra-virgin olive oil
> 1 tablespoon chopped fresh rosemary leaves,
>   or 1 teaspoon dried
> 2 cloves garlic, finely chopped
> Salt, preferably the coarse variety, and freshly
>   ground black pepper, to taste

Prepare the focaccia dough as directed. Preheat the oven to 400F (205C). Lightly oil a baking sheet.

In a medium bowl, toss together the potato, onion, oil, rosemary, garlic, salt, and pepper until well combined. Transfer to prepared baking sheet and spread out in a single layer. Bake on the center rack 10 minutes. Remove from oven and let cool slightly.

Distribute the cooled potato mixture evenly over the top of the risen dough, gently pressing in with your fingers. Bake 20 to 25 minutes, or until lightly golden. Cut into wedges and serve warm or at room temperature, preferably within a few hours of baking for best results. If necessary, cover and store in refrigerator 2 or 3 days before reheating in a low oven. (Do not freeze, as the potatoes will become soggy.)

PER SERVING

Calories 395 ▪ Protein 10g ▪ Total Fat 11g ▪ Sat. Fat 2g ▪
Cholesterol 0mg ▪ Carbohydrate 64g ▪
Dietary Fiber 4g ▪ Sodium 273mg

Quick-Rise Focaccia Dough

MAKES 1 (12 × 7-INCH) LOAF

This recipe can serve as an ideal base for all your favorite focaccia toppings.

> 2¼ to 2½ cups all-purpose white flour,
>   preferably unbleached, plus additional as
>   necessary
> 1 (¼-ounce) package (about 1 tablespoon)
>   quick-acting or rapid-rise yeast
> ½ teaspoon salt
> 1 cup very warm water (120F to 130F; 50C to
>   55C)
> 1 tablespoon extra-virgin olive oil

Preheat the oven to 200F (95C). Lightly grease a 12 × 7-inch or 12 × 8-inch shallow baking dish and set aside.

In a large bowl, combine 1½ cups of the flour, the yeast, and salt. Stir in the warm water and oil. Gradually stir in ½ cup of the remaining flour. Turn the dough out onto a lightly floured work surface and knead for about 10 minutes, incorporating the additional flour as needed, or until a smooth and elastic dough is formed. Shape the dough into a ball. Cover with a kitchen towel and let rest 10 minutes.

Transfer the dough to the prepared baking dish; press and stretch evenly until it covers the bottom of the dish. Set the baking dish on a large baking sheet. Dampen the kitchen towel and drape over the baking dish. Place in the preheated oven and immediately turn off the heat. Let set until the dough has risen to about twice its height, 20 minutes. Remove from the oven.

Remove the kitchen towel and the bottom baking sheet. The dough is ready to be topped and baked as directed in the recipe.

PER SERVING (PER ¼ OF DOUGH)

Calories 305 ▪ Protein 8g ▪ Total Fat 4g ▪ Sat. Fat 1g ▪
Cholesterol 0mg ▪ Carbohydrate 57g ▪
Dietary Fiber 3g ▪ Sodium 269mg

Breads

Baked Garlic Bread

MAKES 6 TO 8 SERVINGS

You can use a French baguette here, but use about three-quarters of a standard 10-ounce loaf and bake on the center rack for the recommended time.

¼ cup extra-virgin olive oil
2 large cloves garlic, finely chopped
2 tablespoons finely chopped fresh flat-leaf parsley, or 2 teaspoons dried (optional)
½ teaspoon coarse salt
½ loaf Italian bread (about 8 ounces), cut lengthwise in half

Preheat the oven to 375F (190C).

In a small skillet, heat the oil over medium-low heat. Add the garlic and cook, stirring often, until softened but not browned, about 3 minutes. Remove the skillet from the heat and immediately stir in the parsley (if using) and salt.

Score the bread into serving pieces, but don't cut all the way through the bread. Place on an ungreased baking sheet and brush evenly with the oil and garlic mixture. Bake in the upper third of the oven 5 to 6 minutes, or until the top is lightly browned. Serve at once.

PER SERVING
Calories 184 ▪ Protein 3g ▪ Total Fat 10g ▪ Sat. Fat 2g ▪
Cholesterol 0mg ▪ Carbohydrates 19g ▪
Dietary Fiber 1g ▪ Sodium 378 mg

Skillet Garlic Bread

MAKES 4 SERVINGS

You can make this quick and easy recipe using pre-sliced Italian bread to save even more time.

2 tablespoons extra-virgin olive oil
1 large clove garlic, finely chopped
4 large slices Italian bread (about 1.5 ounces each)
Coarse salt, to taste

In a large nonstick skillet, heat the oil over medium heat. Add the garlic and cook, stirring constantly, 30 to 45 seconds. Add the bread and cook until undersides are lightly browned, about 2 minutes. Turn over, sprinkle lightly with salt, and cook until undersides are lightly browned, 1 to 2 minutes. Serve at once.

PER SERVING
Calories 147 ▪ Protein 3g ▪ Total Fat 8g ▪ Sat. Fat 2g ▪
Cholesterol 0mg ▪ Carbohydrates 16g ▪
Dietary Fiber 1g ▪ Sodium 186mg

Toasted Bread with Olive Oil and Rosemary

MAKES 6 TO 8 SERVINGS

For delicious variations, try using oregano, thyme, sage, or parsley in lieu of the rosemary. Garlic-flavored olive oil can also be substituted for the plain variety, if desired.

¼ cup extra-virgin olive oil

1 teaspoon chopped fresh rosemary leaves, or ¼ teaspoon dried

1 (10-ounce) French baguette, cut into 1-inch diagonal slices

Coarse salt, to taste

Preheat the oven to broil.

In a small saucepan, heat the oil over medium heat. Add the rosemary and cook, stirring, until fragrant, 1 minute. Remove pan from heat and let cool slightly.

Arrange bread in a single layer on a large ungreased baking sheet. Brush both sides evenly with the oil. Broil 4 to 6 inches from heat source until lightly browned, about 1 minute each side, sprinkling the last side lightly with salt before toasting. Serve warm or at room temperature.

PER SERVING

Calories 209 ▪ Protein 4g ▪ Total Fat 10g ▪ Sat. Fat 2g ▪
Cholesterol 0mg ▪ Carbohydrates 25g ▪
Dietary Fiber 1g ▪ Sodium 288mg

Savory Pies and Tarts

Sicilian Bread Pie with Broccoli

MAKES 6 TO 8 SERVINGS

Known as *impanata* in Sicily, this tasty stuffed bread can be filled with just about anything—cooked frozen chopped spinach, well drained, is excellent here.

2 tablespoons extra-virgin olive oil

1 medium onion (about 6 ounces), chopped

3 large cloves garlic, finely chopped

½ teaspoon dried oregano

⅛ teaspoon crushed red pepper flakes, or to taste

1 (16-ounce) package frozen broccoli cuts, cooked according to package directions, drained well

Salt and freshly ground black pepper, to taste

1 (11-ounce) can refrigerated French bread dough

Preheat the oven to 350F (175C). Lightly oil a 10-inch ceramic pie dish or quiche dish and set aside.

In a large nonstick skillet, heat the oil over medium heat. Add the onion and cook, stirring, until softened and translucent, about 8 minutes. Add the garlic, oregano, and red pepper flakes; cook, stirring, 1 minute. Add the broccoli, salt, and pepper and stir well to combine. Remove from the heat and set aside.

Divide the dough in half. Unfold one half; stretch and press to fit prepared dish, trimming and patching as necessary. Bake on the center rack 5 to 10 minutes, or until just beginning to brown. Remove from oven and fill with the broccoli mixture. Unfold other dough half; stretch and press to fit the top, trimming and patching as necessary. Pinch the edges together to seal. Cut about 5 slits in the top of dough. Bake 15 to 20 minutes, or until top is nicely browned. Let cool 15 minutes before cutting into wedges and serving. Serve warm or at room temperature.

PER SERVING

Calories 240 ▪ Protein 6g ▪ Total Fat 12g ▪ Sat. Fat 2g ▪ Cholesterol 0mg ▪ Carbohydrate 30g ▪ Dietary Fiber 3g ▪ Sodium 589mg

Fresh Tomato and Onion Tart with Basil-Garlic Crust

MAKES 8 SERVINGS

This lovely tart is delicious accompanied by any tossed green salad. Plum tomatoes work best here, as they are less juicy than the round varieties and won't create a soggy crust.

1 recipe Basil-Garlic Crust (right)
4 ounces red onion (about ½ large), cut into very thin rings, separated
Salt and freshly ground black pepper, to taste
2 tablespoons extra-virgin olive oil
8 ounces plum tomatoes (about 4 medium), thinly sliced
2 tablespoons chopped fresh basil

Preheat the oven to 375F (190C).

Fit the dough into an ungreased 10-inch quiche or tart pan. Prick the bottom with a fork in several places. Bake 12 minutes on the center rack. Remove from the oven and let cool about 1 minute.

Line the bottom of the tart shell with the onion rings. Season with salt and pepper and drizzle with half of the oil. Working from the outer edge, arrange the tomatoes over the onion in concentric circles. Season with salt and pepper and drizzle with remaining oil.

Bake in the center of the oven about 25 minutes, or until the crust is golden brown. Cool on a wire rack at least 10 minutes before slicing. Just before serving, sprinkle with the basil. Serve warm or at room temperature.

PER SERVING

Calories 229 ▪ Protein 3g ▪ Total Fat 17g ▪ Sat. Fat 6g ▪ Cholesterol 0mg ▪ Carbohydrate 18g ▪ Dietary Fiber 1g ▪ Sodium 137mg

Basil-Garlic Crust

MAKES 8 SERVINGS

This dough can be used for countless savory pies and tarts. Feel free to substitute other fresh herbs for the basil.

⅓ cup loosely packed fresh basil leaves
1 medium clove garlic, finely chopped
1¼ cups unbleached all-purpose flour, plus additional as necessary
½ teaspoon salt
8 tablespoons vegetable shortening, cut into 8 pieces
4 to 5 tablespoons ice water

Place the basil and garlic in a food processor fitted with the knife blade. Process until finely chopped. Add the flour and salt; pulse to combine. Add the shortening and pulse until the mixture resembles coarse crumbs. Add 4 tablespoons of ice water, 1 tablespoon at a time, pulsing several times after each addition, until mixture comes together into a ball. If mixture is not forming a ball, add remaining 1 tablespoon of water and continue to pulse as necessary. Alternatively, if mixture becomes too sticky, add a bit more flour.

Remove the dough and flatten into a 5-inch disk. Wrap in plastic wrap and refrigerate a minimum of 1 hour, or up to 1 day. (If refrigerated more than 8 hours, let stand at room temperature about 20 minutes before continuing with the recipe.) Using a lightly floured rolling pin, roll the dough out on a lightly floured surface into a 12-inch circle. Follow recipe instructions for filling.

PER SERVING (ONE-EIGHTH OF CRUST)
Calories 189 ▪ Protein 2g ▪ Total Fat 13g ▪ Sat. Fat 5g ▪
Cholesterol 0mg ▪ Carbohydrate 15g ▪
Dietary Fiber 1g ▪ Sodium 134mg

Neapolitan Curly Endive Pie

MAKES 8 SERVINGS

This rustic pie is delicious served with your favorite pasta sauce. If curly endive is not available, substitute with escarole or spinach.

3 large heads curly endive (about 3 pounds),
 leaves separated and trimmed
¼ cup water
2 tablespoons extra-virgin olive oil
3 large cloves garlic, finely chopped
½ cup chopped pitted kalamata or other good-
 quality black olives
½ teaspoon salt
Freshly ground black pepper, to taste
Cayenne pepper, to taste (optional)
2 (10-ounce) cans refrigerated pizza dough
All-purpose flour for dusting

Rinse the endive and briefly drain in a colander. Place the endive and water in a large stockpot, cover, and steam over medium-high heat until stems are tender, about 8 minutes, uncovering the pot a few times and pushing leaves down with a wooden spoon. Transfer to a colander and drain well. Let cool to room temperature. Squeeze between paper towels to rid of excess moisture. Coarsely chop and set aside.

In a large nonstick skillet, heat the oil over medium heat. Add the garlic and cook, stirring, 1 minute. Add the endive and cook, stirring, until very soft, about 5 minutes. Stir in the olives, salt, black pepper, and cayenne (if using). Remove from heat and let cool to room temperature.

Preheat the oven to 400F (205C). Place the oven rack on the lowest position. Lightly grease a 12- to 14-inch pizza pan and set aside.

Unroll one can of the pizza dough onto a lightly floured work surface. Cut off the corners and press into the dough. Using your hands, shape into a circle. Using a rolling pin, roll out into a 12- to 14-inch circle. Place in prepared pan. Prick in several places with a fork. Spoon the filling on top and spread evenly to within ½ inch of rim. Prepare second can of pizza dough as the first and place on top of the filling. Pinch edges together to seal. Prick top in several places with a fork.

Bake 30 to 40 minutes, or until top is lightly browned and bottom is crisp. (After about 25 minutes, if top is browning too quickly, cover loosely with foil until done.) Let cool 10 minutes before cutting into wedges and serving. Serve warm or at room temperature.

PER SERVING
Calories 251 ▪ Protein 6g ▪ Total Fat 9g ▪ Sat. Fat 1g ▪
Cholesterol 0mg ▪ Carbohydrates 36g ▪
Dietary Fiber 5g ▪ Sodium 403mg

Caponata Tart with Basil

MAKES 6 SERVINGS

Frozen puff pastry—the leading commercial brand is dairy-free—makes quick work of this scrumptious tart. Caponata, a sweet and sour eggplant appetizer, can be found in most supermarkets next to the olives.

½ (about 17-ounce) package frozen puff pastry sheets (1 sheet), thawed according to manufacturer's directions
All-purpose flour for dusting
1 (7.5-ounce) jar caponata
2 large cloves garlic, finely chopped
¼ cup finely chopped fresh basil
4 medium plum tomatoes (about 2 ounces each), cut into ½-inch-thick slices
Salt, preferably the coarse variety, and freshly ground black pepper, to taste
1½ tablespoons extra-virgin olive oil

Preheat oven to 425F (220C).

Unfold pastry on a lightly floured surface. Roll into a 12-inch square. Cut off corners to make a circle. Press pastry into an ungreased 9-inch pie plate. Prick pastry thoroughly with fork.

Bake on center rack 10 minutes. Remove from the oven and spread the caponata evenly along the bottom. Sprinkle with the garlic and half of the basil. Working from the outer edge, arrange the tomatoes over the caponata in concentric circles. Season with salt and pepper and drizzle with the oil.

Return to the oven and bake 10 minutes, or until tart is golden. Let cool a few minutes before serving warm, sprinkled with the remaining basil.

Sandwiches, Panini, Calzoni, and Stromboli

Tuscan-Style Pizza Pockets with Beans and Basil

**MAKES 3 TO 4 MAIN-DISH
OR 9 SNACK-SIZE OR APPETIZER SERVINGS**

Adults as well as kids love pizza pockets. Use this recipe as a model for your favorite fillings.

**1 (15.5-ounce) can cannellini or other white
   beans, rinsed and drained**
**⅓ cup prepared pizza sauce, or All-Purpose
   Tomato Sauce (page 131)**
¼ cup finely chopped fresh basil
Salt and freshly ground black pepper, to taste
1 (10-ounce) can refrigerated pizza dough

Preheat the oven to 425F (220C). Lightly grease a standard-size baking sheet.

In a small bowl, combine the beans, pizza sauce, basil, salt, and pepper. Set aside.

Unroll dough onto prepared baking sheet, stretching dough, if necessary, to fit. Cut into 9 rectangles. Spoon about 2 tablespoons of bean mixture on one side of each rectangle, leaving a small border of dough uncovered. Fold dough over to make a pocket. Using a fork, press the sides together. Bake on the center rack 10 to 12 minutes, or until lightly browned. Serve warm.

Panini with Grilled Eggplant, Roasted Peppers, and Spinach-Pesto Sauce

MAKES 4 SANDWICHES

Fortunately, you don't need a panini maker to create this delicious recipe. To mimic the appearance of a sandwich pressed in a panini maker, flatten the bread with a heavy rolling pin before grilling, and grill just one side, if desired.

**1 large round eggplant (about 1 pound), cut
   into ½-inch-thick rounds**
Table salt
**1 medium green or red bell pepper (about 6
   ounces), cut lengthwise into eighths**
**1 medium red onion (about 6 ounces), cut into
   ½-inch-thick rounds**
2½ tablespoons extra-virgin olive oil
½ tablespoon balsamic vinegar
**Salt, preferably the coarse variety, and freshly
   ground black pepper, to taste**
**8 large slices Italian bread (about 1¼ ounces
   each)**
Spinach-Pesto Sauce (page 144)

Sprinkle the eggplant slices with table salt and set in a colander in the sink to drain 30 minutes.

Prepare a medium-hot charcoal grill or gas grill, or preheat a broiler. Position the grill rack or oven rack 4 to 6 inches from heat source. If broiling, lightly oil a large baking sheet and set aside. Or, place a stovetop grilling pan with grids over medium-high heat.

Rinse the eggplant slices under cold-running water and drain well between paper towels.

Brush the eggplant, bell pepper, and onion on all sides with 2 tablespoons of the oil. Grill or broil the vegetables until browned and tender, working in batches as necessary. As a general rule, cook the bell pepper 3 to 4 minutes per side, and the eggplant and onion 2 to 3 minutes per side. Place the vegetables on a large baking sheet with sides as they finish cooking.

When all the vegetables are done, drizzle with the remaining ½ tablespoon oil and the balsamic vinegar, and then sprinkle with salt and pepper. Toss gently with a large spatula to combine. Cover with foil and keep warm while grilling bread.

Grill or broil the bread on both sides until nicely toasted. Divide the vegetables evenly among 4 slices of the bread. Spoon equal portions of the Spinach Pesto Sauce over the vegetables. Top each with a slice of toasted bread and serve at once.

PER SERVING

Calories 393 ▪ Protein 9g ▪ Total Fat 18g ▪ Sat. Fat 3g ▪
Cholesterol 0mg ▪ Carbohydrate 50g ▪
Dietary Fiber 8g ▪ Sodium 549mg

Spinach-Pesto Sauce

MAKES ABOUT ⅓ CUP

This tasty pesto is also wonderful tossed with pasta, gnocchi, boiled potatoes, or steamed vegetables.

1 cup loosely packed fresh basil leaves
1 cup loosely packed baby spinach leaves
3 large cloves garlic, finely chopped
¼ teaspoon coarse salt, or more to taste
2 tablespoons extra-virgin olive oil

Combine the basil, spinach, garlic, and salt in a food processor fitted with the knife blade, or in a blender. Process until finely chopped. Add the oil and process until smooth. If not using immediately, store tightly covered in the refrigerator up to 2 days.

PER SERVING (ABOUT 4 TEASPOONS)

Calories 76 ▪ Protein 2g ▪ Total Fat 7g ▪ Sat. Fat 1g ▪
Cholesterol 0mg ▪ Carbohydrate 3g ▪
Dietary Fiber 0g ▪ Sodium 130mg

Grilled Portobello Mushroom Sandwiches with Lemon-Basil Pesto

MAKES 4 SERVINGS

Nothing beats the taste of a thick and juicy grilled portobello mushroom—unless, of course, it's topped with Lemon-Basil Pesto and placed between a crusty sandwich bun.

4 large packaged portobello mushroom caps, about 2 ounces each
2 teaspoons extra-virgin olive oil
Salt and freshly ground black pepper, to taste
4 large crusty sandwich rolls, about 2 ounces each, preferably whole wheat
Lemon-Basil Pesto Sauce (opposite page)
Spinach leaves (optional)

Heat a nonstick grill pan over medium-high heat. Brush each mushroom on rounded underside and rim with ½ teaspoon of the oil; season with salt and pepper to taste. Place the mushrooms, gill sides down, in pan and grill 3 minutes. Turn and grill 3 to 4 minutes, rotating each mushroom a half turn after 2 minutes, or until the bottoms are nicely browned. Place a mushroom, gill side up, on the bottom half of each roll. Fill each cap with about 4 teaspoons of the pesto, then top with the spinach leaves (if using). Close each roll and serve at once.

Lemon-Basil Pesto Sauce

MAKES ABOUT ⅓ CUP

This tangy pesto is also delightful as a topping for grilled eggplant or zucchini.

- 2 cups loosely packed fresh basil leaves
- 2 large cloves garlic, finely chopped
- ¼ teaspoon coarse salt, or more to taste
- ¼ teaspoon lemon-pepper seasoning
- 2 tablespoons extra-virgin olive oil
- 1 teaspoon fresh lemon juice, or to taste

Combine the basil, garlic, salt, and lemon-pepper seasoning in a food processor fitted with the knife blade, or in a blender. Process until finely chopped. Add the oil and lemon juice; process until smooth. If not using immediately, store tightly covered in the refrigerator up to 2 days.

Stromboli with Red Pepper Puree, Arugula, and Basil

MAKES 4 SERVINGS

These tasty jelly roll–style Italian sandwiches make a quick and easy weeknight supper along with a bowl of soup or salad. Fresh spinach can replace the arugula.

- 1 (11-ounce) can refrigerated French bread dough
- ½ cup sweet red pepper spread or puree (see Cook's Tip, page 146)
- ¼ cup chopped fresh basil
- 1 cup trimmed arugula

Preheat the oven to 425F (220C).

Unroll the dough onto an ungreased standard-size baking sheet, stretching to fit, if necessary, and trimming off any overlap. Cut dough into 4 rectangles. Spread each rectangle evenly with 2 tablespoons of the red pepper spread, then sprinkle with 1 tablespoon basil. Top each with ¼ cup of the arugula. Beginning at short side of each rectangle, roll up the dough, jelly-roll fashion; pinch seam to seal (do not seal ends of rolls). Arrange rolls 4 inches apart on baking sheet. Bake 5 minutes on center rack, or until beginning to brown. Transfer to lower rack and bake 5 minutes or until rolls are lightly browned. Serve warm.

Spinach and Mushroom Calzones

MAKES 4 SERVINGS

During the colder months, I like to serve these tasty calzones for supper with a hot bowl of Roasted Tomato Soup with Basil Puree (page 18). Cut in half, they also make terrific party appetizers.

- 1 (10-ounce) can refrigerated pizza crust
- 4 cloves garlic, finely chopped
- 4 cups fresh baby spinach leaves
- 8 (⅛-inch-thick) slices Vidalia or other sweet onion (about ½ small)
- 4 ounces cultivated white button or cremini mushrooms, thinly sliced
- 2 tablespoons extra-virgin olive oil
- Salt, preferably the coarse variety, and freshly ground black pepper, to taste

Preheat oven to 425F (220C). Lightly oil a standard-size baking sheet.

Unroll dough onto prepared baking sheet, stretching dough, if necessary, to fit. Cut into 4 rectangles. Sprinkle garlic evenly over rectangles. Top each rectangle with 1 cup of the spinach, 2 onion slices, and one-fourth of the mushrooms; drizzle with ½ tablespoon of the oil, then season with salt and pepper. Bring 2 opposite corners to center, pinching points to seal. Bring remaining 2 corners to center, pinching all points together to seal. Bake on the center rack 10 to 12 minutes, or until golden. Serve at once.

PER SERVING
Calories 244 ■ Protein 7g ■ Total Fat 9g ■ Sat. Fat 1g ■ Cholesterol 0mg ■ Carbohydrate 35g ■ Dietary Fiber 3g ■ Sodium 48mg

Desserts

Italian desserts can be daunting, but home cooks in Italy have solved the dessert dilemma by making fruits of all kinds the real stars, saving the tiramisu and cheesecakes displayed on restaurant dessert carts for special occasions. Naturally, fruit desserts are chosen according to what's in season. After all, you don't make Grilled Stuffed Peaches in winter; rather, they are something you enjoy in summer with your fresh-picked raspberries that are used to fill the peaches. But you do have the Compote of Figs with Toasted Walnuts, because you will have dried your figs in autumn. Desserts also reflect the foods that grow well from one region to the next, with oranges and figs in the south, and apples, pears, and peaches in the north. Though not necessarily low in calories or sugar, the majority of the following recipes are low in fat and high in fiber. All can conclude a vegan Italian meal on a happy, healthy note. *Ciao!*

Almond Biscotti

MAKES ABOUT 20 COOKIES

Biscotti are Italian twice-baked cookies, which are typically dunked in coffee or wine, but these are delicious all on their own.

- ¾ cup whole wheat flour
- ¾ cup unbleached all-purpose flour
- ½ tablespoon baking powder
- ¼ teaspoon salt
- ¾ cup sugar
- 6 tablespoons sweetened applesauce
- 1½ tablespoons canola oil
- ½ teaspoon pure vanilla extract
- ½ teaspoon pure almond extract
- ¾ cup slivered almonds

Preheat the oven to 350F (175C). Line a standard-size baking sheet with foil or parchment and set aside.

In a large bowl, mix together the flours, baking powder, and salt until thoroughly combined. In a medium bowl, whisk together the sugar, applesauce, oil, and extracts. Add the sugar mixture and almonds to the flour mixture, stirring to combine. Finish mixing with your hands until thoroughly combined.

With floured hands, shape the dough into 1 (3-inch wide) log about ¾ inches in thickness and transfer to prepared baking sheet. Bake on the center rack 25 minutes, or until firm to the touch. Remove the baking sheet from the oven and let cool 15 minutes. Decrease the oven temperature to 300F (150C).

Using a sharp knife, carefully cut the cooled log crosswise into ½-inch-wide slices. Remove the foil and place the slices, cut-side down, on the baking sheet. Bake about 7 to 10 minutes, or until the bottoms are just golden. Turn the slices over and bake 5 to 8 minutes, or until bottoms are golden. Using a spatula, transfer to a wire rack and let cool completely. Store in airtight containers up to two weeks, or freeze.

PER SERVING (PER COOKIE)
Calories 105 ▪ Protein 2g ▪ Total Fat 4g ▪ Sat. Fat 0g ▪ Cholesterol 0mg ▪ Carbohydrate 16g ▪ Dietary Fiber 1g ▪ Sodium 55mg

VARIATION: *To make **Anise Biscotti**: Omit the vanilla extract and add ½ tablespoon ground anise seed.*

Apple Cake

MAKES 8 SERVINGS

This rustic layered apple cake is an autumn favorite in my house. It actually tastes better the next day, reheated in a warm oven.

- 1½ cups unbleached all-purpose flour, plus additional for dusting
- 1 cup sugar
- 2 tablespoons vegetable shortening
- 2½ teaspoons baking powder
- ½ teaspoon ground cinnamon
- 8 medium Golden or Red Delicious apples (about 6 ounces each), cored and thinly sliced

Preheat the oven to 350 F (175C). Grease a 10-inch springform pan and dust with flour to coat, shaking out excess. In a small bowl, combine ¼ cup of the flour, ¼ cup of the sugar, and the shortening. Using your fingers, pinch and toss until the mixture resembles coarse crumbs. Set aside.

In a large bowl, combine the remaining flour, remaining sugar, baking powder, and cinnamon. Spread one-third of the flour-cinnamon mixture on the bottom of the prepared pan. Cover with one-third of the apple slices, pressing down with your fingers. Repeat layering process, ending with the apples. Sprinkle the top with the reserved shortening and flour mixture.

Cover loosely with foil and bake in the center of the oven 1 hour. Reduce the heat to 300F (150C), remove foil, and bake 30 minutes, or until the top is lightly browned. Remove the sides of the springform pan. Serve warm or at room temperature.

PER SERVING
Calories 285 ■ Protein 3g ■ Total Fat 4g ■ Sat. Fat 1g ■
Cholesterol 0mg ■ Carbohydrate 62g ■
Dietary Fiber 4g ■ Sodium 121mg

Apples Poached in Red Wine

MAKES 4 SERVINGS

From Tuscany, this simple and quick dessert is immensely satisfying on a crisp fall or winter evening. Try to use a Tuscan red wine, if possible.

- 1 cup dry red wine
- ½ cup sugar
- 4 medium Golden Delicious apples (about 6 ounces each), peeled, cored, and sliced into eighths
- 1 cinnamon stick

In a large saucepan, heat the wine and sugar over medium heat, stirring until the sugar dissolves. Add the apples and cinnamon stick; bring to a brisk simmer over medium-high heat. Reduce the heat and simmer moderately, stirring occasionally, until the apples are tender when pierced with the tip of a thin sharp knife, about 10 minutes. Remove and discard the cinnamon stick. (At this point, the mixture can be cooled to room temperature and refrigerated, covered, up to 2 days before gently reheating.) Divide equal portions of the apples and syrup among four serving bowls. Serve warm.

PER SERVING
Calories 221 ■ Protein 1g ■ Total Fat 1g ■ Sat. Fat 0g ■
Cholesterol 0mg ■ Carbohydrate 47g ■
Dietary Fiber 5g ■ Sodium 46mg

Cherry Sorbetto

MAKES 4 TO 6 SERVINGS

Made with frozen sweet dark cherries, this luscious red *sorbetto* from Friuli can be enjoyed any time of the year.

- ½ cup hot water
- ½ cup sugar
- ½ cup orange juice
- ½ teaspoon vanilla extract
- ¼ teaspoon almond extract
- 1 (16-ounce) bag frozen pitted dark sweet cherries, thawed, juices reserved

In a medium bowl, stir together the hot water, sugar, orange juice, and extracts until the sugar is dissolved. In a food processor fitted with the knife blade, or in a blender, process the cherries and reserved cherry juices until coarsely chopped. Add the sugar mixture and process until very smooth. Transfer to a covered container and refrigerate until well chilled, 2 to 3 hours.

Freeze in an ice-cream maker according to the manufacturer's instructions. Alternatively, pour into 2 (16-cube) plastic ice cube trays and freeze until solid, 4 to 6 hours. Transfer the cubes to a food processor fitted with the metal blade; process until smooth, working in batches, if necessary. If not serving immediately, transfer to a covered plastic container and store in the freezer up to 3 days. Serve frozen.

PER SERVING

Calories 214 ▪ Protein 2g ▪ Total Fat 0g ▪ Sat. Fat 0g ▪
Cholesterol 0mg ▪ Carbohydrate 54g ▪
Dietary Fiber 4g ▪ Sodium 2mg

⚘ COOK'S TIP ⚘

To remove the frozen sorbet cubes more easily, dip the bottom of the ice cube tray briefly in tepid water.

Chestnut Cake

MAKES 8 SERVINGS

Ideal with a cup of coffee, *castagnaccio* is an ancient Tuscan unleavened cake made in the fall when chestnuts are in season. Chestnut flour can be located in some Italian and gourmet markets.

**2 cups chestnut flour, plus additional as
     necessary (see Cook's Tip below)**
¼ cup sugar
Pinch salt

1 cup water
3 tablespoons extra-virgin olive oil
**3 tablespoons golden raisins, soaked in warm
     water to cover for 10 minutes, well drained**
1 to 2 tablespoons pine nuts
Confectioners' sugar (optional)

Preheat the oven to 350F (175C). Lightly grease a 9-inch springform pan and set aside.

In a large bowl, mix together the chestnut flour, sugar, salt, and water until thoroughly combined. Add the oil, 1 tablespoon at time, mixing well after each addition.

Dry the drained raisins between paper towels, and flour with some chestnut flour. Add to the chestnut batter, mixing well to combine. Transfer batter to prepared pan. Sprinkle the pine nuts over the top.

Bake 30 minutes, or until a wooden pick inserted in the center comes out clean. Let cool completely in the pan on a wire rack. Remove the sides of the springform pan. Sprinkle with confectioners' sugar (if using). Cut into wedges and serve.

PER SERVING

Calories 212 ▪ Protein 3g ▪ Total Fat 6g ▪ Sat. Fat 1g ▪
Cholesterol 0mg ▪ Carbohydrate 36g ▪
Dietary Fiber 3g ▪ Sodium 18mg

⚘ COOK'S TIP ⚘

Chestnut flour from trees harvested in Washington State can be ordered online from Allen Creek Farm in Ridgefield, WA, at www.chestnutsonline.com or telephone/fax: 360-887-3669. Imported Italian chestnut flour can be ordered online from Dowd and Rogers Inc. in Sacramento, CA, at www.dowdandrogers.com, by telephone: 916-451-6480, or fax: 916-736-2349.

Chocolate Strudel

MAKES 8 SERVINGS

This decadent strudel, called a *strucolo* in Friuli, is divine with a cup of espresso or coffee.

6 tablespoons confectioners' sugar

2 ounces bittersweet baking chocolate, grated

¼ cup blanched slivered almonds or walnut pieces, finely chopped

2 tablespoons water

½ (about 17-ounce) package frozen puff pastry (1 sheet), thawed according to package directions

Unsweetened cocoa powder, for dusting (optional)

Preheat oven to 375F (190C).

In a medium bowl, mix the sugar, chocolate, and almonds until thoroughly combined. Add the water and mix well to thoroughly combine.

Unfold the pastry onto an ungreased baking sheet. Line the middle third of the pastry with half of the chocolate-almond filling. Fold the third of the pastry to your left over the filling; line with remaining filling. Fold the third of the pastry to your right as far over to the other side as it will comfortably stretch, pressing the dough together where it meets to seal. (Do not seal the ends.) Cut about 6 (1-inch long) slits across the top.

Bake in the center of the oven about 25 minutes, or until golden. Cool on baking sheet on a wire rack 30 minutes. Dust with cocoa (if using). Cut into 8 slices and serve slightly warm or at room temperature.

PER SERVING
Calories 230 ■ Protein 4g ■ Total Fat 14g ■ Sat. Fat 4g ■
Cholesterol 0mg ■ Carbohydrate 26g ■
Dietary Fiber 4g ■ Sodium 103mg

Chocolate-Espresso Balls

MAKES ABOUT 20 PIECES

These no-cook chocolate treats are perfect for any occasion.

3 tablespoons unsweetened cocoa powder

¾ cup confectioners' sugar

½ tablespoon instant espresso or coffee powder

3½ ounces bittersweet baking chocolate, grated

1 cup walnuts, almonds, or hazelnuts, finely chopped

1 tablespoon vegetable shortening

1 tablespoon water, plus additional as necessary

Sprinkle a small plate with the cocoa and set aside.

In a medium bowl, mix the sugar and espresso powder until thoroughly combined. Add the chocolate, nuts, shortening, and water; mix until thoroughly combined, adding additional water as necessary to help the mixture hold together. Using your hands, roll the mix into 1-inch balls and roll gently in the cocoa. Transfer to a serving dish, cover, and refrigerate a minimum of 1 hour, or up to 2 days. Serve chilled.

PER SERVING (PER PIECE)
Calories 89 ■ Protein 2g ■ Total Fat 7g ■ Sat. Fat 2g ■
Cholesterol 0mg ■ Carbohydrate 7g ■
Dietary Fiber 1g ■ Sodium 1mg

Coffee Granita

MAKES 4 TO 6 SERVINGS

A granita is an Italian ice, similar to a sorbet, but coarser in texture. If you like iced coffee, you'll love this dessert, perfect on a hot summer's day.

1 cup water
¾ cup sugar
2 cups strong coffee or espresso

In a small saucepan, combine the water and sugar. Bring to a simmer over medium heat, stirring until the sugar is dissolved. Stir in the coffee and remove from the heat. Let cool to room temperature. Cover and refrigerate a minimum of 1 hour.

Meanwhile, place a shallow 2½-quart metal container (such as a large cake pan) in the freezer to chill.

Pour the coffee mixture into the chilled pan. Place in the freezer 30 to 60 minutes, or until ice crystals form around the edges. Stir the ice crystals into the center of the pan and return to the freezer. Repeat every 30 minutes, or until all of the liquid is crystallized but not frozen solid, about 3 hours.

To serve, scoop the granita into chilled dessert bowls or goblets. (If the granita has become too hard, scrape it with a large metal spoon to break up the ice crystals.) Serve at once.

PER SERVING
Calories 148 ■ Protein 0g ■ Total Fat 0g ■ Sat. Fat 0g ■
Cholesterol 0mg ■ Carbohydrate 38g ■
Dietary Fiber 0g ■ Sodium 3mg

> ℘ **COOK'S TIP** ℘
>
> *The granita can be stored, covered, up to four days in the freezer, but it will have become frozen solid. To serve, either let the granita thaw in the refrigerator until you can scrape the crystals, or break it up into chunks and pulse in a food processor fitted with the knife blade until fairly smooth.*

Compote of Dried Figs with Toasted Walnuts

MAKES 6 TO 8 SERVINGS

Figs, harkening back to Biblical times, grow in abundance throughout Italy, particularly in the south. The following baked compote is a tasty way to enjoy the dried variety in winter.

1 cup water
6 tablespoons sugar
1 pound dried figs, soaked in warm water to
**   cover 30 minutes, drained**
⅓ cup chopped walnuts, toasted (see Cook's
**   Tip, page 39)**

Preheat the oven to 350F (175C). In a small saucepan, combine the water and sugar. Bring to a boil over medium-low heat. Cook, stirring occasionally, until the mixture is syrupy and reduced by about one-half.

Meanwhile, arrange the drained figs in a lightly oiled shallow baking dish just large enough to hold them in a snug, overlapping fashion. Pour the sugar syrup over the figs. Cover tightly with foil and bake 20 minutes. Uncover and bake 10 minutes, sprinkling with the nuts the last 5 minutes of cooking. Serve warm.

PER SERVING
Calories 282 ▪ Protein 4g ▪ Total Fat 5g ▪ Sat. Fat 0g ▪
Cholesterol 0mg ▪ Carbohydrate 62g ▪
Dietary Fiber 7g ▪ Sodium 8mg

VARIATION: *Substitute dried apricots, prunes, or dates for the figs, or prepare a combination.*

Italian Fall Fruit Salad

MAKES 6 SERVINGS

This healthy dessert can be enjoyed in the summer by substituting berries, peaches, and/or melon for some or all of the fruit.

2 bananas, sliced

2 ripe pears, cored and sliced

2 apples, cored and sliced

1 dozen seedless grapes

2 tablespoons chopped walnuts

1 tablespoon fresh lemon juice

1 tablespoon sugar

In a large bowl, gently toss all ingredients until thoroughly combined. Cover and refrigerate a minimum of 3 hours, or overnight. Serve chilled.

PER SERVING
Calories 127 ▪ Protein 1g ▪ Total Fat 2g ▪ Sat. Fat 0g ▪
Cholesterol 0mg ▪ Carbohydrate 29g ▪
Dietary Fiber 4g ▪ Sodium 2mg

Macedonia of Melon with Aniseed

MAKES 5 TO 6 SERVINGS

The combination of fresh melon and anise is highly popular in Italy, particularly in the southern regions where cantaloupe and honeydew thrive.

1 cup water

½ cup sugar

1½ tablespoons fresh lemon juice

1 tablespoon aniseed

Pinch salt

5 to 6 cups diced cantaloupe and/or honeydew

In a small nonreactive saucepan, bring the water, sugar, lemon juice, aniseed, and salt to a simmer over medium heat, stirring until the sugar is dissolved. Reduce the heat slightly and simmer, stirring occasionally, until the mixture is reduced to about 1 cup, 10 to 15 minutes. Remove from heat and let cool to room temperature.

Place the melon in a large bowl. Pour cooled syrup through a strainer over fruit; toss gently yet thoroughly to combine. Cover and refrigerate a minimum of 1 hour, or up to 2 days, stirring occasionally. Serve chilled.

PER SERVING
Calories 145 ▪ Protein 2g ▪ Total Fat 1g ▪ Sat. Fat 0g ▪
Cholesterol 0mg ▪ Carbohydrate 36g ▪
Dietary Fiber 1g ▪ Sodium 43mg

Oranges in Marsala

MAKES 4 TO 6 SERVINGS

Sicily produces some of the best oranges in the world. Here, they are paired with its world-class dessert wine for a memorable taste sensation.

6 naval oranges, peeled, white pith and membranes removed, and segmented
2 cups Marsala wine
1 tablespoon sugar
¼ cup chopped walnuts (optional)

In a large bowl, gently toss the oranges, wine, and sugar until combined. Transfer to a serving bowl, cover, and refrigerate a minimum of 2 hours, or overnight. Serve chilled, sprinkled with the walnuts, if using.

PER SERVING
Calories 189 ▪ Protein 2g ▪ Total Fat 0g ▪ Sat. Fat 0g ▪
Cholesterol 0mg ▪ Carbohydrate 29g ▪
Dietary Fiber 4g ▪ Sodium 8mg

Fresh Peach Sorbetto

MAKES 4 TO 6 SERVINGS

Nectarines or strawberries can be substituted for the peaches in this refreshing summertime sorbet.

4 cups sliced fresh peeled peaches
Juice of half a lemon (about 1½ tablespoons)

½ cup freshly squeezed orange juice
2 tablespoons superfine or confectioners' sugar, or to taste

In a large bowl, toss the peaches and lemon juice until combined. Spread the fruit in a single layer on a baking sheet. Freeze, uncovered, until the peaches are frozen solid, about 2 to 3 hours.

Place the frozen fruit, orange juice, and sugar in a food processor fitted with the knife blade, or in a blender. Process until smooth, working in batches if necessary. (If fruit seems too hard to process, let thaw about 10 minutes at room temperature.) If not serving immediately, cover and hold in the freezer up to 1 hour before serving.

PER SERVING
Calories 103 ▪ Protein 1g ▪ Total Fat 0g ▪ Sat. Fat 0g ▪
Cholesterol 0mg ▪ Carbohydrate 26g ▪
Dietary Fiber 4g ▪ Sodium 0mg

Peaches in Chianti

MAKES 6 SERVINGS

Chianti is often used to macerate peaches in Tuscany, creating the perfect no-cook summertime dessert.

4 large ripe yet firm peaches, peeled (see Cook's Tip, opposite page), pitted, and each sliced into eighths
Juice of half a medium lemon (1½ tablespoons)
3 tablespoons sugar
2 cups Chianti or other dry red wine

Place the peaches in a medium bowl and add the lemon juice and sugar; toss gently yet thoroughly to combine. Let stand about 10 minutes at room temperature, and then toss again. Add the wine and mix gently to combine. Cover and refrigerate a minimum of 8 hours, or overnight. Serve chilled.

Peaches in Spiced White Wine

MAKES 4 TO 6 SERVINGS

For an elegant presentation, serve this summertime dessert in chilled wine goblets garnished with fresh raspberries, strawberries, blackberries, and/or blueberries.

2 cups dry white wine, such as Pinot Bianco or Pinot Grigio

½ cup sugar

1 teaspoon grated dried orange peel

2 cinnamon sticks

6 medium ripe yet firm peaches, peeled (see Cook's Tip, right), pitted, and sliced

In a small saucepan, bring 1 cup of the wine, the sugar, orange peel, and cinnamon to a brisk simmer over medium heat, stirring often until the sugar dissolves. Reduce the heat slightly and simmer, stirring occasionally, until the mixture is reduced by half, about 10 to 15 minutes.

Strain the wine syrup into a large bowl and add the remaining 1 cup wine. Add the peaches, stirring gently to combine. Cover and refrigerate a minimum of 3 hours, or overnight. Serve chilled.

> **⌘ COOK'S TIP ⌘**
>
> *To peel peaches, bring a medium stockpot filled with water to a boil over high heat; drop in peaches and boil for 20 seconds. Drain and rinse under cold-running water. Peel off the skins.*

Grilled Stuffed Peaches with Raspberries

MAKES 4 SERVINGS

Italians have a penchant for grilling fruit as well as vegetables. Any berry, fresh or frozen, can be used in lieu of the raspberries.

4 large peaches, peeled (see Cook's Tip, above), halved, and pitted

1 cup fresh or frozen raspberries or blackberries

⅓ cup packed light brown sugar

4 teaspoons fresh lemon juice (the juice from 1 medium lemon)

Prepare a medium charcoal grill or gas grill. Position the grill rack 6 to 8 inches from heat source. Or, place a stovetop grilling pan over medium heat.

Place each peach half on a piece of lightly oiled aluminum foil large enough to enclose and seal the peaches. Spoon 2 tablespoons of the berries into each peach half. Sprinkle each with

2 teaspoons of the brown sugar and ½ teaspoon of the lemon juice. Fold up foil and seal. Grill 15 to 18 minutes, rotating a half-turn halfway through cooking. Serve at once, directly from the foil.

PER SERVING

Calories 123 ■ Protein 1g ■ Total Fat 0g ■ Sat. Fat 0g ■
Cholesterol 0mg ■ Carbohydrate 32g ■
Dietary Fiber 3g ■ Sodium 7mg

Baked Pears with Chocolate Sauce

MAKES 4 GENEROUS OR 8 SMALL SERVINGS

Chocolate sauce is seldom paired with fruit in Italy, with the exception of baked pears, where the combination is heavenly.

**4 ripe yet firm Bosc pears, peeled, cut in half
lengthwise, and stems and cores removed
½ cup unsweetened pear or apple juice
2 tablespoons sugar
Chocolate Sauce (right)**

Preheat the oven to 375F (190C). Lightly oil a baking dish just large enough to hold the pears in a single layer.

Arrange the pears, cored sides down, in the prepared baking dish. Pour the juice around the pears. Sprinkle evenly with half the sugar. Cover and bake 20 minutes. Turn over, cored sides up, and sprinkle evenly with the remaining sugar. Cover and bake 20 minutes, or until the pears are tender when pierced with the tip of a sharp knife. Transfer to individual serving plates, cored sides down. Spoon the cooking juices evenly over each serving. Drizzle evenly with the chocolate sauce and serve at once.

PER SERVING

Calories 308 ■ Protein 3g ■ Total Fat 12g ■ Sat. Fat 7g ■
Cholesterol 0mg ■ Carbohydrate 58g ■
Dietary Fiber 7g ■ Sodium 20mg

Chocolate Sauce

MAKES ABOUT ⅔ CUP

Happily, bittersweet baking chocolate is not only delicious, but contains no dairy products or by-products. Use this versatile sauce as a dip for both fresh and dried fruit, and biscotti.

**¼ cup light corn syrup
3 ounces (3 squares) bittersweet baking
chocolate, chopped**

In a small saucepan, bring the corn syrup to a simmer over medium heat. Remove from heat and immediately add the chocolate; stir until completely melted. Serve at once.

PER SERVING (PER TABLESPOON)

Calories 68 ■ Protein 1g ■ Total Fat 5g ■ Sat. Fat 3g ■
Cholesterol 0mg ■ Carbohydrate 9g ■
Dietary Fiber 1g ■ Sodium 7mg

Baked Pears with Currants and Cinnamon

MAKES 4 AVERAGE-SIZE OR 8 SMALL SERVINGS

This delightful pear dessert is ideal for stress-free entertaining, as it can be assembled up to twelve hours before baking.

- ⅓ **cup granulated sugar**
- ⅓ **cup packed dark brown sugar**
- ½ **teaspoon ground cinnamon**
- ⅓ **cup zante currants**
- 4 **ripe yet firm Bosc pears, unpeeled, cut in half lengthwise, cored**
- ⅓ **cup water, plus additional as needed**

Preheat the oven to 350F (175C). Lightly oil a baking dish just large enough to hold the pears in a single layer. In a small bowl, combine the sugars and cinnamon. Add the currants, tossing well to combine. Set aside.

Arrange the pears, cored sides up, in the prepared baking dish. Fill the pear cavities with about half of the sugar mixture. Stir the water into the remaining sugar mixture; pour around pears. (At this point, dish can be stored, covered, in refrigerator up to 12 hours before proceeding with the recipe; don't worry if they darken.)

Bake 40 to 45 minutes, uncovered, or until the pears are tender when pierced with the tip of a sharp knife, basting occasionally and adding more water to the dish as necessary if the syrup becomes too thick. Serve pears warm with the syrup.

PER SERVING

Calories 218 ▪ Protein 1g ▪ Total Fat 1g ▪ Sat. Fat 0g ▪
Cholesterol 0mg ▪ Carbohydrate 56g ▪
Dietary Fiber 5g ▪ Sodium 1mg

Pears Poached in Amaretto

MAKES 6 SERVINGS

From Lombardy, where the famous amaretto liqueur was created in the city of Saronno, these almond-scented poached pears are an elegant conclusion to any special meal.

- 2 **cups water**
- 1 **cup sugar**
- 4 **large ripe yet firm Bosc pears, peeled, quartered, and cored**
- 2 **cinnamon sticks**
- 2 **to 3 whole cloves**
- ½ **cup amaretto liqueur**
- 2 **tablespoons slivered almonds (optional), toasted if desired**

In a large saucepan or medium stockpot, heat the water and sugar over medium heat, stirring until the sugar dissolves. Add the pears, cinnamon sticks, and cloves; bring to a simmer over medium-high heat. Reduce the heat to low and simmer, covered, until the pears are just tender, 10 to 15 minutes, stirring occasionally. Stir in the amaretto and simmer, covered, 2 minutes.

With a slotted spoon, transfer the pears to a serving platter or individual serving bowls. Strain the poaching liquid into a small saucepan and reduce over medium-high heat until reduced to 1 cup, about 10 minutes. Pour the syrup evenly over the pears. Serve warm or at room temperature, sprinkled with the almonds (if using). Alternatively, cover and refrigerate completely cooled pears up to 2 days, and serve chilled or return to room temperature.

Pears Poached in Grappa

MAKES 4 TO 6 SERVINGS

This is an ideal winter dessert to serve company. If you don't have grappa—a potent Italian spirit distilled from the residue of grapes left behind in the wine press—kirsch, a clear cherry brandy, is a fine substitute here.

- 2 cups water
- ½ cup sugar
- 2 large ripe yet firm Bosc pears, peeled, quartered, and cored
- 1 cinnamon stick
- 4 whole cloves
- ½ teaspoon grated dried lemon peel
- ⅔ cup dried apricots
- 1 cup raisins
- 4 to 6 tablespoons grappa

In a large saucepan, heat the water and sugar over medium heat, stirring until the sugar dissolves. Add the pears, cinnamon stick, cloves, and lemon peel; bring to a simmer over medium-high heat. Reduce the heat to low, cover, and simmer gently, turning occasionally, 5 minutes. Add the apricots and raisins and simmer, covered, until the pears are just tender, about 10 minutes.

Using a slotted spoon, transfer the fruit to a serving dish. Strain the poaching liquid into a small saucepan and reduce it to 1 cup over high heat. Remove from the heat and stir in the grappa. Pour the syrup over the fruit and let it cool to room temperature. Serve at room temperature, or cover and refrigerate a minimum of 1 hour or up to 2 days, and serve chilled.

Prunes in Marsala

MAKES 6 TO 8 SERVINGS

A wonderful company dessert that can be made several days ahead of serving, this simple prune compote is one of my favorites.

- 1 pound pitted prunes
- 2 cups Marsala, port, or Madeira wine
- ½ cup water
- 1 tablespoon sugar

In a medium saucepan, combine the prunes, wine, and water; bring to a boil over medium heat. Immediately reduce the heat to a gentle simmer. Simmer, uncovered, for 15 minutes, stirring occasionally.

Stir in the sugar, remove the saucepan from heat, and let cool to room temperature before serving. Alternatively, cover and refrigerate a minimum of 2 hours, and serve chilled.

PER SERVING

Calories 219 ■ Protein 2g ■ Total Fat 0g ■ Sat. Fat 0g ■
Cholesterol 0mg ■ Carbohydrate 44g ■
Dietary Fiber 5g ■ Sodium 7mg

Strawberry Crostini

MAKES 6 TO 8 SERVINGS

Your brunch or dinner guests will love this delicious dessert variation of the classic appetizer.

- **24 (½-inch-thick) slices French baguette**
- **2 tablespoons orange marmalade, preferably the bitter Seville style**
- **1½ cups sliced fresh strawberries**
- **4 tablespoons sugar**

Preheat the oven to broil.

Arrange the bread in a single layer on a large ungreased baking sheet. Broil 6 to 8 inches from the heat source until very lightly toasted, 1 to 2 minutes. Remove the baking sheet from oven and spread the marmalade evenly over each piece of baguette. Top with equal portions (about 1 tablespoon) of strawberries. (Entire surface should be covered with fruit.) Sprinkle evenly with the sugar.

Broil until the sugar is melted and beginning to caramelize, 3 to 5 minutes. Serve immediately.

PER SERVING (PER 4 CROSTINI)

Calories 125 ■ Protein 2g ■ Total Fat 1g ■ Sat. Fat 0g ■
Cholesterol 0mg ■ Carbohydrate 28g ■
Dietary Fiber 2g ■ Sodium 148mg

Tuscan-Style Strawberries in Rosé

MAKES 4 SERVINGS

Any good-quality rosé wine can be used in this simple yet elegant dessert.

- **4 cups fresh sliced strawberries**
- **¼ cup sugar**
- **2 cups rosé wine, preferably a Tuscan variety**

In a large bowl, gently toss all ingredients until thoroughly combined. Cover and refrigerate a minimum of 1 hour, or overnight. Serve chilled, preferably in chilled long-stem red-wine wineglasses or goblets.

PER SERVING

Calories 177 ■ Protein 1g ■ Total Fat 1g ■ Sat. Fat 0g ■
Cholesterol 0mg ■ Carbohydrate 25g ■
Dietary Fiber 3g ■ Sodium 8mg

Tangerines with Cherry Liqueur and Candied Fruit, Sicilian Style

MAKES 4 TO 6 SERVINGS

Sicilians have a penchant for candied fruit, especially around the holidays. This elegant dessert looks particularly festive with candied red and green cherries and pineapple. Maraschino is an Italian liqueur that is sweeter and lower in alcohol content than kirsch, a colorless cherry brandy. If using the latter, it's better to start out with the lesser amount called for in the recipe, then add according to taste.

8 tangerines or clementines

2 tablespoons sugar

¼ cup maraschino liqueur or 2 to 3 tablespoons of kirsch

1 tablespoon fresh lemon juice

¼ cup chopped mixed candied fruit

Reserve 2 of the tangerines. With a sharp paring knife, remove the peel and white pith from the remaining 6 tangerines, working over a bowl to collect their juices. With a serrated knife, working on a flat surface with a lip to contain the juices, cut the fruit into ¼-inch-thick slices crosswise against the membrane. Place the slices in a shallow serving bowl, along with any accumulated juices. Sprinkle evenly with the sugar and set briefly aside.

Juice the remaining tangerines into a small bowl (you should have about ¼ cup of juice). Stir in the liqueur, and the lemon juice. Pour the juice mixture over the tangerine slices and add the candied fruit; toss very gently to combine so as not to break apart the tangerine slices. Cover and chill in the refrigerator a minimum of 30 minutes, or overnight, tossing occasionally. Serve chilled.

PER SERVING (MADE WITH 2½ TABLESPOONS KIRSCH)
Calories 142 ▪ Protein 1g ▪ Total Fat 0g ▪ Sat. Fat 0g ▪ Cholesterol 0mg ▪ Carbohydrate 30g ▪ Dietary Fiber 4g ▪ Sodium 9mg

Metric Conversion Charts

Comparison to Metric Measure

When You Know	Symbol	Multiply By	To Find	Symbol
teaspoons	tsp	5.0	milliliters	ml
tablespoons	tbsp	15.0	milliliters	ml
fluid ounces	fl. oz.	30.0	milliliters	ml
cups	c	0.24	liters	l
pints	pt.	0.47	liters	l
quarts	qt.	0.95	liters	l
ounces	oz.	28.0	grams	g
pounds	lb.	0.45	kilograms	kg
Fahrenheit	F	⁵⁄₉ (after subtracting 32)	Celsius	C

Fahrenheit to Celsius

F	C
200–205	95
220–225	105
245–250	120
275	135
300–305	150
325–330	165
345–350	175
370–375	190
400–405	205
425–430	220
445–450	230
470–475	245
500	260

Liquid Measure to Liters

¼ cup	=	0.06 liters
½ cup	=	0.12 liters
¾ cup	=	0.18 liters
1 cup	=	0.24 liters
1¼ cups	=	0.30 liters
1½ cups	=	0.36 liters
2 cups	=	0.48 liters
2½ cups	=	0.60 liters
3 cups	=	0.72 liters
3½ cups	=	0.84 liters
4 cups	=	0.96 liters
4½	=	1.08 liters
5 cups	=	1.20 liters
5½ cups	=	1.32 liters

Liquid Measure to Milliliters

¼ teaspoon	=	1.25 milliliters
½ teaspoon	=	2.50 milliliters
¾ teaspoon	–	3.75 milliliters
1 teaspoon	=	5.00 milliliters
1¼ teaspoons	=	6.25 milliliters
1½ teaspoons	=	7.50 milliliters
1¾ teaspoons	=	8.75 milliliters
2 teaspoons	=	10.0 milliliters
1 tablespoon	=	15.0 milliliters
2 tablespoons	=	30.0 milliliters

Index